CHARLES HADDON SPURGEON

Charles Haddon Spurgeon

The People's Preacher

J. Ritchie

40 Beansburn, Kilmarnock, Scotland

ISBN-13: 978 1 910513 01 9

Copyright © 2014 by John Ritchie Ltd.
40 Beansburn, Kilmarnock, Scotland

www.ritchiechristianmedia.co.uk

All rights reserved. No part of this publication may be reproduced, stored in a retrievable system, or transmitted in any form or by any other means – electronic, mechanical, photocopy, recording or otherwise – without prior permission of the copyright owner.

Typeset by John Ritchie Ltd., Kilmarnock
Printed by Bell & Bain Ltd., Glasgow

CONTENTS.

CHAPTER I.
LIFE'S BEGINNINGS 9

CHAPTER II.
PREPARATION AND SERVICE 21

CHAPTER III.
NEW PARK STREET CHAPEL . . . 34

CHAPTER IV.
MARRIAGE, FAME, TROUBLE, AND USEFULNESS . 51

CHAPTER V.
IN LABOURS MORE ABUNDANT 78

CHAPTER VI.
THE OPENING OF THE TABERNACLE . . . 91

CHAPTER VII.
THE PASTORS' COLLEGE 104

CHAPTER VIII.
THE WORK AT THE TABERNACLE . . . 120

CHAPTER IX.
SPURGEON AND HIS STUDENTS 139

CHAPTER X.
WORK AND REST 161

CHAPTER XI.
A HELPMEET'S WORK 171

CHAPTER XII.
YEARS OF GOOD 184

CHAPTER XIII.
THE STORY OF THE STOCKWELL ORPHANAGE . . 197

CHAPTER XIV.
AFTER FIVE-AND-TWENTY YEARS . . . 217

CHAPTER XV.
SPURGEON'S PHILOSOPHY 235

CHAPTER XVI.
TO THE JUBILEE YEAR 248

CHAPTER XVII.
SPURGEON AS A COMMENTATOR . . . 265

CHAPTER XVIII.
GREATLY BELOVED 293

CHAPTER XIX
REST FOR THE WARRIOR . 314

APPENDIX . 327

LIST OF ILLUSTRATIONS.

House at Kelvedon in which Mr. Spurgeon was born . 11

High Street, Kelvedon, where Mr. Spurgeon was born 19

Mr. Spurgeon's Birthplace, as it appeared in 1834 . . 27

Portraits of Mr. Spurgeon 53

Interior of the Metropolitan Tabernacle . . 123

The Metropolitan Tabernacle 137

Mrs. Spurgeon 173

C. H. Spurgeon . . . 185

Stockwell Orphanage . . 199

Mr. Spurgeon's School and Almshouses . 211

Westwood House, Residence of Mr. Spurgeon . . 249

Mr. Spurgeon's Study 267

Portrait of Mr. Spurgeon and the Tabernacle . . . 293

At the Gates of the Cemetery 315

Memorial Service in the Tabernacle 323

Spurgeon: The People's Preacher.

CHAPTER I.

LIFE'S BEGINNINGS.

"A PRINCE has fallen in Israel!" Such was the exclamation of thousands when they heard the news of the death of Charles Haddon Spurgeon, who had for more than thirty years occupied among the preachers of the era a position absolutely unique. "The last of the Puritans," said many, and in that phrase described the man, his faith, his character, and his works. For the greatest modern preacher was scarcely modern in his thoughts, and he drew the crowds, not because he chose to be abreast of the age, but because he held the living present to the living past with the force of a strong resolution. How great he was, and how good, more than a few are trying to show by lip and pen; but though there is much to tell, the most will never be known of the marvellous influence which he had on the religious faith and life of his times. His spoken and his written words have proved to be, in the language which he often used, "like apples of gold in pictures of silver," and the man will live when most of his compeers have been forgotten, because of the strong vivid faith and the large-hearted benevolence which were his marked characteristics.

It is to show what a fine example to young men Spurgeon presents that this testimony is written.

Charles Haddon Spurgeon was born at the village of Kelvedon, in Essex, on the 19th of June 1834. He inherited the honour and the blessing of a pious ancestry. His great-grandfather was a God-fearing man, and his great-grandmother was a woman of eminent piety. Both took a lively interest in the spiritual welfare of their children, and ordered their household according to the will of God.

Mr. Spurgeon's grandfather was born at Halstead, and in early life became a Christian, and joined the Congregational church in that town. At the age of twenty-six he devoted himself to the ministry of the Gospel, and entered Hoxton Academy, to prepare himself for the great work. At the completion of his studies he settled at Clare, in Suffolk. After a short but useful pastorate there, he removed to Stambourne, in Essex. He entered on the pastorate of this church in the year 1810, and continued in the office upwards of half a century. Invitations were sent from other churches, but such were the peace and prosperity reigning at Stambourne, that he declined them all. When more than eighty years old, he could say, "I have not had one hour's unhappiness with my church since I have been over it." His usefulness continued to the last; and this led him to reply to some friends who advised his retirement, "No! I will never give up so long as God inclines people to come and souls are saved." During the last two years of his life he preached only occasionally, as his health permitted; but he presided at the communion of the Lord's Supper to the end. On the 12th of February 1864, in his eighty-seventh year, he entered upon his heavenly rest; and nine days after his remains were committed to the grave, in the presence of a large number of endeared and sorrowing friends.

Grandfather Spurgeon is described as a staid, quiet

HOUSE AT KELVEDON IN WHICH MR. SPURGEON WAS BORN

(From Photo by Howard Bentham.)

man, wearing a dress cravat, a frilled shirt, knee-breeches, buckled shoes, and silk stockings. He wore also, Stevenson says, "a vest with deep pockets, as if provided for large collections." His manners were benignant and full of old-time courtesy, and the clergyman of the parish church was as much his friend as any Nonconformist minister. He was remarkable for his spirituality and blameless life; and he was aided in his labours by a wife who was after his own heart. During his last illness he desired to preach the Gospel; and the peace and triumph of his death-bed greatly impressed those who were with him when the end came.

Mr. Spurgeon's father was born at Stambourne in 1811. For many years he was engaged in business in Colchester. For sixteen years, while occupied with business during the week, he preached on the Sunday to a small Independent church at Tollesbury. This led to his full entrance on ministerial work; and after he had reached the prime of life, he accepted a call to the pastorate of the Congregational church at Cranbrook, in Kent, where he remained five years. Thence he removed to London, and became, in succession, minister of the Fetter Lane Church, Holborn, and the Upper Street Church, Islington. The latter position he resigned at the end of the year 1876, after which time he did good service as an occasional preacher in various parts of the kingdom. The mother of Mr. Spurgeon was esteemed wherever she was known for her sincere piety and her Christian usefulness.

While yet a child, Mr. Spurgeon was removed to his grandfather's house at Stambourne, and here for a few years he resided under the watchful care of a loving aunt. He early manifested a love for books; and it is said that he would sit for hours together turning over the pages of *Robinson Crusoe* or *The Pilgrim's Progress*. Even at this period his mind displayed its natural vigour and bias; and the lessons thus learnt have influenced the matter and method of his own teaching in after years.

There are not many stories told of his boyhood. He was a decidedly precocious child, who thought for himself as much as he read the thoughts of other men.

At one time while staying with his grandfather he was reading the Scriptures at family worship, and it came to his turn to read the verse in the Book of Revelation which speaks of the bottomless pit.

"Grandpa, what can this mean?" asked the boy. "How can a pit be bottomless?"

"Charlie, go on with your reading," was the answer.

"But I want to know, grandpa."

"Pass on," continued the old man.

Charlie, however, was not to be quenched so easily. Every morning he read the same passage until the repetition became tiresome, and at last the grandfather said, "Now, my boy, what is it that puzzles you?"

"Grandfather," he said, "when the bottom of a fruit-basket is worn out the fruit falls through to the ground: where do all the people fall who drop out through the bottomless pit?"

The grandfather was not quite prepared with an answer to that question, and the solemnity of the family was rather disturbed on that occasion.

One remarkable incident connected with the boyhood of the great preacher is often referred to.

It was at Stambourne that, what Mr. Spurgeon called, "The Rev. Richard Knill's Prophecy" was delivered. Mr. Knill was for several years a minister of the Gospel in St. Petersburg; and during the latter part of his life pastor of a church in the city of Chester. He was a man full of zeal for the glory of God—of love to Jesus Christ—of compassion for perishing men. The young especially engaged his warmest interest. Wherever he went, he sought to do good; and he had such a wise and holy art of Christian usefulness, that he was honoured above most in saving souls. On one occasion, during a visit of young Spurgeon to his grandfather's house, Mr. Knill stayed there a few days, being engaged to preach at Stambourne on behalf of the London Missionary Society. Naturally, the precocious boy of ten years of age became the object of his attention. After talking to him for a while, he asked him to read; and was so pleased that, laying his hands on the child's head, he said, "I have heard old ministers and young ones read well, but never did I hear a little boy read so correctly before. I hope he will one day fill Rowland Hill's pulpit." The little boy and the preacher had pleasant talks in the garden, where, in a large yew arbour, they knelt down together, and the preacher poured out fervent and earnest intercession for the boy's salvation. Mr. Knill's stay extended from Friday to Monday, during which time he and his young friend were almost always together; and the talk for the most part was about Jesus, and the importance and advantages of becoming His disciple while young. On the Sunday, the sermons for the Missionary Society were preached; and the next day the man of God took his departure, but not before he had uttered his strange prediction.

Mr. Spurgeon was himself greatly affected by this incident, and often referred to it. On one occasion Mr. Knill said in the presence of the family that he felt a profound presentiment that the little boy whom he held on his knee would one day preach the Gospel to many thousands of people. Mr. Spurgeon always thought that Mr. Knill's prophecy helped its own fulfilment. He believed what the good man said of him, and his thoughts were therefore turned in the direction of that which was to be his future life-work.

Another story that is told of Spurgeon's boyhood is that when he was not quite seven years old, he saw, when walking through the village street, a man whom he knew to be a professor of religion standing with rough and loose loungers, laughing and talking as if he were one of them. The boy went swiftly to the side of the man, and in his clear, ringing voice—the voice which was hereafter to wing its way to so many hearts—he put the startling question, "What doest thou here, Elijah?"

He had from his childhood the quick eyes that see, and the heart that sympathises with all life. He was witty and observant from the first; and the after-years of his life prove how deep were the impressions made upon him in his earliest years. It was good for him, as it is for any man whose work is to be among the crowds, to spend the growing years among the fields and woods and all the sweet influences of nature.

During Mr. Spurgeon's first residence with his grandfather and maiden aunt at Stambourne, the latter, who had special charge of him, took great pains to train his character aright, and to inspire him with a love for all that was good. We are not, therefore, surprised to find that he took a deep interest in religious books, and cherished an early attachment to the house of God. He never indulged in untruth. His familiarity in childhood with the stories and pictorial illustrations of religious persecution, in the past history of our country, begat in him an early hatred of religious intolerance. While yet a youth he was often found reading aloud alone; or he would address, in imitation of a preacher, his brothers and sisters. In spite of all this, he gave evidence of the possession of strong passions and a determined will. This occasioned at times considerable anxiety to his parents, and constrained them earnestly to pray that God would bring him under the gracious and subduing influences of his Holy Spirit.

Spurgeon's grandfather and the rector of the parish were exceedingly good friends. Indeed, they were sensible people at Stambourne, who never thought that they did God service by hating instead of loving each other. It was quite a common thing for the inhabitants to go to church in the mornings, and the Independent Chapel in the evenings; and Mr. Spurgeon used to tell how he and his grandfather and the vicar went to tea together to the squire's, and "the great treat of the tea-party was that the four, the three old gentlemen and the little boy, all ate sugared bread and butter together." The Anglican pastor showed many kindnesses to the Dissenting one; and a story is told of how on one occasion, when there was a great joint of beef on the rectory table, the vicar cut it in two, and sent one, all smoking hot as it was, to the home of the Dissenting parson.

Only a few months before his death Mr. Spurgeon published a delightful little book called *Memories of Stambourne*, which will be read with increased interest now, because it gives some interesting particulars of his own life with his grandfather. In the *Methodist Recorder* the Rev. John Telford, B.A., says in a sympathetic article on "Mr. Spurgeon's Boyhood: A Study of Origins"—"It is no wonder that Stambourne had a singular attraction for Mr. Spurgeon. It was there that the foundation of his character was firmly laid. His father and mother had seventeen children, with but scant means for their support. It was no doubt some little relief for the boy to pay long visits to his grandfather's parsonage. There he found himself in an old Puritan world. James Spurgeon was a man of sparkling wit, in whom local tradition afterwards discerned the original of John Ploughman. He was a preacher of rare spiritual force, about whom one hearer said quaintly that a sermon from his lips made 'his wing-feathers grow afoot. He could mount as eagles, after being fed with such heavenly food.' A devout working-man paid him a grand tribute. 'He was always so experimental. You felt as if you had been inside of a man.' When Charles became a preacher there were people who said, 'I heard your grandfather, and I would run my shoes off my feet any day to hear a Spurgeon.'

"The little fellow was early initiated into the throes of sermon-making, for on Sunday mornings he was taken into the best parlour with his grandfather whilst the sermon was receiving its finishing touches. The *Evangelical Magazine*, with a portrait of a preacher and of a mission station, was put into the boy's hands with sundry admonitions to be quiet, as he 'had the *Magazine*.' If these arguments failed, the boy was reminded that perhaps grandpa would not be able to preach if he were distracted, then how would poor people learn the way to heaven."

The Rev. John Spurgeon, the venerable father of the great preacher, was visited soon after his son's death by a member of the staff of the *Daily Chronicle*, and he gave in conversation some very pathetic little touches to the history of his illustrious son. "It has been said that Charles was brought up by his grandfather and grandmother," he said. "The fact is that my father and mother came to see us when Charles was a baby of fourteen months old. They took him to stay with them, and he remained with them until he was between four and five years of age. Then he came home to stay with us at Colchester, where now I was residing, at the same time carrying on my ministerial work at Tollesbury, some miles distant. Afterwards he often went to spend his holidays with his grandparents, who were very fond of him. . . . Charles was a healthy child and boy, having a good constitution, and he was of an affectionate disposition, and very studious. He was always reading books—never digging in the garden or keeping pigeons, like other boys. It was always books and books. If his mother wanted to take him for a ride she would be sure to find him in my study poring over a book. He was clever, of course, and clever in most directions of study. He learned to draw very well.'

PLAYING AT PREACHING.

When he was a very little boy he used to preach to his brothers and sisters in the stable. Charles got up into the rack, his brother James sat in the manger, and his little sisters on the trusses of straw below. Then Charles would preach to his small congregation as vigorously, if not as eloquently, as later he preached to the large one.

Charles went to school at Colchester when he was seven years old, first to a private school kept by a captain's wife, Mrs. Cook, and afterwards to one of which Mr. Lewis was the master. He was an excellent scholar, and was always first at every examination. He learned French, Latin, and Greek. His chief tutor was Mr. Leeding, who considered young Spurgeon one of the best scholars of his years to be met with, and who always declared that he could with ease have taken honours at the University. When he was a boy of fourteen he could read the Greek Testament, and his mathematical ability was exceptionally good. Mr. Leeding used to tell a story of how he once gave him a mathematical book to study, but Spurgeon did not like it, and declared then that mathematics had no attraction for him. Leeding did not insist, but, like a wise man, took the book back and put it on the shelf. "Ah, you will be glad to do it next term," he remarked, and he was right. The next term Spurgeon asked for the book, and soon mastered it.

He was a little more than fourteen when he and his brother James went to an agricultural college at Maidstone. The time was not lost; for the teaching which the boy received in educational matters remained with him in after life, and no doubt often furnished him with illustrations. At this college three clergymen came to teach the boys religion, for it was a Church of England school, and one of them presented Spurgeon with a copy of the *Christian Year*, as a reward for his proficiency in religious knowledge.

When he was fifteen years old he went to be an usher in

a school in Newmarket. In his father's diary there is this entry, under date the 17th of August 1849:—"Charles started for Newmarket this morning. His mother went with him. The Lord go with him and keep him and bless him."

This very pathetic little record tells, for it reveals both his father's piety and his mother's tenderness. The Rev. John Spurgeon was a worthy descendant of a long line of spiritually-minded men who prayed for their children. His mother was a devoted Christian woman, who ever showed the greatest solicitude for her children, whom she would gather around her in order to pray for them individually. She was especially fervent in asking for God's blessing upon her youngest son.

"Ah, Charlie," she said to him once, "I have often prayed that you might be saved, but never that you might be a Baptist."

"God has answered your prayer, mother, with His usual bounty," promptly replied her son, "and has given more than you asked."

The Newmarket school was kept by Mr. Swindell. Charles was to assist in teaching, and in return he was to receive instruction in Greek.

Professor J. D. Everett, F.R.S., of Queen's College, Belfast, who was also a teacher in the same school, gave some interesting early reminiscences in the *Christian World*, in which he says:—

"From a shorthand diary which I kept at Mr. Swindell's I transcribe the following items. There is not much in them, but they may have some interest as genuine contemporary records:—

"'On Friday evening (August 17, 1849), as we expected Mr. Spurgeon, the new teacher, to arrive by the coach at half-past five, we went to the heath to see the coach in. It came, and as it passed us we saw that there was no one

HIGH STREET, KELVEDON, WHERE MR. SPURGEON WAS BORN.
(From Photo by Howard Benham.)

outside, and only a few ladies and a boy inside; so we concluded the teacher had not come. However, the boy in question was Mr. Spurgeon. He is fifteen years old, and is a clever, pleasant little fellow. He comes from a collegiate school at Maidstone, in which he obtained the first prize, but he knows very little Latin and Greek, and in mathematics has done five books of Euclid, and only as far as equations and the Binomial Theorem in Algebra.

"'*Sunday, August* 19.—Mr. Spurgeon is a nice lad.

"'*Monday, August* 20.—After the twelve o'clock interval, Mr. Spurgeon and I went, with Mr. Swindell's permission, into our own room and read Horace. He knows, I think, more Latin than any of the boys, but not quite so much as I know.

"'*Tuesday, October* 9.—After dinner I took Percy and four other boys to see the races. We saw the Cesarewitch, the most celebrated race of Newmarket; thirty-one horses ran. We also saw four other races. I saw quite enough to gratify my curiosity, and did not wish to stop to see any more races. Mr. Spurgeon did not go, as he thought he should be doing wrong if he went.'"

Professor Everett thus describes him as he was at that time:—

"He was rather small and delicate, with pale but plump face, dark brown eyes and hair, and a bright, lively manner, with a never-failing flow of conversation. He was rather deficient in muscle, did not care for cricket or other athletic games, and was timid at meeting cattle on the roads.

"He had been well brought up, in a family with strong Puritanical tendencies, and was proficient in the subjects taught in the middle-class schools of those days. He knew a little Greek, enough Latin to gather the general sense of Virgil's *Æneid* without a dictionary, and was fond of algebra. He had a big book of equation problems (by Bland, I think), and could do all the problems in it, except some two or three which I was proud to be able to do for him. He was a smart, clever boy at all kinds of book learning; and, judging from the accounts he gave me of his experiences in his father's counting-house, he was also a smart man of business. He was a keen observer of men and manners, and very shrewd in his judgments. He enjoyed a joke, but was earnest, hard-working, and strictly conscientious.

"He had a wonderful memory for passages of oratory which he admired, and used to pour forth to me with great gusto, in our walks, long screeds from open-air addresses, of a very rousing description, which he had heard delivered at Colchester Fair by the Congregational minister, Mr. Davids. His imagination had evidently been greatly impressed by these services, at which, by-the-bye, his father was selected to give out the hymns on account of the loudness of his voice—a quality which would appear to have run in the family, but which had not at that time shown itself in my young friend. I have also heard him recite long passages from Bunyan's 'Grace Abounding.'

"He was a delightful companion, cheerful and sympathetic, a good listener, as well as a good talker. And he was not cast in a common conventional mould, but had a strong character of his own."

CHAPTER II.

PREPARATION AND SERVICE.

THE story of Mr. Spurgeon's conversion has been often told. He delighted to speak of it himself. It occurred in a Primitive Methodist chapel in Colchester, on Sunday morning, December 15th, 1850. The Baptist preacher had always a kindly regard for the Primitive Methodists; and the memory of his conversion was doubtless the reason of it. His father, in the interview before referred to, said: "Those circumstances are all very clearly in my mind, and I'll relate them to you. As you know, I was, as I remain, in the Congregational Church, and it was to my independent church that I drove over every Sunday from Colchester to Tollesbury. Charles and other members of the family went with me—always some of them—and Charles was going on the Sunday with which I am concerned. This particular Sunday turned out stormy, and Charles could not go. 'You cannot,' his mother said, 'go to Tollesbury; therefore you had better go to the Primitive Methodist chapel'—the Primitive Methodist chapel in Colchester. The preacher in the Primitive Methodist chapel was a local man—a local preacher, who also worked at digging, planting cabbages, and so on.

"There being few people present, on account of the bad day, the local preacher wondered if he would go on. 'I don't think I'll preach,' said the local preacher, but nevertheless he did, and from the text, 'Look unto me,' etc. Everybody knows the words of the extended text which is here meant. Charles heard the sermon and came home, and in the evening attended the Baptist Chapel in Colchester with his mother. We were all together at home later in the evening, when something happened.

"We spent the evening as an evening should be spent, reading the Bible and so on. Then by-and-by I said, 'Come, boys, it's time to go to bed.' 'Father,' remarked Charles, 'I don't want to go to bed yet.' 'Come, come,' said I, whereupon he told me that he wanted to speak with me. We sat up long into the night, and he talked to me of his being saved, which had taken place that day, and right glad was I to hear him talk. 'In the text, "Look, look, look," Charles said to me, holding up his hands, 'I found salvation this morning. In the text, "Accepted in the beloved," preached at the Baptist Church in the evening, I found peace and pardon.' These, I think, were his words, and so was his conversion to salvation brought about."

Many years after Mr. Spurgeon often told the story of his longing after salvation, that never-to-be-forgotten snowy Sunday referred to by his father, his attempt to reach his own chapel and failure to do so, and his walk along the wintry road. He found rather an obscure street, and turned down a court, and there was a little chapel. He wanted to go somewhere, but he did not know this place. It was the Primitive Methodists' chapel. He had heard of these people from many, and how they sang so loudly that they made people's heads ache; but that did not matter. He wanted to know how he might be saved, and if they made his head ache ever so much he did not care. So, sitting down, the service went on, but no minister came. At last a very thin-looking man came into the pulpit, and opened his Bible and read these words: "Look unto me, and be ye saved, all the ends of the earth." It seemed to Spurgeon that he fixed his eyes on him. He said, "Young man, you are in trouble." "Well, I was, sure enough. Says he, 'You will never get out of it unless you look to Christ.' And then lifting up his hands, he cried out, as only I think a Primitive Methodist could do, 'Look, look, look! It is only look,' said he. I saw at once the way of salvation. Oh, how I did leap for joy at that moment! I know not what else he said; I did not take much notice of it—I was so possessed with that one thought. Like as when the brazen serpent was lifted up, they only looked and were healed. I had been waiting to do fifty things, but when I heard this word, 'Look,' what a charming word it seemed to me! Oh, I looked until I could almost have looked my eyes away, and in heaven I will look on still in my joy unutterable." It was the thought of his own conversion, and the manner of it, that made Mr. Spurgeon always in each of his sermons make a special appeal to the unconverted. He thought it a preacher's duty.

Fourteen years after his conversion, on the 11th of October 1864, Mr. Spurgeon preached in the Colchester Chapel, on the occasion of the anniversary of its opening. He took for his text Isaiah xlv. 22. "That," said the preacher, "I heard preached from in this chapel, when the Lord converted me." And pointing to a seat on the left hand, under the gallery, he said, "I was sitting in that pew when I was converted."

Mr. Spurgeon had been brought up among the Independents; both his father and grandfather, as we have seen, being ministers in that denomination. His views, however, of Christian baptism had undergone a change since he had taken up his residence at Newmarket. He had identified himself with the Baptists, believing that their theory and practice as to this ordinance accorded most fully with the teaching of the New Testament. Now that he was converted, he felt it his duty to make a public profession of his faith in Jesus Christ, by being baptised and uniting himself to the Baptist body. On Friday, therefore, the 3rd of May 1851, he was publicly baptised at Isleham, seven miles from Newmarket, by Mr. Cantlow, the Baptist minister of that village. The day was the anniversary of his mother's birth. He arose early to have a couple of hours for quiet prayer and dedication to God. Then he walked eight miles to the spot where he was to be immersed. "What a walk it was!" he said. "What thoughts and prayers thronged my soul during that morning's journey!"

The young soldier of the Cross soon began to fight his Lord's battles. He saw the enemy of God and man busy around, and he resolved to do his best, in Divine strength, to frustrate his designs. He could not be content to be an idler in the Master's vineyard while there was so much work that needed to be done. By various methods of usefulness he sought to spread the Gospel and save souls from death. He became a tract-distributer, and whenever he walked out carried tracts with him for the purpose of giving away. He gave himself to Sunday-school instruction, and not only won the attention and love of the children, but his addresses in the chapel vestry, reported by his youthful hearers in their homes, soon brought the parents to attend and hear. The cause of Foreign Missions engaged his thought. It is said that "at one of the examinations of the school he had consented to deliver an oration on missions. It was a public occasion, and in the company was a clergyman. As the examination proceeded news was brought to the clergyman of the death of his gardener, and he was about to return, but hesitated, and his thoughts ran thus: 'The gardener is dead; I cannot restore his life—I will return and hear what the young usher has to say on missions.' He returned, heard the oration, and was pleased to show his approval by presenting Mr. Spurgeon with a sovereign.' About this time, too, he wrote an essay on Popery, entitled, "Antichrist and her Brood; or, Popery Unmasked." It has not been printed; but the gentleman who offered the prize for which the essay competed sent the writer a handsome sum of money, stating that though the production was not deemed entitled to the premium, yet the donor approved of his zeal, and hoped he might employ his talents for the public good.

From Newmarket Mr. Spurgeon removed to Cambridge, and became teacher in the school of Mr. Henry Leeding, in that university town. He immediately became a member of the Baptist community in Cambridge, and entered upon Christian work there and in the surrounding districts. He was then sixteen years old. He joined a Lay Preachers' Association, and soon had an appointment to preach. His first sermon was preached in a thatch-roofed cottage in the village of Taversham, about four miles from Cambridge. There are several interesting reminiscences of his preaching in those early days. One person remembers a sermon at Somersham, from the text, "Fear not, thou worm Jacob." The boyish voice of the preacher afforded a striking and impressive contrast to the tones of the aged minister who was accustomed to occupy the pulpit. Another person remembers him preaching at Houghton. The sermon was a very impressive one, and any one who could have heard it without seeing the juvenile preacher, would have taken it to be the discourse of a staid and experienced Christian. A village schoolmaster of those days, who was regarded as an authority, was so impressed with the precocious talent of the young preacher, and his style of preaching, that he foretold something of his future renown. His discourses then, as in later years, abounded in illustrations gathered from all sources; especially illustrations derived from history, geography, astronomy, and other branches of his school occupation. These rendered them at once interesting and instructive.

Having set his hand to the plough, Mr. Spurgeon was determined not to look back. His universal acceptance with the people who constituted his congregations encouraged him. Every evening, after his school duties for the day were ended, he gave himself to the work of preaching. Already, at this early period of life, he seemed to feel that preaching was the great business of his life; and could say with Paul, "Necessity is laid upon me; woe is me if I preach not the Gospel." Sometimes he preached in a chapel, at other times in a cottage, and occasionally in the open air. In this way thirteen villages were supplied by this young evangelist with the bread of life. Some idea of the extent of his labours may be formed from a knowledge of the fact that in one year he preached three hundred and sixty-four sermons.

Speaking of this period, in an address delivered to the Metropolitan Tabernacle Country Mission, Mr. Spurgeon said:—" I was for three years a Cambridge man, though I never entered the university. I could not have obtained a degree, because I was a Nonconformist; and, moreover, it was a better thing for me to pursue my studies under an admirable scholar and tender friend, and preach at the same time. I was, by my tutor's own expressed verdict, considered to be sufficiently proficient in my studies to have taken a good place on the list had the way been open. 'You could win in a canter,' said he to me. I had, however, a better college course, for I studied theology as much as possible during the day, and then at five in the evening I became a travelling preacher, and started into the villages to tell out what I had learned. My quiet meditation during the walk helped me to digest what I had read, and the rehearsal of my lesson in public, by preaching it to the people, fixed it on my memory."

MR. SPURGEON'S BIRTHPLACE, AS IT APPEARED IN 1834.

It was indeed most excellent training and practice for the young man; and it had answered so well in his own case that Mr. Spurgeon advised other men to try it. God and His world of nature! What better could there be to fill the young student's thoughts and inspire his imagination? It was no easy task to which he gave himself. He had often to walk seven or eight miles over country fields or muddy roads. He dressed himself in waterproof leggings and a mackintosh hat and coat; and when the night was very dark he carried a lantern so that he might not lose his way. So he trudged on; and, as he afterwards said, " I thought my reading over again while on my legs, and thus worked it into my very soul."

A little company of villagers would be present in a cottage, or a barn, or a farmer's kitchen; and here the boy, for he was no more, broke the bread of life to the people. He used often to smile as he thought of these times. He feared that he had said many odd things, and made many blunders; but his audience was not hypercritical, and he had, as he said, a happy training school, in which by continual practice he attained the degree of ready speech which he afterwards possessed.

His services were very acceptable in many villages; but there was one, a pleasant country place with the pretty name of Waterbeach, about five miles from Cambridge, which has become famous because the boy-preacher of seventeen years was its pastor.

Then, and afterwards, his father urged him to enter Regent's Park College in order the better to prepare for the ministry. He felt the force of the arguments brought to bear upon him; and although he did not wish to take time from his already beloved work of preaching, he yielded to the advice of his elders so far as to make an appointment with Dr. Angus, the tutor of the college which was then at Stepney. The house of Mr. Macmillan, the publisher, was fixed upon as the rendezvous; and thither went young Spurgeon at the appointed time.

He was shown into a room, and there he waited two hours. He did not like to ring the bell for the servant, and so summoned what patience he could, and indeed, as he afterwards said, he "let patience have her perfect work," wondering very much what could be the meaning of the long delay.

The meaning was this. The servant had said nothing of his arrival. Dr. Angus had been shown into another room, and he too waited two hours for his would-be student, of whom we may be sure that he formed no high opinion as to his habits of punctuality.

If an earthquake or lightning flash, or something else, had knocked down the wall that divided the two men, one wonders what effect it would have had upon the man who was to be the greatest preacher of his age.

After he had waited two hours he summoned courage to ring the bell, and the mystery was explained to him; for he was told that Dr. Angus had also arrived promptly at the time agreed upon, but he had grown tired a little earlier than Spurgeon, and had left the house about ten minutes.

"I was disappointed for the moment," said Spurgeon, when relating the occurrence; "but I have a thousand times since then thanked the Lord very heartily for the strange providence which forced my steps into another and far better path."

He went away from Mr. Macmillan's house resolved to write to the College Institution, and make application for admission; but it was on the afternoon of that day that a singular thing occurred, which influenced him strongly, not only at the time, but afterwards.

He had a preaching engagement at Chesterton; and, full of thought and meditation, he walked over Midsummer Common to keep it. When he was about half-way across the common he was startled by a loud voice which seemed to be speaking to him. He heard the words distinctly—"Seekest thou great things for thyself? Seek them not!"

"It may have been a singular illusion," said Mr Spurgeon, years afterwards when referring to it; "but the impression was vivid to an intense degree."

And he never lost it! Even the most carping critic could not accuse Charles Haddon Spurgeon of seeking great things for himself.

As he went on over the wooden bridge to Chesterton he reviewed the situation; and decided that although obscurity and poverty might be before him, he would renounce the idea of collegiate instruction, and work for the souls which he believed God had given into his charge.

For though he was everywhere popular, Waterbeach was enthusiastic. Just before the time when the idea of going to college had been impressed upon him, the little Cambridgeshire village was without a pastor; and the people, seeing, as they thought, in this young man one suited to their requirements, gave him an invitation to settle among them. The success of his labours, under God, justified the wisdom of their choice. The congregation increased till the chapel was crowded to excess; and the church membership rose from forty to nearly one hundred. These were days of hard work, but work faithfully and cheerfully wrought, under the influence of love to Christ and the souls of men. In this obscure field the juvenile pastor was being prepared by the Chief Shepherd for wider and more distinguished usefulness. Events, under the guiding providence of God, were hastening on the day when the prophecy of Richard Knill was to receive its fulfilment. This village preacher, heard only by a few poor and unlettered agricultural congregations, was destined in a few years to become the most extensively known and useful preacher of the Gospel in the world.

How happy he was at Waterbeach may be told in his own words, written at the time:—

"God sends such sunshine on my path, such smiles of grace, that I cannot regret if I have forfeited all my prospects for it. I am conscious I held back from love to God and His cause; and I had rather be poor in His service than rich in my own. I have all that heart can wish for; yea, God giveth more than my desire. My congregation is as great and loving as ever. During all the time I have been at Waterbeach I have had a different house for my home every day. Fifty-two families have thus taken me in; and I have still six other invitations not yet accepted. Talk about the people not caring for me, because they give me so little! I dare tell anybody under heaven 'tis false! They do all they can. Our anniversary passed off grandly; six were baptised; crowds on crowds stood by the river; the chapel was afterwards crammed, both to the tea and the sermon."

Dearly as they loved him the people at Waterbeach soon began to fear that they must lose him, for so great a genius could scarcely be held by so small a place. There are still people left who can remember him, and who say that he preached like a man a century old in experience. He spoke with a straightforwardness that was positively terrible, and uttered terrific warnings to those who were indulging in sin.

One day Mr. Spurgeon was attending the anniversary of the Cambridgeshire Sunday School Union, and as usual he made a speech fluent and racy, but earnest and convincing. Among his hearers was a man who was especially struck by his appearance and ability. A short time after this man met a friend who told him a doleful story of the decay of the church of which he was a member—the Baptist Church meeting in New Park Street Chapel, Southwark, which then stood in great need of a man sent from God to raise it from its dejected condition.

Then did the listener to Spurgeon's Sunday-school address tell what he knew of the young preacher of Waterbeach.

"That is the man for you," he said. "If any one can heal the breaches and restore the waste places, Charles Spurgeon can do it."

But the hint was not acted upon until it had been repeated during a second interview between the two friends. Then the New Park Street man began to have hope; and soon after a strange thing happened to the young preacher.

He had walked one Sunday morning from Cambridge to Waterbeach as usual. The day was cold, and the walk of four or five miles was turned to the best possible account as a preparation for the day's services.

Arrived at the chapel, he sat down for a few minutes' rest in the table pew. A letter was brought to him bearing a London postmark. The young man opened the letter with some curiosity. It contained an invitation to him to preach at New Park Street Chapel, Southwark, and occupy the pulpit which had formerly been occupied by Dr. Rippon.

Dr. Rippon's hymn-book was before him; he had been about to choose the hymns for the service from it, and the name of the great compiler thus brought into connection with young Spurgeon filled him with awe.

"There must be some mistake here!" he said, as he passed the letter to the deacon who would presently give out the hymns.

"I am afraid there is no mistake," replied the deacon, shaking his head. "I have always known that some big church or other would try to run away with our minister before long."

But it was time to commence the service, into which the preacher entered so heartily that, as he afterwards said, he put both the letter and the thought of it so completely away that he forgot all about it until the day was over

On the following morning he answered the letter. He told the writer that he had fallen into an error in directing his invitation to Waterbeach, as the Baptist minister of that village was only about nineteen years of age, and quite unfitted to bear the responsibility of a London pulpit.

The reply to that was to the effect that the writer of the first letter was quite aware of what he had done, that he had made no mistake, and knew the correct age of the Mr. Spurgeon to whom he had addressed his letter. He repeated the invitation, and named a date, giving at the same time the address of some lodgings in London at which it would be convenient for him to stay.

Mr. Spurgeon accepted the invitation, and on a memorable Saturday afternoon in December 1853 he made his way to the boarding-house in Queen's Square, Bloomsbury, to which he had been directed, in order to spend the night, and prepare to preach his first sermon in London.

The young man from the country did not enjoy that first night in the great city.

There were other young men in the boarding-house, and he felt as if they quizzed him. Perhaps they did, for he confessed that he wore a huge black satin stock, and used a blue handkerchief with white spots. He told them that he had come up to preach, and they appeared greatly amused at the idea. They told him a little about the great preachers of London, their learning, their matchless oratory, and the large congregations of great men who thronged to hear them. Poor Spurgeon! He never forgot the depressing effects of that Saturday evening, and he thus recalled its discomforts—"On the narrow bed he tossed in solitary misery, and found no pity. Pitiless was the grind of the cabs in the street, pitiless the recollection of the city clerks, whose grim propriety had gazed upon our rusticity with such amusement, pitiless the spare room, which scarce afforded space to kneel, pitiless even the gas-lamps which seemed to wink at us as they flickered amid the December darkness. He had no friend in that city full of human beings, but feeling among strangers and foreigners, hoped to be helped through the scrape into which we had been brought, and to escape safely to the serene abodes of Cambridge and Waterbeach, which then seemed to be Eden itself."

Many a young man has had the same feelings on coming first to London; but was ever young man before sent to the city to do so grand a work of salvation for it as the Waterbeach Baptist little minister?

CHAPTER III.

NEW PARK STREET CHAPEL.

THE history of the New Park Street Chapel may be almost said to be the history of Nonconformity in London; and an excellent historian is the Rev. Godfrey Holden Pike. He was not, however, the first Baptist historian, for "Thomas Crosby, teacher of mathematicks upon Horsleydown," wrote *The History of the English Baptists*, from which it appears that the Society at Southwark comes from a very ancient stock indeed.

The first Baptists, "grave professors, and very severe moralists," were compelled by the dangers and persecutions of their time to meet in private houses, but they had a pastor, William Rider, who is claimed by the Tabernacle Church as its first minister. He was followed by Benjamin Keach, who took charge of the Baptists of Southwark in 1668. He was at that time twenty-eight years old, and was already known as an able evangelist. He was several times seized and bound and imprisoned for preaching. He wrote a book called *The Child's Instructor; or, A New and Easy Primer*, which gave great offence, and for which he was summoned to the Aylesbury Assizes, and charged with being a seditious, schismatic person, evilly and maliciously disposed. The sentence passed on him was that he should go to gaol for a fortnight, stand upon the pillory at Aylesbury in the open market for two hours on two occasions,

DR. GILL AT NEW PARK STREET.

pay twenty pounds, have his book burnt before his face by the common hangman, and renounce his doctrines. The sentence was completed upon him, all excepting the last part of it; but Keach never renounced his doctrines, and it was past the power of any one to make him. Mr. Pike says, "The chapel in Southwark in Keach's time presented to the casual observer anything but an unpicturesque appearance. In front of the meeting-house was a court bounded by a brick wall, and a peep through the iron gates would have shown a pretty avenue of limes leading to the principal entrance." Crosby, the historian, married one of the daughters of Keach, and another became the wife of Benjamin Stinton, who succeeded him. Next to him came John Gill, of Kettering, the author of the *Exposition of the Whole New Testament*, a very learned scholar and divine. His removal from Kettering to London was a distinct Nonconformist gain to the city. It was in 1724 that Gill commenced the Commentary that fills nine folio volumes. He preached one hundred and twenty-two sermons from the texts of Solomon's Song on consecutive Sunday mornings, and these were afterwards published. Their merits were so great that Hervey formed a friendship with their author on account of them. Gill was acknowledged to be the greatest divine of the Baptist body. He was witty as well as profound. There is a story told of an old lady who came to the Doctor to complain of the tunes which were used.

"What tunes would you like, madam?" asked Dr. Gill.

"I should like some of David's tunes," was the reply.

"Well, madam, if you will get David's tunes for us we will try to sing them," was the rejoinder.

Dr. Gill died in 1771, at the age of seventy-four, and in the fifty-third year of his ministry.

John Rippon was Dr. Gill's successor, and he laboured for sixty-three years in Southwark. During his pastorate the almshouses were founded. Rippon's Hymn-Book, in use in many Dissenting churches to-day, had an immense success, and realised great profits. But other works of his were less successful. It is to be regretted that he did not complete one which he commenced, "A History of Bunhill Fields Burial-Ground," for this would have been of great historical value.

After Dr. Rippon's death, at the age of eighty-five, in the year 1836, Dr. Angus became the minister of the church, but he resigned the position in 1841 for other work in Regent's Park College, and he was succeeded by the Rev. James Smith, and then by the Rev. W. Walters.

But it seemed that the church had passed its zenith. Many other Nonconformist places of worship abounded; the old supporters removed from the neighbourhood; "the pews were forsaken, the aisles were a picture of desolation, the exchequer was empty." That which might have been expected came; for, as Mr. Pike says, "The process of decay had bred apathy in the few remaining members, and sadness in the breasts of the deacons, who could devise no means of staying the catastrophe they dreaded—the disappearance from Southwark of a dear old Christian landmark."

Such was the state of things on that never-to-be-forgotten morning when the young minister from Waterbeach walked along Holborn Hill toward Blackfriars and Southwark Bridge, "praying, fearing, hoping, believing." The first sight of the New Park Street Chapel dismayed him, it looked so large and fine. It was capable of seating twelve hundred people; but it was six times too large for the congregation which first listened to Charles Spurgeon. Perhaps the very smallness of the number gave him courage. In any case, he enjoyed his first Sunday in London, and as he returned at night to his lodgings in Southwark he "wanted no pity from any one, and cared not a penny for the young gentlemen lodgers and their miraculous ministers, nor for the grind of the cabs, nor for anything else under the sun."

He was asked to go again, and he did so, and in less than a month was invited to preach for six months; but when three of these had passed he received a cordial and unanimous invitation to become the pastor. The letter in which he wrote his acceptance deserves to be printed in letters of gold. It is to be found in Mr. Pike's *Sketches of Nonconformity in Southwark*, where it was reproduced by permission of its writer. It breathes a spirit of beautiful humility. We quote but one sentence: "Remember my youth and inexperience; pray that these may not hinder my usefulness."

It was indeed his youth that seemed to be his great charm. "The Boy Preacher" soon began to be talked of everywhere. But they gave him more than a youth's work to do; and if he had been a thousand men instead of one, he could soon have found a thousand chapels in which to preach. Deacons went up to London from all parts of the country to hear him, and they all took back the same report. "Young Spurgeon is wonderful! We must get him, if possible, to preach at our anniversary services!"

As for the deacons of New Park Street, it was little wonder that they loved the young man who had brought them such a marvellous return of prosperity, though they loved him quite as much for himself as for what he did. But it was a grand sight to see the people who flocked to hear him from week to week. The congregation had so increased that "the chapel in the evening, when the gas was burning, was like the Black-hole of Calcutta. One evening, in 1854, the preacher exclaimed, 'By faith the walls of Jericho fell down, and by faith this wall at the back shall come down too!' An aged and prudent deacon, in somewhat domineering terms, observed to him at the close of the sermon, 'Let us never hear of that again!' 'What do you mean?' said the preacher; 'you will hear no more about it *when it is done*, and therefore the sooner you set about doing it the better.'"

At length it became absolutely necessary that something should be done to provide increased accommodation for the crowds who came, not only as occasional hearers, but who desired to form part of the regular congregation. A meeting was held to consider the matter; enlargement was decided on; and a fund was forthwith started to meet the required cost. The chapel was closed, and Exeter Hall, Strand, taken for Sunday services during the alterations. The first sermon was preached in the hall on Sunday, 11th February 1855, and Mr. Spurgeon continued to preach there till the last Sunday in May following. The place was crowded to overflowing Sunday after Sunday; and newspaper paragraphs announced that the Strand was blocked up by the multitudes who flocked to hear "a young man called Spurgeon preaching in Exeter Hall." A writer in *The Friend*, who was himself a member of the Society of Friends, but had been to hear the "young man," thus speaks of him and his preaching:—"The crowds which had been drawn to hear him, the interest excited by his ministry, and the conflicting opinions expressed in reference to his qualifications and usefulness, have been altogether without parallel in modern times. It was a remarkable sight to see this round-faced country youth thus placed in a position of such solemn and arduous responsibility, yet addressing himself to the fulfilment of its onerous duties with a gravity, self-possession, and vigour that proved him well fitted to the task he had assumed. In a few weeks the empty pews were crowded; every sitting in the chapel was let; and ere twelve months had elapsed the eagerness to hear him had become so great that every standing-place within the walls was occupied on each Sabbath; and it soon became evident that increased accommodation must be provided."

AN OVERCROWDED CHAPEL.

In the early part of June, New Park Street Chapel was re-opened. It had been enlarged to the fullest extent of the ground; and accommodation for upwards of three hundred additional persons had been furnished, in addition to which a large and commodious vestry and schoolroom had been erected—the schoolroom being erected along the side of the chapel, with windows which could be let down, to allow those who were seated in the school to hear the preacher. Notwithstanding all the enlargement, Mr. Spurgeon and his friends were more inconvenienced than ever. Every Sunday hundreds had to be turned away; and those who gained admission were so tightly packed, and the heat was so excessive, that the distraction was most destructive of peaceful and devout worship. It was obvious at once that soon something further would have to be done.

Various journals began to call attention to this new metropolitan sensation. Paragraphs and letters appeared both for and against. Enemies were sometimes very bitter. Absurd stories were freely circulated at the preacher's expense; and in some cases base and cruel falsehoods were invented and passed from one to another to do their deadly work. Gross pictorial caricatures were exhibited in the print-sellers' windows. The fury of the foolish was vain. God made the wrath of men to praise Him by overruling it for the increased fame and usefulness of His servant.

It was at this time, when he was in the midst of his early popularity, that he paid his first visit to Scotland. He preached in Glasgow on Sundays, 22nd and 29th July 1855. Long before the hour of beginning service the spacious churches in which he preached were in each case crowded, and thousands anxious to gain admission were unable. The *Glasgow Examiner* was at that time ably edited by a gentleman who published in its columns, week by week, critiques on the "Scottish Clergy," with reports of a sermon or two by each preacher. The following article, written by this gentleman, appeared in the *Examiner* the second week after Mr. Spurgeon preached. It is a masterly and discriminating review by an impartial and competent judge, and is worthy of preservation in connection with this record of the great preacher's life.

The writer thus begins:—" The way moth-eaten routine generally settles off any one who dares to break away from its old time-worn tracks is by pronouncing him an empiric. Galileo, Columbus, Luther, Knox, the Apostle Paul, even the Author of Christianity Himself, were, by the accredited orthodoxy of their day, stigmatised as empirics; and so will it be with any one who ventures to do or say otherwise than according to the existing modes and fashions. We are not to be understood as saying that routine is in itself bad, or that every departure from it is wise or commendable. On the contrary, the highest effort of human wisdom is to methodise, whether it be the menial duties of a household, the discoveries of science, or the speculations of philosophy. To rail against routine merely because it is routine, is to arraign that wisdom, and contemn those Divine laws, which have tracked infinitude with orbits, which have appointed each star its appointed times and seasons, and have sustained the sublime harmony of the universe from ages lost in the depths of a past eternity. To depart, or to attempt to depart, from a well-established routine, is much oftener an act of ignorance or folly than of sound judgment; yet, as man's knowledge and experience are always limited, the best system of routine must therefore be imperfect, and will, at certain periods, require to be broken up and revolutionised. Routine in religious services is extremely liable to beget a listless, lukewarm compliance with its prescribed forms, while the spirit or *animus* gradually subsides. The preacher speaks his usual time; the people sit patiently enough, perhaps; a few may even listen; the usual number of verses are sung, and the business of the day is over; there is generally no more about it. No one can deny that this is more or less than a simple statement of the real state of matters in the majority of our churches at the present day. Should the minister during his discourse sharpen his intellect with a sprinkling of snuff, let fall his handkerchief on the Psalm-book, or give one thump louder than usual with the fist ecclesiastic, that will be noted, remembered, and commented on, while there is all but total oblivion of the subject and the nature of the discussion. To break up this deadening process, to shake the dry bones and make them live, ought to be the great aim of the preacher of the present day; but it is not every one who can do it. Affectation of manner or style won't do it; talent, we may say genius, of a peculiar nature is required; and we have no hesitation in saying that Mr. Spurgeon possesses the requisites in an unusual degree.

"No doubt many respectable and sensible men, when hearing only of the odd, and to them uncanonical, expressions of this young preacher, would be very apt to find the word 'empiric,' or 'quack,' upon their tongue's end. We must ourselves plead guilty to some such expression when we first heard of this youth, unsystematic training, and official boldness. We, in common with our fellow-citizens, had seen and heard so much of boy-preaching, lay-preaching, and bold-preaching, that there was nothing uncharitable in entertaining some doubts of his intrinsic excellence; still, that large London audiences daily waited on his ministry was a fact that could not be stifled with a sneer. It could not be any novelty in the theme itself, as there were thousands of preachers, and millions of books and tracts, dilating on it before Mr. Spurgeon made his appearance; it could not be any new doctrine, for this was the same as John Calvin preached centuries ago, and circumstantially the same as that preached by all the evangelical denominations around him; neither could it be his youth, as there are in the churches of Britain scores of preachers as young as he is; neither could it be the few *outré* sentences that were scattered through his discourses, for there are many in London who say stranger and odder things than any that he has yet uttered. But what was the character of these crowds that went to hear him? Were they the profane, the ignorant and illiterate, the light-hearted and frivolous young people of the metropolis? There might have been some of these among the many; but, as far as we can learn, they were fair examples of the respectable church-going community, perfectly capable of judging rationally on all subjects that engross public attention. We maintain that no man could have sustained such excitement, and kept together such crowds of people for two or three years, unless he was possessed of more than ordinary gifts. But we do not now require to judge him by the effects of his preaching on a metropolitan crowd.

"He has appeared amongst us, and the London verdict has been fully confirmed by immense audiences, that have been equally spell-bound by his oratory. According to reports, he indulged somewhat freely in the out-of-the-way expressions on the first Sabbath of his sojourn in this city; but such was not the case last Sabbath, and the last Sabbath's discourses were still more fascinating and attractive. In the first place there is about him that hearty, open, English frankness which has no hesitation in giving full and free utterance to its opinions, loves, and dislikes. Then there is the ready, acute perception which never fails to bring out fresh and striking illustrations from any text on which the attention is directed. Again, there is an extensive acquaintance with literature, which, by the aid of a retentive memory, can at a moment's notice furnish the speaker with choice and appropriate material. And lastly, there is a power of voice, and volubility of utterance, which enable him to get on with great ease, and at the same time to give powerful effect to his sentiments. We may have heard many preachers who could reason more correctly and profoundly, who displayed more classical elegance and polish, but we have not heard one who can more powerfully arrest the attention and carry the sympathies of an audience along with him."

After giving a full report of the two sermons preached on the previous Sabbath, the reviewer thus proceeds:—

"We have deemed it necessary to give a pretty full report of the preceding discourses for various reasons. There are many under the impression that the discourses of Mr. Spurgeon are remarkable only for bold and daring assertions, for oddities and eccentricities, for vapid declamation and rodomontade, and for an absence of all the higher qualities of pulpit instruction. This notion has been communicated partly by anecdotes of his preaching on their rounds in ecclesiastical society, and partly by certain notices in various periodicals. Though such ideas are dissipated by a perusal of the various published discourses of this preacher, many of our readers may not have seen his discourses, and have necessarily derived all their knowledge of him through the channels stated. We find it therefore necessary, in the outset, to report what he said in our city last Sabbath, and we can give most satisfactory evidence—the evidence of thousands of our fellow-citizens who heard these discourses —that we have kept back nothing, but have given a fair, though a necessarily abridged report of the services, assuring them that these discourses are faithfully reported. We shall deal with them as they are given, and those who may marvel that there is so little singular or *outré* in them, have only to procure his published discourses, and they will find their contents similar. The candid reader, whatever may have been his prepossessions, will, after perusing the above, admit that there is little or nothing objectionable either in the subject, matter, or style. If there be any who assume that orthodox theology is so stereotyped as to forbid all originality of illustration, or too sacred to allow the fair things and lovely of nature to shadow it forth, then is it evident that to such the preceding will appear objectionable. Those, too, who think that preaching the Gospel is the harping on one or two cardinal points, or the repetition of some favourite dogma in language strictly ecclesiastical, must be offended with the freedom, independence, and variety of the preacher's style and thoughts. Instead of limiting himself to commonplace illustrations, he opens his eyes on nature, on science, on society, and gathers from them all that he reckons suitable to illuminate his subject Instead of confining himself to the language of the schools, and of divines and theologians, he ransacks all the stores of literature, and reckons not a sentence disqualified to take a place in his discourse because it was coined or used by a Shakespeare, a Scott, a Johnson, or even a Burns. Language hitherto reckoned fit only for plays, novels, and songs, is seized by this preacher, and oftentimes most ingeniously and aptly brought into his discussions. We do not inquire whether in every case the sentiments and language are appropriate, but refer to the fact that such is his independence, that he, with equal freedom, selects from sacred writers; and such is his miraculous power of assimilation, that what would come from others as a motley, incoherent mass, becomes in his hand unique, complete, and beautiful.

"The arrangement of his discourses is simple, rememberable, and textual. The outline arises naturally out of the text, and is scarcely less striking than the facts, anecdotes, and arguments employed in the illustration of the different parts of the discourse; as he uses no notes, he is occasionally tempted to depart from the straight line of argument, but he recovers his position with a miraculous ease and grace. Nor will the judicious critic find much to censure in the sentiments. Doctrines are stated broadly and plainly, and some disputed points are settled very unceremoniously

The doctrine of election, effectual calling, and perseverance are very frequently, and, occasionally, somewhat unnecessarily introduced; but as the preacher deems them essential, he feels that he must use great plainness of speech. Though it has been extensively circulated that his prayers are irreverent, presumptuous, and blasphemous, there was nothing in them on Sabbath last which could with truth be so characterised. On the contrary, they were correct, appropriate, and beautiful. He certainly has not followed the usual pulpit style, but has opened his eyes on the state of society in all its forms and phases, and adapted his confessions, and petitions, and thanksgivings. He confesses the peculiar sins of the times, as well as the inherent and changeless depravity of man's nature; the sins of the parlour, of the counting-house, and public assembly; the sins of individuals, families, and nations. He offers petitions for various classes and characters—for the profligate and careless, for the old, the young, and for little children; petitions for churches, for nations, for the world, all in a somewhat novel manner. While he gives thanks for special blessings, and employs language which none but the genuine believer can appropriate, and which even *he* must sometimes acknowledge with hesitancy, he forgets not the common benefits which all share, and the common blessings with which all are crowned.

"We have heard much of undue familiarities and daring impieties, but witnessed none of them. There were an earnestness, an unction, a fluency, and an urgency, which are but too seldom imitated.

"His reading and exposition of the Word of God we reckon exceedingly good. Every word receives its proper emphasis and tone, and his remarks are generally terse, original, and instructive. We prefer to hear the chapter read first, and the remarks afterwards; but though he expounds as he goes along, he does it in a style which is almost unobjectionable, as the remarks are mostly designed to call attention to the precise and delicate shades of meaning which he wishes to bring out.

"His preaching is altogether peculiar, and not very easily described. Probably the following may convey to the reader some idea of it. Some preachers owe much to their *personnel*, or presence in the pulpit. Before they open their mouths, there is something about them which causes a sort of awe and respect to creep over the audience. The appearance of this preacher may be said to be interesting rather than commanding. He is quite a youth, and his countenance boyish. He is under, rather than over, the middle size, and has few or none of the physical advantages of the orator in his appearance. But what he lacks in appearance he has in reality. Soon as he commences to speak, tones of richest melody are heard. A voice full, sweet, and musical falls on every ear, and awakens agreeable emotions in every soul in which there is a sympathy for sounds. That most excellent of voices is under perfect control, and can whisper or thunder at the wish of its possessor. And there is poetry in every feature and every movement, as well as music in the voice. The countenance speaks—the entire form sympathises. The action is in complete unison with the sentiments, and the eye *listens* scarcely less than the ear to the sweetly flowing oratory. But among the thirty thousand English preachers, and the three thousand Scotch ones, there are many sweet voices as well as this, and many who have studied the art of speaking with the greatest assiduity, and yet they fail to attract an audience. Mr Spurgeon is more than a 'voice crying'; he has rare powers of observation, recollection, assimilation, and creation. His field of observation is wide and varied. He seems to have opened his eyes to *nature* in all its varieties, to *science* in all its discoveries, and to *literature* in all its departments. Everything which the eye of man can look upon, or the ear hear, seems to have made an indelible impression on his mental powers. The impression is not only distinctly made, but ineradicably maintained. Every mountain, every valley, every book, every sentence, which has once come in his way, becomes for ever fixed in his recollection. And not only fixed, but becomes the material on which marvellous powers of assimilation vigorously operate. Out of the forms of beauty which his eyes see, other still lovelier forms are created. The loveliest natural landscape is adorned with additional beauty by the aid of a refined and chastened fancy. The thoughts that have come floating down from the long bygone ages are placed in the crucible of his mind, and, purged of the objectionable, come out bearing his own image and superscription. There is evidently in him great power of *assimilative* genius, and occasional indications of even a higher order of genius—even that which creates fresh and new forms of beauty, which bear the distinct mark of his own mind.

"These higher qualities are evidently greatly aided by a close study of the graces of speaking. The natural had been aided by study—the gifts of the orator by the graces. Despite an occasional neglect of all the laws of logic and ratiocination, there are evidently a thorough knowledge and appreciation of both. The *negligée* sometimes forms a pleasing contrast with the precise. The bow drawn at a venture may send the arrow more direct to the mark than the bow drawn according to the strictest rules.

"Do we then pronounce the eloquent occupier of Park Street Chapel pulpit faultless as an orator? We shall never attempt anything so incongruous as to measure him according to the standard of others. The man that, at all hours of the day, and all days of the week, has allured by his preaching thousands of the London citizens, where all sorts of extravagance has been so long doing its utmost, is not to be tied down in details to the routine of others. His popularity gives him no licence to utter error or to conceal the truth; but it does allow him a licence of illustration, of manner, and of action, peculiarly his own. Nor do the multitudes at his feet warrant him to look up to Jehovah with feelings one whit less reverent than the beggar on the dunghill. There is danger in such a case as his of neglecting to cultivate the humble, hallowed, and contrite heart; of forgetting the immeasurable distance between the creature and the Creator—the lofty One who inhabiteth eternity and the creatures of His hand. Beyond all things, there is a danger of speaking of sacred as of common things, and of naming that august name, at which angels bow, as we name an earthly friend. Constant familiarity with holy things requires a constant watch on the spirit, and he who speaks of Jehovah and of the Redeemer of man as he would of his acquaintance, is deficient in his ideas of himself and of his relationship with the universe and its Maker.

"The English press has gone the entire length in both its praise and its censure. He has been denounced as mean in stature, inexpressive in countenance, and contemptible in intellect. On the same day his *personnel* has been extolled as attractive, his intellectual power tremendous, and his oratory overwhelming. He has heard voices innumerable denouncing him, and voices innumerable admiring him. Many a pen has been dipped in gall by jealous rivals, and many a pen in honey by generous critics. All this has been said, and all this written, and Mr. Spurgeon still lives, and lives in the affection of thousands. The crowds which congregated on Sabbath last to hear him in this city were not greater than the crowds that every Sabbath flock to his meeting-house in London. He heeds not his accusers; he has no time to receive the gratulations of his friends, but preaches on; and as he preaches, the printing-press takes up the subject, and gives it a circulation much wider than human voice can reach. Sentences picked from his discourses have been printed for the not very enviable purpose of damaging his popularity; but the effect is the reverse. That popularity steadily increases, and has already risen from the humbler to the higher classes. One has gone away from hearing him, professing to be very much disgusted with his *egotism;* another with his ignorance; a third with the impudence of the *young man;* a fourth with the profanity and daring impieties that he uttered; but he preached on, and the crowds were greater than before.

"Some have said, 'Oh, it is very easy getting up a crowd in London.' Let such try the experiment, and they will find fact correct theory. There have been few clergymen in England able to attract crowds for any length of time; and not one, either at present or in the past, has for so many months allured daily such immense congregations We state this as a fact, and allow his detractors to account for it as they best can. Those who have nothing to say against him but his youth might profit by a perusal of the reply of William Pitt, when a similar charge was brought against him. He said: 'The atrocious crime of being a *young* man, which the honourable gentleman has, with such spirit and decency, charged upon me, I shall neither attempt to palliate nor deny, but content myself with wishing that I may be one of those whose follies may cease with their youth, and not of those who continue ignorant in spite of age and experience.'"

A writer in another paper, the *Glasgow Daily Bulletin*, says of him in connection with the other two sermons preached during this visit:—"Mr. Spurgeon owes his celebrity to the possession of first-class oratorical gifts, which seem to have attained maturity of development at a very early age, so that he has established a reputation at a period of life earlier than that at which ordinary men enter upon a profession. His appearance indicates him somewhat beyond his actual age; and, like his great model, Whitfield, he seems blessed with 'no constitution'; that is, he is endowed with a voice strong, clear, bell-like, which could be heard by an audience of very many thousands; and with a physical frame equal to a vast amount of hard work. In contour of face he reminds us somewhat of the Rev. John Caird, and the eye has the lustrous light of genius in it. You cannot listen for a few minutes to the bright-eyed boy, whether he be preaching or pleading in prayer, without feeling that no mere clap-trap rhetorician is before you. There is a force and massiveness about his thoughts and language, a touching, compelling sincerity, which give us the best idea we have ever had of the great early preachers. Like some of these —like Rowland Hill, or like Whitfield, of later times—he descends to a homeliness of illustration, to anecdotage, even to mimicry—a dangerous style, for great taste must be always exercised along with it; but in the ability to pass from the homely or the grotesque to the dizzy heights of the imagination, the real power of the orator is seen. The impression is too vivid to permit of our entering on any critical review of the discourses of the day—the subject of the one, 'The Saviour on the Tree,' and of the other, 'The Lamb upon the Throne'—suffice it to say, that, as most brilliant and thrilling appeals, we have rarely heard them equalled—certainly, in some points of effect, never surpassed."

The newspapers were compelled, whether they wished or not, to notice the new preacher who was moving everywhere he went immense congregations to earnestness; and every newspaper article, whether written in a sympathetic or antagonistic spirit, increased the desire of those who read to hear the man for themselves.

CHAPTER IV.

MARRIAGE, FAME, TROUBLE, AND USEFULNESS.

ON the 8th of January 1856, Charles Haddon Spurgeon was married to Miss Susanna Thompson, the daughter of Mr. Robert Thompson, of Falcon Square, London. The service was in his own chapel, in the presence of a large company of his own personal friends, and was conducted by Dr. Alexander Fletcher. It is said that two thousand tried and failed to get in. The service was simple, but very interesting. First they sang "Salvation! oh, the joyful sound," and Dr. Fletcher's prayer for them was especially fervent. Never had young couple more hearty good wishes than these two; for the people loved them greatly. After the ceremony they went away for their honeymoon to the Continent and had a royal time, though even from the first Mr. Spurgeon did not take as long holidays as he needed; and the young people were home and at work again after a few weeks.

His marriage was a very happy one so far as love could make it so; but Mrs. Spurgeon, though she has survived her husband, has been a sufferer during nearly the whole of their married life.

Mr. Spurgeon was soon hard at work again. In March he was preaching in Hanover Square Rooms on behalf of the Ragged Schools in that neighbourhood. The month after he lectured for the Young Men's Christian Association at

Newington. On this occasion he described his own method of getting at the meaning of hard texts of Scripture. He said that when books failed him, he offered this prayer: "O Lord, teach me what this means."

At this period he was preaching daily, often twice a day, and sometimes thrice, travelling throughout the length and breadth of the land. For months together he preached twelve sermons every week, often travelling many miles between the services held. Weak churches, and pastors with small incomes, found in him, in this way, a generous helper and friend. It is said that, when preaching for his poorer brethren in different parts of the country, he declined to receive even his personal expenses, except where the church could afford to pay them. All this time there was great division of opinion as to his merits and motives; and while the common people especially heard him gladly, many and grave were the predictions of some of the leaders of the Christian church, affirmative of speedy failure and collapse.

The way in which he was received at first by his own denomination may be learnt from the following review of the first volume of *The New Park Street Pulpit*, which appeared in the Baptist newspaper, *The Freeman*, of 27th February 1856:—"We are not fond of criticising sermons. There is a sacredness about the messages delivered under the authority of Christ that should protect them in general, not only from animadversions, but altogether from the ordinary sentences of the judgment. They are appeals to the heart, suggested and commanded by the Spirit of God; and when the matter is so weighty, and so vastly beyond the powers of the human intellect to estimate, it seems an unworthy, if not a sinful cavilling to dwell upon the peccadilloes of the preacher's manner. So that we are entering on a task to-day which we would rather have avoided.

"Particularly would we have shunned it in the present

AGE 21.   AGE 36.

AGE 30.   AGE 54

PORTRAITS OF MR. SPURGEON.
(By permission of the Proprietor of the *Strand Magazine*.)

instance, for the complaint rings loudly in our ears, resounding from various circles in society, and echoed by some portion of the press, that Mr. Spurgeon has not been fairly dealt with; that his own denomination is more unjust than any; and that the leading men of it are amongst his foremost detractors. It is a dangerous task, under such circumstances, for a critic to speak candidly all that he thinks. However, this volume has been sent to us for review; and though we would rather have preserved silence, we do not feel that it would be right to shrink from the challenge that has thus been given. We shall speak honestly what we think, and speak it, we hope, in the spirit of Christian charity.

"Mr. Spurgeon is unquestionably a phenomenon, a star, a meteor, or, at all events, something strange and dazzling in the horizon of the 'religious world.' The old lights have gone down, and since Irving, and Hall, and Chalmers 'fell asleep,' there has been no preacher that has created a 'sensation' at all compared with the young preacher of New Park Street Chapel. But do not let our readers imagine that they have found here a luminary of the same class with those we have just named. Whatever Mr. Spurgeon's merits may be—and he has some rare ones—they are of a very different order from those which distinguished the mighty preachers of the last generation. They were all men of gigantic reasoning powers, of refined taste, of profound scholarship, and of vast theological learning. Of all these qualities Mr. Spurgeon has little enough; nor, to do him justice, does he pretend to any of them, except, perhaps, in some unlucky moments, to the last. But it will probably be agreed to by all competent judges, that neither Irving, nor Hall, nor even Chalmers, was so well fitted to carry the Gospel to the poor and ignorant as is this modern orator of the pulpit. Their writings will last for many generations and will be as fresh to the latest as they are to-day; Mr.

Spurgeon's sermons will, perhaps, soon be forgotten for ever, but they go to the hearts of the multitude; and as he has the good sense to know the direction in which his talent lies, he promises to be incomparably useful in a class of society which preachers too often complain is utterly beyond their reach.

"A lively imagination, sometimes rising to the region of poetry, but more frequently delighting in homely and familiar figures of speech; a free colloquial manner of address, that goes directly to the understanding of the simplest; and an enthusiastic ardour, that must prove catching to all his hearers, unless they are more than usually insensible, are the chief legitimate attractions of Mr. Spurgeon's style; and they are qualities so rare in their combination, and are in him so strongly developed, as to stamp him, in our judgment, with the decided impress of genius. We should suppose that it must be impossible to hear him without acquiring for him a sentiment of respect; for, if offended by his extravagances, as the thoughtful certainly will be, the offence is so immediately atoned for by some genuine outburst of feeling, that you remember that his extravagances are but the errors of a youth, and that the material on which these excrescences appear is that out of which apostles and martyrs have, in every age, been fashioned. You pardon his follies, for they are nothing else, for the sake of his unquestionable sincerity and impassioned zeal. You wish it had been possible that a mind so gifted might have received more culture before it was called into its present dangerous position; but finding it as it is, you accept it with gratitude, and pray God, the All-wise, to be its guide and protector.

"We rejoice so heartily in Mr. Spurgeon's success, and so thoroughly desire to see it prolonged and increased, that we trust we shall be pardoned if we point out some of the flaws which we perceive in these printed discourses, where they are less likely to abound than in their actual delivery from the pulpit, but which are so serious, even here, that we doubt not they have given rise to much of that hostile criticism of which Mr. Spurgeon, or his admirers, so bitterly complain. We shall not speak of his fluent eloquence, sometimes rushing into rant, nor of his imaginative flights that sometimes soar so high, that they only reach sublimity and fall on 't'other side;' these are but trivial blemishes that a few more years will inevitably efface. The faults we speak of are rather moral than intellectual, and need the more to be corrected, because they else will grow more palpable and grievous with the lapse of time. Even his doctrinal inconsistencies—so ably exposed of late in the *Christian Spectator*, in a paper which we hope he has read and prayed over—are of inferior moment, for they also would doubtless disappear as study and reflection came to his assistance. The faults we deplore are faults which have their seat elsewhere, and must be sources of weakness as long as they continue, and, if indulged, will prove disastrous to the last degree.

"Perhaps, indeed, we should be right in summing them all up in one—the vice of vanity; for they all seem to spring from this fruitful root. This may originate his daring method of expounding Holy Writ, his intense egotism, and his habit of decrying his fellow-Christians and fellow-ministers. And these, we fear, are the illegitimate attractions which help to swell his popularity; though we sincerely believe that Mr. Spurgeon would be the first himself to rebuke the followers who loved him for such faults. It is amusing, but it is also painful, to hear a young man of twenty-one speaking of his experience, as if he had lived threescore years and ten. Surely some sort of glamour must invest him when he says, 'I have always found through life,' or his audience would burst into a titter; but 'tis far worse to find him denouncing 'Arminians' (whose creed he evidently does not understand) in almost every sermon. Our blessed Lord did, indeed, denounce the Pharisees, but then they were hypocrites, which Mr. Spurgeon does not even fancy the Arminians to be; and if they were so, this young pulpit orator is not quite armed with the authority of inspiration. It is sad to see so young a man so deeply imbued with the *odium theologium.* And though we cannot but hope that as his knowledge increases his charity will grow larger, yet when we remember how such popularity-baits are nibbled at, we tremble lest the growth should be all the other way. If, already, he can not only preach but print mere vulgar abuse of men who, in the sight of God, may be as sincere as he, and as holy, to what lengths of ribaldry may he not descend, when he finds that this knack of ' cordially-hating ' brings around him a crowd of fulsome flatterers ?

"But we hope better things. We see in Mr. Spurgeon a soul-loving preacher of Christ's gospel. Few have his peculiar gifts for arresting the attention of the thoughtless, or inspiring the cold with fervour. These are high endowments; high, but awfully responsible. Of that responsibility we believe, too, that Mr. Spurgeon has no mean sense. And, therefore, we hope, not without confidence, that his usefulness will continually augment, and that whatever detracts from it will gradually disappear. We admire the boldness with which he dashes down some of the idols of the pulpit, and we pray that he may be saved by God's grace from ever bowing down to others."

Mr. Spurgeon's success was not dependent on critics and reviewers. His hope and help were, from the first, in God. And he could bear joyful testimony to the fact that God stood by him continually, even in the most trying seasons, and so prospered his way. In June 1856 it was again found necessary to resort to Exeter Hall on Sunday evenings, the chapel being used in the mornings. This, however, was felt to be extremely inconvenient; and the necessity of finding, by some means or other, a larger building was pressed on the attention of himself and his friends more than ever.

About this time he preached at Stambourne, in connection with the jubilee of his grandfather's ministry. One of the newspapers of the day thus reports the proceedings on the occasion:—" On Sunday week a large concourse assembled by public invitation at the Hill Farm, Stambourne, to celebrate the jubilee of the Rev. James Spurgeon, who has just attained the forty-sixth year of his ministry in this village, as pastor of the Independent Chapel. Considerable preparations had been made, and there were probably from fifteen hundred to two thousand persons present at the services. The public duties were conducted by members of Mr. Spurgeon's family; the Rev. C. H. Spurgeon, of London, being the preacher, assisted by his younger brother (a student) and his father in leading the devotions of the meeting. Many of the surrounding ministers of churches, with their congregations, came from great distances to testify their respect for the venerable pastor of Stambourne meeting. The devotional exercises and the sermons, on the whole, were suitable to the occasion. The collections were liberal. In the course of his sermon the preacher animadverted very severely on the Rev. Thomas Binney's book, *On making the Best of both Worlds*, which he denounced as a specimen of the 'new heretical theology.' At the close a minister rose up and protested against Mr. Spurgeon's remarks on Mr. Binney. A general state of confusion ensued in the congregation. Some clapped, some shouted 'Hear, hear,' others cried, 'Turn him out.' The reverend gentleman, however, persisted in defending Mr. Binney, and explained that the design of Mr. Binney's book was to prove and illustrate the Scriptural doctrine that 'Godliness is profitable unto all things, having promise of the life that now is, and of that which is to come.' He said, 'I charge Mr. Spurgeon with having uttered a public falsehood.' In reply, Mr. Spurgeon denounced the speaker for wishing to gain public notoriety by means of his popularity; and in his subsequent prayer at the close of this painful scene, he petitioned that the Lord would forgive him for the sin he had committed, and make him sensible of the wrong he had done in not having first gone privately and reproved him, according to the Scriptural rule."

In August 1856 Mr. Spurgeon's people began to establish a fund to provide for the erection of a new place of worship. Meanwhile, the proprietors of Exeter Hall intimated to them that they did not feel at liberty to let their building continuously to one congregation; they, therefore, had to look around for another place. Just at that time a large hall was finished in the Royal Surrey Gardens, for the monstre concerts conducted by Mons. Jullien; and they secured it for Sunday evening services. On the evening of the 19th October the church and congregation assembled there for the first time for the worship of God. A large number of persons, amounting to about seven thousand, were present, and the service was begun in the usual way, by singing, reading the Scriptures, and prayer. Just as the preacher began his prayer, a disturbance was caused by some evil-disposed persons, and the whole congregation was seized with a sudden panic. There was a fearful rush to the doors, particularly from the galleries. Several persons were trampled to death, and a much larger number were removed to the hospitals seriously injured.

The following account of the catastrophe, taken from the columns of *The Freeman*, is the most reliable that appeared, and therefore the most suitable for these pages:—" On Sunday evening last an awful calamity occurred at the Surrey Gardens, which has formed the topic of conversation in all circles of London ever since. It will be known to many of our readers that the Rev. C. H. Spurgeon, of New Park Street Chapel, having been refused permission to continue his Sunday evening services in Exeter Hall, had made arrangements with the Surrey Gardens Company for the use of their large music hall for four consecutive Sundays. Last Sunday was the first occasion of his taking possession of the Gardens, and half-past six was the hour announced for the commencement of the service; but long before that time, indeed as early as four o'clock, there was an assemblage of persons more than sufficient to fill the hall, and this number was considerably augmented before the doors were opened. At six o'clock the doors were opened, and the hall, including the various balconies and side galleries, speedily became filled. The outer gates were then closed, leaving vast crowds of people, both inside the Gardens and also in the adjoining streets. It is estimated that there were not less than twelve or fourteen thousand persons in the building, and five or six thousand standing outside. At about half-past six o'clock Mr. Spurgeon ascended the pulpit, and commenced the service. The service began by singing a hymn, which was followed by the reading of a chapter, and a somewhat lengthened exposition. This done, Mr. Spurgeon stood up to pray, and had prayed at some length, when an alarm of danger was given, and in a few moments the whole of the vast assembly was seized with a feeling of consternation.

"'The accounts vary as to the exact words used to sound the alarm. Some say it was a cry of 'Fire,' which proceeded from a person in the uppermost gallery; others that the words used were 'The roof, the roof!' that they emanated from some people on the basement storey, and were accompanied by the tinkling of a bell. But whatever the cry, the people in all parts of the hall rose *en masse* in a state of the greatest terror, and made for every point of outlet from the place with the most frantic eagerness. The scene is said to have been one of indescribable agony and confusion. Mr. Spurgeon, indeed, with his stentorian voice, implored the excited multitude to keep their seats, assuring them there was no danger, and that the alarm was false. This assurance was repeated by the officials and others at every point of the building; but, unfortunately, it had no effect upon those to whom it was addressed. Those in the rear of the doors pressed heedlessly upon those in front, and carried all before them, like a raging flood.

"Soon the hall and its staircases and passages presented a scene which baffles description. The shrieks of frightened women and children utterly drowned the deeper voices that vainly exhorted them to dismiss their fears and retain their seats. Rushing in terror-stricken masses they sought a precipitate escape. Of course, the only safe ways of egress were speedily gorged and choked up; while many, unable to reach the doors, wildly dashed through the windows, or leaped from the galleries to the floor, cutting and wounding themselves in their frenzied efforts. On the circular stone staircase leading from the front gallery the crush was awful, and the catastrophe lamentable. The strong iron balustrade by which it was protected gave way before the tremendous pressure, and a heap of persons were precipitated to the pavement below. Here occurred the most serious and fatal effects of this deplorable catastrophe. Urged on, driven, pushed down by the surging crowd above, those below came on, as it were with certain death before their eyes, and, ere they could restrain themselves, fell over the side, down the wall-staircase, on to the stone floor beneath. The first that tumbled over was a well-dressed woman, who struck upon her head, and died without even a sound; another respectably-dressed female fell screaming in an agony, with a child clasped in her arms; then came a third woman; then two men, clutching eagerly at each other, at the stones, at air,

THE TERRIBLE CATASTROPHE. 61

as they sank into the abyss. Others followed, falling over one another; while above, a fierce fight was furiously raging for life; some still striving to come down, others struggling to stand still, or get upwards.

"As soon as the shrieks of the unfortunate sufferers were heard by those who had obtained ingress into the Gardens, but could not obtain admission into the hall, they made a desperate rush for the outer gates; but by a strange arrangement they could find no means of getting outside the gates, they having been firmly closed, to prevent the great crowd which had been outside all the evening from entering the Gardens. Men, women, and children climbed, were drawn, and thrown over the iron railings, many of them being seriously injured in consequence. As soon as it was known by those outside that a terrible accident had occurred, the wildest rumours prevailed. Some asserted that the entire building had fallen in, burying all beneath; others that the galleries had given way, carrying their occupants upon those below. Then the most fearful excitement prevailed outside. Fathers, whose wives and daughters were in the building; mothers, whose children were there; and, in fact, every person who knew of a relative of any kind that had gained admission, raised their wildest lamentations for those whom they believed were lost to them for ever.

"With the assistance of a large body of police which had arrived, and were under the direction of Mr. Superintendent Lund, every help was now rendered to the wounded. Such of those who were not too badly wounded were at once conveyed in cabs to their own dwellings; others, through the kindness of the inhabitants of Penton Street, Amelia Street, Carter Street, and Manor Street, were received, and promptly attended to, by the medical men in the neighbourhood.

"Of course, while all this was going on, it was impossible

for the service to proceed. Several attempts were made to sing, in order to allay the excitement, but, as might be expected, they were all in vain. Mr. Spurgeon's conduct appears to have been most judicious. He repeatedly raised his voice to calm the excitement, but with very little success. When the first alarm was over, he addressed the assembly, saying, 'Will our good friends retire as quickly as possible, and may God forgive those who have been the authors of this confusion! I cannot preach to you now, but we will sing you out, and go as gradually and as quietly as possible.' The announcement that he would not preach appeared to give great dissatisfaction, and cries arose from every part of the hall of 'Go on, preach.' After a short delay Mr. Spurgeon said:—'My friends, what shall I preach about? You bid me preach to-night. I am ready to do all I can, but in the midst of all this confusion, what shall be my subject? May God's Holy Spirit give me a subject on this solemn occasion! My friends, there is a terrible day coming, when the terror and alarm of this evening shall be as nothing. That will be a time when the thunder and lightning and blackest darkness shall have their fullest power; when the earth shall reel to and fro beneath us; and when the arches of the solid heavens shall totter to their centre. The day is coming when the clouds shall reveal their wonders and portents, and Christ shall sit upon those clouds in glory, and shall call you to judgment. Many men have gone away to-night, in the midst of this terrible confusion, and so shall it be on that great day. I can, however, believe that the results of that day will show that there will be a great many—not a less proportion than those who now remain to those who have left—who will stand the ordeal of that great day. The alarm which has just arisen has been produced, in some measure, by that instinct which teaches us to seek self-preservation. But in the more numerous of the cases it is not so much the dread

A HEROIC ENDEAVOUR. 63

of death which has influenced them, as the dread of something afterwards—"That undiscovered country from whose bourne no traveller returns." 'Tis conscience that makes cowards of them. Many were afraid to stop here, because they thought it was to stop and be damned. They were aware—and many of you are aware—that if you were hurried before your Maker to-night, you would be brought there unshriven, unpardoned, and condemned. But what are your terrors now to what they will be on that terrible day of reckoning of the Almighty, when the heaven shall shrink above you, and hell open her mouth beneath you? But know you not, my friends, that grace, sovereign grace, can yet save you? Have you never heard the welcome news that Jesus came into the world to save sinners? You are the chief among sinners. Believe that Christ died for you, and you may be saved from the torments of hell that await you. Do you not know that you are lost and ruined —that none but Jesus can do the sinner good? You are sick and diseased. Jesus can do you good, and will. I thought this night of preaching from the text, "The curse of the Lord is in the house of the wicked, but he blesseth the habitation of the just." I feel I cannot preach as I wish. You will have another alarm yet, and I would rather that some of you would seek to retire gradually, in order that no harm may be done. My text will be found in the third chapter of Proverbs, at the 33rd verse.' The reverend gentleman had just repeated the words of the text, when another pause ensued, and the most terrific confusion took place.

"Comparative silence was again obtained, after singing part of another hymn, when Mr. Spurgeon proceeded to comment upon his text, and after saying that, although his congregation might suppose that there were fifty classes of persons, there were, in the eyes of God, but two—the righteous and the wicked. 'God knows nothing,' he added, ' of any class save the righteous and the wicked, the wicked and the just.' Here the agitation and tremor of the preacher became painfully visible, and he broke off his discourse by saying, 'You ask me to preach, but how can I after this terrible scene? My brain is in a whirl, and I scarcely know where I am, so great are my apprehensions that many persons must have been injured by rushing out. I would rather that you retired gradually, and may God Almighty dismiss you with His blessing, and carry you in safety to your homes. If our friends will go out by the central doors, we will sing while they go, and pray that some good may yet come out of this great evil after all. Do not, however, be in a hurry. Let those nearest the door go first.' The second verse of the hymn previously announced, 'His sovereign power without our aid,' was sung, and Mr. Spurgeon then addressed a few words to the audience. Having pronounced the benediction, Mr. Spurgeon, accompanied by several of his deacons, withdrew, exhausted and agitated, as may well be supposed, after the extraordinary scene which he had witnessed.

"We regret to add that eight persons were killed, and not less than fifty wounded in this dreadful affair.[1] The wonder, however, is that the number killed and injured was not larger. The aspect of the hall, after the departure of the audience, too sadly told the tale of the fearful struggle which must have occurred during the endeavours of the unfortunate people to escape. There was scarcely any description of garment worn by male or female but what was to be found in the building—boots, shoes, legs of trousers, tails and arms of coats, petticoats, shawls, bonnets, hats, victorines, capes, coats, and other articles of wearing apparel to a great extent.

"Of course a coroner's inquest is to be held, and a careful investigation is being made also by the police. On

[1] It was ascertained that *seven* persons were killed and twenty-eight seriously injured.

THE CORONER'S VERDICT.

Monday morning, Mr. Superintendent Lund, to whose energy and presence of mind a great number of persons owe their lives, stated that he was present in the hall from the commencement of the service until the fatal occurrence took place. He occupied a position on the platform, very near to Mr. Spurgeon, and had an uninterrupted view of the whole body of the hall. He asserts that, about the time stated above, he distinctly saw three persons in the body of the hall suddenly rise, and lifting their arms towards the roof, shout, 'Fire, fire!' He is convinced they were not swell-mobsmen, as was first supposed, as he states thieves never occupy so prominent a position as the persons he saw, but generally station themselves near the doors, in order to rob people as they make their exit. He believes, and is supported in his opinion by many other persons, that the alarm was raised by some opponents of Mr. Spurgeon, who had repaired to the hall for the purpose of disturbing the proceedings."

A coroner's inquest was held, and the jury brought in a verdict of "accidental death." The lamentable calamity produced the most serious effects on Mr. Spurgeon's nervous system. He was entirely prostrate for some days, and compelled to relinquish all his preaching engagements. Through God's goodness, however, he was so far restored by the last Sunday in October as to be able to occupy the pulpit at New Park Street on that day. A great many persons were admitted by ticket before the doors were opened to the public; and when the preacher entered, every nook and corner, as well in the body of the chapel as in the galleries, was densely crowded by an eager auditory. When Mr. Spurgeon appeared, it was with difficulty that a passage could be made for him to the pulpit, and when he at length entered it every step in the staircase was taken possession of. He was conducted to the pulpit by the deacons, and seemed quite recovered from his recent affliction. He began the service by offering a singularly solemn and affecting prayer, expressive of thanksgiving, on the part of himself and friends, for preservation in the late calamity.

The reporter of the *Morning Post* supplies the words of the prayer. After invoking a blessing upon his flock, the preacher proceeded as follows:—"We are assembled here this day with mixed feelings of joy and sorrow—joy that we meet each other again, and sorrow for those who have suffered bereavements. Thanks to Thy name—thanks to Thy name! Thy servant feared he should not have addressed this congregation again; but Thou hast brought him from the fiery furnace, and not even a smell of fire has passed upon him. Thou hast, moreover, given Thy servant strength, and he desires now to confirm those great promises of free grace which the Gospel affords. Thou knowest, O God, our feelings of sorrow. We must not open the sluices of our woe. O God, comfort those who are lingering in pain and suffering, and cheer those who have been bereaved. Let a blessing rest upon them, even the blessing of the covenant of grace and of this world. And now, Lord, bless Thy people. We have loved one another—we have rejoiced in each other's joys—we have wept together in sorrow. Thou hast welded us together, one in doctrine, one in practice, and one in holy love. Oh, that it may be said of each that he is bound up in the bundle of life. O Lord, we thank Thee for all the slander, calumny, and malice with which Thou hast allowed the enemy to honour us; and grant we may never give them cause to blaspheme with reason!" Mr. Spurgeon concluded with a personal reference to the various classes of his hearers, calling on despisers to tremble, scoffers to weep, and bidding all true penitents rejoice.

The sermon that morning was from Phil. ii. 9—"Wherefore God hath highly exalted Him, and hath given Him a name which is above every name." He commenced with

A COMFORTING TEXT. 67

the following statement:—"Now, my dear friends, 1 almost regret this morning that I occupy this pulpit. I regret it, because I feel myself utterly unable to preach to you for your profit. I have thought, during the period of relaxation I have had since that terrible catastrophe which has befallen us, that I had thoroughly recovered; but on coming back to this spot again, I feel somewhat of the same feelings which well-nigh prostrated me before. You will, therefore, excuse me this morning if I make no allusion, or scarcely any at all, to recent circumstances; for, were I to enter into the subject, and to bring to your remembrance that solemn scene, I should speedily be forced to be silent. It might not have been the malice of men so much as some have thought. It was probably the intention of the parties to disturb the congregation, but not to commit the terrible crime which resulted in the death of several individuals. God forgive those who did it! They have my forgiveness from the bottom of my soul. I may say, however, dear brethren, that we shall not be daunted at what has taken place; and I shall preach again in that place yet! God shall give us souls there, and Satan's empire shall tremble more yet—for I believe that God is with us, and who is he that can be against us? The text which I have selected is one which has comforted me, and enabled me to come here to-day, in order to try to comfort you. I shall not attempt to preach from the text; I shall only make a few remarks; for I have been utterly unable to study, and I trust your loving hearts will excuse me."

After this introduction the preacher entered into the theological and practical aspects of his text, showing how the Christian should rejoice in the exaltation of Jesus Christ. During the early portion of the service he was evidently scarcely able to overcome his emotion; but, as he proceeded with his discourse, he resumed his usual tone, and appeared almost altogether to get the better of the powerful feelings by which he was at first agitated. In the course of his observations he referred to the attacks which some of the papers had made upon him in the midst of his affliction; but he did so in a most mild and Christian-like manner. He said he sought not flattery for himself, but glory for God, and he cared not for all the obloquy which might be heaped upon him, so long as his Divine Master was not rejected but honoured. This, he said, was the lofty position he wished always to take; but when selfishness crept in, it was impossible to maintain it. He had found that whenever he had yielded to the slightest pleasure when praised, he had become effeminate and weak, and unable to resist, with proper calmness and dignity, the attacks of those who were opposed alike to him and the gospel which he preached. But when he had been able to say to the praises of men, "What are you? worthless things!" then he could feel equally unmoved by slander and abuse. He could say to his enemies, "Come along with your arrows; they may strike my coat of mail, but they shall not—cannot—reach the flesh." He very feelingly and forcibly impressed the desirability of cultivating those feelings whenever men were persecuted by the bigoted, and wicked, and uncharitable, on account of their religious belief.

The critics of the press were divided in their judgments on this sad catastrophe. One popular newspaper said:—
"Mr. Spurgeon is a preacher who hurls damnation at the heads of his sinful hearers. Some men there are who, taking their precepts from Holy Writ, would beckon erring souls to a rightful path with fair words and gentle admonition; Mr. Spurgeon would take them by the nose and bully them into religion. Let us set up a barrier to the encroachments and blasphemies of men like Spurgeon, saying to them, 'Thus far shalt thou come and no farther.' Let us devise some powerful means which shall tell to the thousands who now stand in need of enlightenment—This

man, in his own opinion, is a righteous Christian, but in ours, nothing more than a vaunting charlatan. We are neither straightlaced nor Sabbatarian in our sentiments; but we would keep apart, widely apart, the theatre and the church—above all, would we place in the hand of every right-thinking man a whip to scourge from society the authors of such vile blasphemies as, on Sunday night, above the heart-rending cries of the dying, and louder than the wails of misery from the maimed and suffering, resounded from the mouth of Mr. Spurgeon in the music hall of the Surrey Gardens."

The *Times*, after some unjust observations on Mr. Spurgeon's conduct during the terrible scenes of that memorable evening, goes on to say:—"Let Mr. Spurgeon be at least content with as many as the Surrey Music Hall was intended to hold sitting in comfort, and with sufficient means of exit. It appears that he has the means of controlling the admission, since his own special flock is secured places before the proselytes and strangers are let in. We do not say this from any desire to stint Mr. Spurgeon of his audience. We have no wish to criticise his style of oratory, which severe critics affirm to be of the familiar, bold, and irreverent sort. On the contrary, we are delighted to hear that there is one man in the metropolis who can get people to hear his sermons from any other motive than the fulfilment of a religious obligation. The men who have awakened slumbering generations, shaken idols or Popes, or huge vices from their thrones, have not been uniformly characterised for severity of language, sobriety of illustration, and chasteness of style. Luther, Latimer, and many others, were remarkable for the contrary. Mere faults of style are no concern of ours, and, apparently, are tolerated by the British public when the substance finds an echo in their understandings or their hearts. But there is a certain moderation to be observed in all things—even in the size of congregations. Would Mr. Spurgeon be so good as to attend to the subject at once?"

One more critique we give, from the *Evening Star*:—"Other questions than that of the structure of the buildings, or the self-protection of startled assemblages, are raised by the Surrey Gardens calamity. The vocation of the preacher, and the secret of his power, are brought by it within the range of every man's thoughts, and, therefore, of newspaper discussion." After some observations on the grades of people that constitute the ordinary church and chapel-going congregation, the writer proceeds:—"But where are the artisan classes?—that keen-eyed, strong-minded race who crowd the floor at political meetings or cheap concerts, fill the minor theatres, and struggle into the shilling gallery of the Lyceum or Princess's. So very scanty is their attendance upon the most noted preachers, that it is their adhesion to Mr. Spurgeon which has made that gentleman a prodigy and a phenomenon. The first that we heard of him, two or three years since, was, that the Bankside labourers went to hear him on Sunday and week nights. The summer before last we found the artisans of Bethnal Green —a much more fastidious race—flocking around him in a field at Hackney. And in the list of the killed and wounded at the Music Hall are journeymen painters, tanners, and milliners' girls. Is it worth while to ask the reason why?

"A single hearing is sufficient to answer the question— supposing that the hearer can also see. He never yet was a popular orator who did not talk more and better with his arms than with his tongue. Mr. Spurgeon knows this instinctively. When he has read his text, he does not fasten his eyes on a manuscript and his hands to a cushion. As soon as he begins to speak he begins to act—and that not as if declaiming on the stage, but as if conversing with you in the street. He seems to shake hands with all around, and put every one at his ease. There is no laboured exordium making you wonder by what ingenious winding he will get back to his subject; but a trite saying, an apt quotation, a simple allegory, or two or three familiar sentences, making all who hear feel interested and at home. Then there is no philosophical pomp of exposition; but just two or three catchwords, rather to guide than confine attention. Presently comes, by way of illustration, a gleam of humour—perhaps a stroke of downright vulgarity—it may be, a wretched pun. The people are amused, but they are not left at liberty to laugh. The preacher's comedy does but light up his solemn earnestness. He is painting some scene of death-bed remorse, or of timely repentance; some Magdalene's forgiveness, or some Prodigal's return. His colours are taken from the earth and sky of common human experience and aspiration. He dips his pencil, so to speak, in the veins of the nearest spectator, and makes his work a part of every man's nature. His images are drawn from the homes of the common people—the daily toil for daily bread, the nightly rest of tired labour, the mother's love for a wayward boy, the father's tenderness to a sick daughter. His anecdotes are not far-fetched, and have a natural pathos. He tells how some despairing unfortunate, hastening with her last penny to the suicide's bridge, was stopped by the sound of psalmody, and turned into his chapel; or how some widow's son, running away from his mother's home, was brought back by the recollection of a prayer, and sits now in that pew. He does not narrate occurrences, but describes them with a rough graphic force and faithfulness. He does not reason out his doctrines, but announces, explains, and applies them. He ventures a political allusion, and it goes right to the democratic heart. In the open air some one may interrupt or interrogate, and the response is a new effect.

"In short, this man preaches Christianity—his Christianity at any rate—as Ernest Jones preaches Chartism, and as Gough preaches temperance. Is it any wonder that he meets with like success? or is he to be either blamed or scorned? Let it be first remembered that Latimer was not less homely when he preached before the king; nor South less humorous when he cowed Rochester; nor Whitfield less declamatory when he moved Hume and Franklin; nor Rowland Hill less vulgar, though brother to a baronet. To us it appears that dulness is the worst fault possible to a man whose first business it is to interest; that the dignity of the pulpit is best consulted by making it attractive; and that the clergy of all denominations might get some frequent hints for the composition of their sermons from the young Baptist preacher who never went to college."

On the morning of Sunday, 23rd November 1856, Mr. Spurgeon and his friends assembled again in the Surrey Music Hall for divine worship. As the hour of service drew near, streams of human beings, intent on seeing Mr. Spurgeon again occupy the pulpit at the scene of the deplorable calamity which attended his former appearance in the hall, poured from all quarters to the place, and excited the wonder of the neighbourhood. No person was admitted within the hall until half-past ten o'clock, unless provided with a shilling ticket, which entitled the bearer to four services. After that time all were indiscriminately admitted. The number present was about six thousand. The preacher commenced by prayer, in which he said that the hall in which they were assembled was quite as sacred as any other place whilst used for religious purposes, inasmuch as God is in every place. He prayed that there might be heard within its walls that morning music more sweet than had ever been heard there before—the music of penitential sighs. After prayer he read the fifteenth chapter of St. Mark's gospel, and interspersed his reading with various expositions. In his exposition of the history of the crucifixion, he said it seemed to him that the dream of Uncle Tom, in which he thought he saw each of the thorns in our Saviour's crown of thorns turn into diamonds, and the crown itself glisten with pearls, was a great fact. Before he proceeded with the delivery of his sermon he referred to the "ten thousand rumours" about his church and congregation, among them the rumour that they were to build a tabernacle to hold fifteen thousand people. He said that they had never conceived the idea of attempting such an undertaking, but had thought that it was absolutely necessary to erect a building to hold five thousand people. He said that he himself had no wish for such a place, but could not bear the thought of so many people, owing to want of accommodation, being debarred from hearing him; that they were not justified in continuing in so small a place as the present one. He protested against the suggestion that all should be admitted by ticket, their great object being to admit all —whether or not they could afford to pay for a seat—that the Gospel might be preached to them; and that they would admit as many of the public as possible without tickets.

After some further remarks he preached on the text, "But God commendeth His love towards us in that while we were yet sinners Christ died for us." It was anticipated that he would make some distinct allusion to the catastrophe which attended his former appearance in Surrey Hall, but he abstained from doing so. An intelligent hearer thus gives his impressions of what he saw and heard at the hall on the third Sunday morning of this period of occupancy by Mr. Spurgeon's congregation:—"Last Sunday morning we visited the scene of the late awful catastrophe, and worshipped with the vast assemblage congregated within the walls of a place of popular amusement. The interior, however, of the building could hardly be better adapted than it is to the purposes of divine worship; for if, on the one hand, there was nothing of the 'dim religious light,' on the other, there was nothing suggestive of vain thoughts, and nothing incongruous with sacred service. For hearing, its adaptation seems perfect. At the remotest part of the second gallery we could distinguish every syllable. The sight from that position—the floor and three spacious galleries thronged with seven or eight thousand of our immortal fellow-creatures—was truly imposing; and when they rose and joined in singing 'Before Jehovah's awful throne,' to the Old Hundred, it was difficult to suppress visible emotion. One can hardly conceive the impression of a full Roman Catholic cathedral service, of which we have heard so much, surpassing that of thousands of human voices praising their God under the guidance of one unpretending leader.

"But we pass to the youthful preacher, and to the service—which, it is mere justice to say, was all that could be wished. We left, indeed, with the hope that those thousands did not all quit the place as they entered it; not only because we had heard that upwards of forty communicants would be added that night to the church, nor merely because of the numbers present; but partly because, scanning the vast crowd as closely as we could, we felt confident that great numbers of both sexes were *not* of the class who frequent our usual places of worship, and partly because a solemn subject had been placed before them in a mode which not only ought to awaken them, but was likely to do it. The remarks, during reading, on the closing part of the twenty-fifth chapter of Matthew, were natural and impressive; the prayers were in harmony with them; and the text, from Psalm vi. 12, '*If he turn not he will whet his sword,*' indicated the class whom the preacher intended to address. Bad as the weather was, the place was as full as it was permitted to be; and the attention of the promiscuous multitude, whom we could see to full advantage, never flagged. We saw not one sleeper.

At every longer cessation of the preacher's voice, suppressed coughs obtained relief; and immediately the deep silence, broken only by the speaking from the pulpit, was again resumed. Each ear seemed on stretch, not to catch the sounds of sweet music or of mirth, but to imbibe every word of faithful warning.

"We have heard Mr. Spurgeon declaim illogically and unseemly to his congregation on his peculiar creed, and also indulge in humour; but of that presently. Last Sunday there was not a word which could provoke a smile, and nothing that any caviller could describe as extravagant or unbecoming in diction; *yet* the attention was unflagging. What was the secret of this? The answer is to us very easy, and it is instructive, too. Mr. Spurgeon has one of the finest voices, perhaps, in England for addressing a large multitude; he has great facility in expressing his meaning; his fancy is quick, and ranges on the level of human things; his manner gives full effect to all he says; his style is forcible, homely, and pointed; his thoughts, as a rule, are just, often striking, and sometimes beautiful—such a description is at least appropriate to what we heard last Sunday morning; but there is something more than all this, something in great part of a moral kind, in which, we are persuaded, lies the secret of his power. Mr. Spurgeon, having all these qualifications, is pre-eminently a man of heart, and thoroughly unaffected and natural.

"A mere reader of his sermons might easily think he detected the language of vanity; a hearer, at least a discriminating hearer, would not think so. The preacher evidently is intent, not on himself, but on his audience. He centralises all his mind in theirs. You never hear him uttering the most beautiful, or the most striking, or even outrageous figure or illustration, without perceiving that he is not indulging in the admiration of his hearers, but aiming to get hold of them. He does not care, like too many, to display his taste or his oratory, but to make it tell. Power over the minds of his audience, power to be used for good, power by almost any means, is his object; and therefore he attains it. We have heard humour, puns, almost jokes in some of the few other discourses to which we have listened; but we are bound to state that, to us, they seemed honest in purpose; sometimes the mere by-play of an active fancy; sometimes that natural tendency to blend humour with the most solemn occasions, which did not desert Sir Thomas More even on the scaffold, and which our great bard so often illustrates.

"Indeed, though we do not defend, or care to defend, what scandalises our more stately preachers so much, this condemned 'humour' is a part of that great merit of Mr. Spurgeon—*naturalness*. He would not speak as *he* felt, if, amidst the most serious things, the contrast of humour did not sometimes crop out. It would be outrageous, and almost wicked, to *aim* at such a thing; it would misbecome forty-nine preachers out of fifty; but it does not, in the same manner or degree, misbecome Mr. Spurgeon, and just because it is a part of the soul his Maker gave him. Hence, so far as we have observed, it was merely a ripple or a bubble on the flow of serious thought; you were borne along quite as powerfully as if the superficial disturbance had not occurred."

Mr. Spurgeon continued to preach in the Surrey Music Hall, every Sunday morning, till December 1859. The company owning the hall resolved, at that time, to open the Gardens for amusement on the Sunday evenings; and Mr. Spurgeon and his friends felt bound, in honour, to leave the place. During the three years they had assembled there, multitudes of all ranks flocked to hear the Gospel. Sunday after Sunday, members of the aristocracy, representatives of the people in the House of Commons, literary and scientific men, as well as the trading and artisan classes, helped to form the audience, and joined in the worship of God. At length, on the 18th December 1859, the New Park Street Church and its pastor began their third and longest sojourn at Exeter Hall, which ended on the 1st of March 1861.

On leaving that place for good, Mr. Spurgeon made the following remarks:—"In the providence of God we, as a church and people, have had to wander often. This is our third sojourn within these walls. It is now about to close. We have had, at all times and seasons, a compulsion for moving—sometimes a compulsion of conscience, at other times a compulsion of pleasure, as on this occasion. I am sure that when we first went to the Surrey Music Hall, God went with us. Satan went, too, but he fled before us. That frightful calamity, the impression of which can never be erased from my mind, turned out, in the providence of God, to be one of the most wonderful means of turning public attention to special services, and I do not doubt that, fearful catastrophe though it was, it has been the mother of multitudes of blessings. The Christian world noted the example and saw its after-success; they followed it, and to this day, in the theatre and in the cathedral, the Word of Christ is preached where it was never preached before. In each of our movings we have had reason to see the hand of God, and here particularly; for many residents in the West End have, in this place, come to listen to the Word, who, probably, might not have taken a journey beyond the river. Here, God's grace has broken hard hearts; here have souls been renewed, and wanderers reclaimed. 'Give unto the Lord, O ye mighty, give unto the Lord glory and strength; give unto the Lord the glory due unto His name.' And now we journey to the house which God has, in so special a manner, given to us; and this day would I pray as Moses did, 'Rise up, Lord, and let thine enemies be scattered, and let them that hate Thee flee before Thee.'"

CHAPTER V.

IN LABOURS MORE ABUNDANT.

Such were the crowds that flocked to hear Mr. Spurgeon, both at New Park Street and Exeter Hall, in 1856, that the necessity of providing for the erection of a larger place of worship was pressed most forcibly on himself and his friends; and in the month of August of that year a fund was commenced for the purpose. The following October the first great meeting was held to consider what steps should be taken for erecting a suitable edifice, and meeting its cost. It was proposed to build a large chapel, capable of holding five thousand persons. The proposal was heartily taken up and supported by the preacher's friends, and in all parts of the country practical sympathy was largely shown with the movement. There were those who laughed at the idea as absurd, impracticable, Quixotic; there were those who looked upon it as presumptuous and altogether wicked. But the work went on.

Mr. Spurgeon travelled all over the land, preaching daily, with the promise of half the proceeds of the collection being devoted to the new tabernacle. At the same time, he frequently allowed the whole proceeds to be applied to the local objects of needy churches and institutions. While it would be out of place here to follow him in all his wanderings, certain visits may be named, as indicating the character and extent of his itinerant labours.

In January 1857 he preached at Birmingham. A correspondent of the time says:—" There are not many names in England which have attraction enough to draw together, at three o'clock on a week-day afternoon, three thousand people to hear a sermon. But this the Rev. C. H. Spurgeon did last Tuesday, in the large hall of Birmingham. The feeling in anticipation of his visit, which had been growing for three or four weeks, had become intense, so that multitudes from town and country flocked to the place of meeting, and long before the service commenced the spacious building was crowded in every part."

On the appearance of the youthful preacher all eyes were arrested, and a solemn silence ensued. He began by a prayer, uttered in a clear, sonorous voice, which was heard in the remotest part of the vast edifice. After commenting on the 103rd Psalm, and offering another prayer, he took for his text, "Thou shalt call his name Jesus, for he shall save his people from their sins." He began by saying that, as he was a stranger in Birmingham, he did not wish to appear among them under false colours, but plainly to announce to them the truths he believed, and the doctrines he preached, so that should he ever come again they would know what they had to expect. And then, for three-quarters of an hour, he unfolded the distinguishing peculiarities of the Gospel, and the power of Christ to save, with great earnestness and effect. In the evening a still larger assembly was convened, when he preached from the text, "To know the love of Christ, which passeth knowledge," a sermon which is described as full of eloquence, illustration, and power.

The next day he preached again twice, in Mount Zion chapel. Persons were admitted by ticket. The morning subject was "Self-examination." The evening discourse was based on seven texts, each of which contained the same sentence, "I have sinned"—a sentence which was uttered by seven individuals, Pharaoh, Balaam, Saul, Achan, Judas,

David, and the Prodigal, who were considered as types of different characters. The sermons again were most powerful, and the desire to hear so great that numbers were unable to obtain admission. The amazing popularity of the preacher drew to these services persons of all denominations—Episcopalians, Wesleyans, Independents, Baptists, Unitarians, men of all creeds and no creed. Merchants, manufacturers, clergymen, dissenting ministers, lawyers, doctors, professors, students, artists and artisans, literary men and illiterate men were all there; pleased or displeased, according to the variety of their tastes, their habits of thought and feeling, and their views on the great question of religious faith and obligation. The visit was, in some respects, one of the most important of Mr. Spurgeon's engagements at this period.

While engaged in incessant labours during the week in various parts of the provinces, he was at his post Sunday after Sunday in London, where his popularity continued to increase. On the first Sunday of March 1857 there were present, among the vast throng, the Marquis of Lansdowne, Baron Bramwell, and thirty members of Parliament. The Marquis evinced great interest in the service, and was much impressed by the aspect of such an immense congregation. At the close he sought an interview with the preacher, and strongly urged him to take care of his health, that he might the longer employ the talents which had been given him for usefulness. The following Sunday the Music Hall was again crowded, and among the congregation were Lord John Russell, Lord Stanley of Alderley, Sir James Graham, and a number of other distinguished persons. The two lords had a lengthened conversation with Mr. Spurgeon on retiring, and expressed their unqualified admiration of his talents. It was at this time that Mr. John Ruskin was among his hearers, and at the close of a morning service presented him with £100 to add to the fund for building the tabernacle.

AT THE CRYSTAL PALACE

While the common people heard him gladly, the great ones of the land, either influenced by curiosity, or drawn, as no doubt they were in many cases, by other considerations, attended his ministry at the Music Hall. There were seen the Duchess of Sutherland, the Duchess of St. Albans, the Duke of Athol, the Marquis of Stafford, the Earl of Carlisle, Lord and Lady Blantyre, Lord Grosvenor, Lady Craven, Lord and Lady Coote, Lady Mowbray, Lady Truro, Lady Peel, Lady Courtney Boyle, Lady Franklin, Lord John Hay, Lord Calthorpe, Lord Bolton, Lord Shirley, Miss Florence Nightingale, Mrs. Harriet Beecher Stowe, Sir Joseph Paxton, and sometimes between sixty and seventy members of Parliament. Some of these distinguished persons sought and obtained interviews with the preacher. It was reported that some members of the royal family also were occasionally present at his services. It would be an easy task to lengthen this list of persons of distinction and learning who once, or oftener, went to hear him.

On Wednesday, 7th October 1857, Mr. Spurgeon preached to the largest audience that has assembled in modern times to listen to the exhortations of a minister of the gospel. It was the day appointed for humiliation and prayer in connection with the Indian Mutiny; and Mr. Spurgeon consented to preach in the Crystal Palace, Sydenham. The palace was opened to the public at nine o'clock, and by noon every seat within earshot of the preacher had its occupant. The pulpit, which was brought from the Surrey Gardens, was placed at the north-east corner of the central transept, at its junction with the nave, and the thousands of seats which had been here disposed were soon engaged. Those portions of the galleries, also, which were within range of the speaker's voice were speedily filled, and the large orchestra was crowded even to the backmost bench. Mr. Spurgeon ascended the pulpit at five minutes past twelve, and immediately proceeded to open the service with a brief invocation, the congregation exhibiting the most reverential decorum. This was followed by the singing of the well-known hymn, "Before Jehovah's awful throne," etc., to the tune of Old Hundred.

Mr. Spurgeon then read a Scripture lesson, consisting of a part of the ninth chapter of Daniel, relating to the sins of the Israelites, and the judgments which befell them in consequence—the reading being accompanied with an exposition, and an application of several passages to the past conduct and present position of the English nation. The prayer, which followed the reading and exposition, contained many emphatic allusions to the Indian Mutiny. In one of the most remarkable, the minister, invoking the Almighty, said, "Thou couldst not endure the sin of Sodom, and we are sure Thou canst not endure the sins which have been committed in the cities of Ind;" and then, after briefly glancing at the atrocities perpetrated by the mutineers upon the wives and daughters of Britain, he besought the Almighty that our avenging soldiers in India might remember that they were not warriors merely, but executioners. After the prayer came another hymn, consisting, as Mr. Spurgeon announced, of verses selected by himself from different psalms, on account of their appropriateness to the occasion, the first verse being—

> "Our God, our help in ages past,
> Our hope for years to come;
> Our shelter from the stormy blast,
> And our eternal home."

The preacher selected for his text the words of the prophet Micah—"Hear ye the rod, and who hath appointed it;" from which he delivered a most animated address. A liberal collection was made at the close for the Indian Relief Fund.

With reference to this service, the *Morning Advertiser*

deemed it necessary to publish the following statement:—
"As we find that misconception exists in the minds of some
of the public relative to the circumstances under which Mr.
Spurgeon consented to preach in the Crystal Palace on
Wednesday last, it is right to state that, in agreeing to the
proposal made to him to preach for the Indian Relief Fund
on that day, he merely stipulated that the company should
act liberally towards the fund. His sole inducement to
preach on the occasion was a desire to do all in his power
towards increasing the fund for the relief of our countrymen
and countrywomen, who had suffered from the Indian
Mutiny. This benevolent wish must have been gratified to
an extent he could hardly have anticipated; for the total
amount, including the £200 contribution made by the company, produced by Mr. Spurgeon's sermon was £680. This
splendid donation was handed over to the Lord Mayor by
the reverend gentleman. After what we have stated it is
unnecessary to add that Mr. Spurgeon, individually, has
not received one farthing for his services on Wednesday
last. Those, indeed, who are personally acquainted with
him know that a more disinterested or generous-minded
man does not exist, and that no consideration on earth
would have induced him to receive any gratuity from the
directors on the occasion, had it been offered to him.
It is due, however, to them to state, that, as an expression
of their sense of the value of his services, and of the disinterested manner in which he acted, they have given £50
towards the fund now being raised for his new tabernacle."
It will be seen from this statement that there were evil-
disposed persons who attributed the young preacher's
noblest efforts to selfish and interested motives. He knew,
however, that he could well afford to leave his righteousness
and his reputation with his God.

At the close of 1857 a bazaar, in aid of the funds for the
erection of the new tabernacle, was held in the Surrey

Music Hall. On the opening day Mr. Spurgeon delivered a lecture on the pleasures that might be enjoyed by Christian persons. He recommended that asceticism should be avoided; but, at the same time, he warned his hearers against those things that were called pleasures, but which the conscience told were not pleasures which should be indulged in by a Christian person. Of this class he instanced evening parties, where persons met together in white kid gloves, stared at one another, and talked nonsense; and declared that, for his part, he would rather stop at home than undergo the misery of such amusements. He believed that if some person advertised bottles of water as a most delectable drink, the draught would soon be considered a great delicacy, and that many things pleased merely because they were called pleasures. With regard to dancing, his opinion was that it was a most healthy exercise, and should be freely indulged in; but he thought males and females should dance apart, the ordinary practice of coupling the sexes in the dance being productive of unholy thoughts. Games of skill he saw no objection to, but games of chance could be said to be productive of no beneficial result; and, as in the case of Messrs. Palmer and Cooke, had led to evil consequences which the countenance of Lord Derby could not counteract. The rattle of dice-boxes always reminded him of the casting of lots at the foot of the cross for the vesture of the Saviour, and he did not think it became any Christian to touch them. But it was no use giving advice on these matters, for most persons had made up their minds upon them, and only sought some authority to excuse that which their consciences told them was not right. Religion, he declared, was never intended to make our pleasures less, and he advised all to despise conventionalism in their enjoyments, but to avoid those pleasures which the conscience condemned. Referring, in conclusion, to the object with which the meeting had taken place, he thanked those who were in attendance for their assistance, and stated that, up to the present time, £5200 had been raised towards the erection of the tabernacle. The suggestion that the sexes should dance separately excited the great amusement of *Punch*, who, the following week, gave a woodcut, descriptive of a number of staid and grave-looking deacons dancing, in what looks like a chapel vestry, the "Newington Polka" and "Spurgeon Quadrilles."

By January 1858 the sum of £6100 was in hand towards the projected tabernacle. Large as this amount was in itself, it was small compared with what was necessary to complete the undertaking to which Mr. Spurgeon and his friends had committed themselves, and which they felt sure would be crowned with success. Mr. Spurgeon's enemies were meanwhile as busy and malevolent as ever, predicting his speedy downfall, yet mad because he continued to rise. The *Univers*, in March 1858, rejoicing over various symptoms of the decline of Protestantism in England, regarded him as "going down." "The star of this famous preacher," it said, "has commenced to pale. Since the day of fasting and humiliation we have not heard much of his misadventures. The services at Westminster Abbey threw him into the second rank, while a certain anecdote which represented him as a great consumer of beer and cigars also deprived him of much of the consideration he had enjoyed." This is a specimen of the foul slanders and falsehoods put into circulation by those who sought to injure him and hinder the truth he preached with such power and success.

This year was one of the busiest and most laborious in the distinguished preacher's life. North and south, east and west, he travelled day after day, from week to week and month to month, incessantly. He seemed ubiquitous; and everywhere—alike in large cities and towns, and in remote country districts—the people gathered in crowds to hear the Gospel from his lips. One of the towns visited in 1858 was Halifax. On the 7th of April he preached there twice in aid of the new Baptist chapel which had been erected for the Rev. W. Walters. A wooden structure had been put up, of immense size, capable of accommodating eight thousand persons. Owing to the unfavourable state of the weather—the snow falling incessantly for the whole day—the congregations were not equal to expectation; still, they were very large. As the congregation was dispersing in the evening, some confusion was created by one of the supports of the gallery giving way, and two persons had each a leg broken, and had to be removed to the infirmary. A few hours after the close of the service, too, the structure fell in, with a tremendous crash. The snow collected in large masses on the canvas roof, and the weight was greater than could be borne. Had the accident taken place three hours earlier, when Mr. Spurgeon was conducting the service, the consequences to the audience would have been most serious.

The gracious providence of God manifest in connection with this service was felt and acknowledged by thousands beside the preacher himself. Numbers who had travelled miles across the Yorkshire hills and dales to hear his gospel message, rejoiced on their return for his and their wonderful preservation.

This year he preached the annual sermon for the Baptist Missionary Society, at the Surrey Hall. There were seven thousand persons present—the largest congregation that ever listened to a missionary sermon. The text was Psalm xlvi., last four verses. The former part of his subject—the desolations God had wrought among kingdoms, different forms of idolatry, false philosophies, especially the mushroom philosophies of the present day—was illustrated with vigour, frequently with poetic beauty; and the practical appeals at the close were very powerful and effective. The preacher threw himself heart and soul into the missionary cause.

THE FIRST ILLNESS.

On the 11th of June, in the same year, Mr. Spurgeon preached in the saloon of the Grand Stand at Epsom. Shortly after noon, numbers of vehicles, of every imaginable description, were to be seen traversing the various roads leading to the Downs. The afternoon and evening services were largely attended, and were most impressive in their character. The next month we find him preaching two sermons in the open air at Old Sarum, to large and deeply interested congregations, gathered from all parts of the surrounding district. A few days after his visit to Wiltshire he addressed a crowded audience in St. James's Hall, London, preaching a "Centenary Sermon" on behalf of the Haverstock Hill Orphan Working School. In the early autumn he visited the north of Ireland. At Belfast the Botanical Gardens were selected as a suitable locality for his services; but, in consequence of the opposition of one of the proprietors, he had to preach elsewhere. The May Street Presbyterian Church, in which he officiated, was crowded in every part, and the preacher received a most enthusiastic Irish welcome.

Mr. Spurgeon's constant and extraordinary labours were beginning, thus early in his career, to tell on his health. Towards the close of 1858 he was prostrated by a serious illness. Mr. Spurgeon felt his illness very keenly; his love for his work was so great that he could not bear to be silent even for a few Sundays. And he entreated his friends not to believe that his illness was caused by his labours for his beloved Master. He besought the prayers of his people on his behalf; and we can well believe that they were offered as earnestly during his first illness as they were during his last.

This sickness was not of long duration; and as soon as possible he was again as busy as ever.

By January 1859 the amount raised for the new tabernacle was £9639. A suitable site had been procured near the Elephant and Castle, Newington, Southwark, and £5000 set aside to pay for it. On the 16th of August that year the foundation-stone of the building was laid, amid great rejoicing, by Sir Samuel Morton Peto. It was thought at one time that this site could not be secured; the providence of God, however, was seen in the matter. "We feel constrained," said Mr. Spurgeon, in his *History of the Metropolitan Tabernacle*, "to mention the singular providence which placed Mr. Spicer and other friends upon the Court of the Fishmongers' Company, so as to secure the land; next, the fact that the Company was able to sell the freehold; and next, that the late Mr. William Joynson, of Mary Cray, deposited the amount to pay for an Act of Parliament to enable the Company to sell, in case it turned out that they had not the legal power to do so. Singularly happy, also, was the circumstance that a gentleman in Bristol, who had never heard the pastor, nevertheless gave no less a sum than £5000 towards the building. Eternity alone can reveal all the generous feeling and self-denying liberality evinced by Christian people in connection with this enterprise—to us, at any rate, so gigantic at the time that, apart from divine aid, we could never have carried it through."

This year, again, was a year of incessant travel and preaching in all parts of the country. Among other places, he paid a second visit to Halifax. On the 9th of November he preached two sermons in the Mechanics' Hall, to overflowing and delighted congregations. The morning subject was, "God's delays in answering prayer," from the text, "Go again seven times"—1 Kings xviii. 43. The evening sermon was from Rom. i. 16—"For I am not ashamed of the gospel of Christ." Mr. Walters, the minister of Trinity Road Chapel, Halifax, who was present on both occasions, seeing that the preacher used a scrap of paper each time, laid on the Bible, asked for them as a memento of the visit.

One is written with ink, the other only in pencil; both on half-sheets of note-paper. The sermons were each about three-quarters of an hour long, and were most fluently and powerfully delivered. Here are the outlines:—Morning sermon—Text, 1 Kings xviii. 43, "Go again seven times."

    I. EXPLANATIONS—
        Sovereignty.
        Make sense of need deeper
        Stir up fervent prayer.
        Cleanse out sin.
        Qualify for future work.

    II. EXHORTATIONS—
        This is your only hope.
        This failing, you perish.
        The great mercy.
        Your great unworthiness.
        The sureness of success.

    III. DIRECTIONS—
        Ignorance to be removed
        Sin to be avoided.
        Christ to be simply regarded.

Evening sermon—Text, Rom. i. 16, "For I am not ashamed of the gospel of Christ."

    I. What is the gospel?
        Good news. This tells us what it is not
        1. In its germ.
        2. In its incarnation.
        3. In its development.

    II. Who are ashamed of it?
        1. In the pulpit—
        Half-hearted, timid, crack-jaw ministers.
        2. Out of the pulpit—
        Those who do not profess it; who never carry it out, or are silent.

III. Why not ashamed?
   1. It is wise in itself.
   2. It is divine.
   3. It is all my life.
   4. I see its results.
      1. Out with it.
      2. Hope in it.
      3. Get it within.

CHAPTER VI

THE OPENING OF THE TABERNACLE.

"We will not go into debt for this house of our God. I decline to preach in the place until it is paid for." So said Mr. Spurgeon, and he always meant what he said.

They were good times for England. The enthusiastic preacher never said Nay to an invitation if he could help it. He went north, south, east, and west; only stipulating that the collections taken after each of his sermons should be divided, and that half should be for the church in connection with which he preached, and half for the tabernacle which was being built for the New Park Street Church. How the man worked! It is a wonder that he did not even then work himself to death. Wherever he went the places were packed. It was always a matter of wonder among the crowds that waited for him, how he was ever to get through them and find his way to the pulpit. But he was uniformly cheery and kind, and had a pleasant word for the people whom he had to push in his efforts to force his way.

A story is told of a big meeting in a little village in Kent. The chapel was crammed; and the deacons, mindful of the fact that the congregation, chiefly engaged in agricultural pursuits, were used to plenty of fresh air, had taken the precaution to open the windows. While Mr Spurgeon was preaching a breeze sprang up, which presently rather inconvenienced him. It blew the leaves of the open Bible, and made them rustle; and it also blew Mr. Spurgeon's hair into his eyes, and over his forehead. Everybody will remember that he wore his hair parted nearly, but not quite in the middle, and that there was a lock which was certain to respond to any breeze.

He stopped suddenly in his talk, and said, "Will some one kindly close the window?"

A deacon who was sitting at the back of the chapel immediately went quietly out. He felt that it would be a moral impossibility to make his way through the people and get to the offending window from the inside; he therefore went to the outside and reconnoitred. The only way he could think of was to get a broom and push up the window.

In the meantime the wind was becoming still more playful. "Please shut the window," said Mr. Spurgeon again.

The deacon outside was short, and even when the broom was fetched he needed a chair or stool, and there was not such a thing in the whole place unoccupied. He must run to the nearest cottage and borrow one. The second appeal of Mr. Spurgeon had sent forth two other deacons, and yet the thing was not accomplished.

Again the preacher stopped, and in his own whimsical way, as he pushed back the teazing lock of hair, he said, "Really, I am not like Burton beer, best on draught." The people laughed; up went the window, and in a few minutes the laughter of mirth was changed to tears of feeling.

There was a good collection after that sermon and the one preached in the evening. Indeed, it may be said that Mr. Spurgeon first taught the people how to give. Certainly they opened their purses for him as they did for no one else. And he always did what he could to make them happy and comfortable. The writer of these words remembers an occasion when he declined to preach in a stuffy little chapel.

"It is cruelty to animals," he said, "and very unnecessary cruelty too, when there is a beautiful apple-orchard with soft green grass and plenty of shade quite close."

The orchard belonged to a churchman, but he did not refuse the request sent in Mr. Spurgeon's name that he would grant the use of it to the Baptists for the day. And never did the preacher's words seem more eloquent and beautiful than then. The green grass, the blue sky, the distant hills, and the little meandering stream were as an inspiration to him.

And nobody grudged him his share of the collection at the close. The people who enjoyed his services had always themselves need of funds, and these were far more augmented through Mr. Spurgeon than they could have been by any other means.

So successful was Mr. Spurgeon in collecting funds for the Tabernacle, that, by January 1860, £16,868 was in hand, or more than half the amount required. In addition to home labours this year, he preached in Paris in February, and in Geneva in June. Meanwhile the spacious structure, on the erection of which his heart was set, was steadily going forwards. Mr. Stevenson notices[1] a very interesting incident in connection with the progress of the building:—"One evening while the works were in progress Mr. Spurgeon visited them after the men had left, and he there encountered Mr. Cook, one of his deacons. They walked about together for some time, and then Mr. Spurgeon proposed that they should kneel down and ask God's blessing upon the work. They did so; and there in the twilight, with the blue sky above them, and the piles of bricks and timber all around them, they knelt where no eye but that of God could see them, and the pastor and his friend each

[1] *Pastor C. H. Spurgeon.* Passmore & Alabaster.

poured out most earnest supplications for the prosperity of the work, the safety of the men engaged on the building, and a blessing on the church. Their prayers were not offered in vain, but were abundantly answered. Out of so large a number of men engaged on the work, not one of them suffered harm; the divine protection was over them."

Towards the close of the year a large and enthusiastic meeting was held in the Tabernacle before it was completed. The floors were laid, but there were no pews. Notwithstanding the discomforts, much money was given there, and more promised. Mr. Spurgeon was much cheered; for not only was the building in which he longed to proclaim the unsearchable riches of Christ approaching its completion, the money to pay for it was also nearly all obtained. At the beginning of the year the following statement of affairs was made:—"This church needs rather more than £4000 to enable it to open the new tabernacle free of all debt. It humbly asks this temporal mercy of God, and believes that for Jesus' sake the prayer will be heard and the boon bestowed. As witness our hands." God heard the prayer, and honoured the confidence of His servants.

The first service in connection with the opening of the Tabernacle for divine worship was conducted at seven o'clock in the morning on Monday, 18th March 1861, when more than a thousand persons assembled to offer praise and prayer to God. Mr. Spurgeon presided, and it was he who offered the first prayer. During that week a most successful bazaar was held in aid of the building fund, the clear proceeds of which was £1200. On Monday, the 25th, a second prayer-meeting was held, presided over by the Rev. G. Rogers, who also spoke to the assembly on "The House of God the Gate of Heaven." In the afternoon Mr. Spurgeon preached to a large congregation the first sermon, on Acts v. 42, "And daily in the temple, and in every house, they ceased not to teach and to preach Jesus Christ."

A second sermon was preached in the evening by the Rev. W. Brock, from Phil. i. 18, "Christ is preached, and I therein do rejoice; yea, and will rejoice." On the following evening there was a public meeting, limited exclusively to the contributors to the building fund, of whom more than three thousand were present. Sir Henry Havelock took the chair; and, in the course of his opening address, said they could not look around that magnificent building without feeling that it was entirely of God's doing. The progress which had been made in that work of God was the most extraordinary thing in modern church history. Mr. Spurgeon, Revs. F. Tucker, J. Russell, and C. Stovel, with others, addressed the meeting.

One evening of the opening services was devoted to friends of the neighbouring churches. The invitation to the ministers and members of these churches, to show their sympathy in the opening of the new house of God, by attending especially at this meeting, was most cordially accepted, and the number present proved the heartiness of the response. An audience numbering four thousand people assembled on the occasion, whilst on the platform and pulpit were met a goodly array of ministerial brethren. The chair was occupied by the Rev. Dr. Steane. In his speech he adopted a striking method of asking the audience to give further proof of their sympathy with the pastor of the tabernacle and his work. He asked the pastors of the churches to rise, as an expression of their congratulations and affectionate love; when they all rose at once. He then requested the entire assembly, if they really and heartily wished Mr. Spurgeon "God-speed," to rise also; when every person in the building rose. "Nothing," he said, "could have been more unanimous and more delightful;" and then, turning to his young brother, he gave him the right hand of brotherly fellowship on behalf of all. The meeting was subsequently addressed by Revs. C. H. Spurgeon, W. Howieson.

P. Turquand, G. Rogers, R. W. Betts, and Newman Hall.

On the Good Friday of that year, March 29th, Mr. Spurgeon preached in the Tabernacle twice; in the morning from, "Christ Jesus whom God hath sent forth to be a propitiation through faith in His blood;" and in the evening from, "My beloved is mine, and I am His." The sermon he preached on the evening of Easter Sunday was published in the *Metropolitan Tabernacle Pulpit*, under the title of "Temple Glories." It was one of the most animated and powerful of the preacher's discourses at that period. He drew a graphic picture of the effect on a church of the descent of the Holy Spirit upon it; how previously the services were lifeless and badly attended, loveless, without zeal, without interest; but how afterwards, when "the fire had come," the minister was in a glow, and the people were stirred to the most intense earnestness. It is impossible to read this sermon, especially the latter part of it, without feeling that the preacher was describing his own experience. His remarks upon the prayer-meeting of the church he was picturing were most forcible. The sermon concluded with the words, "This is the effect of the fire. O God, send the fire here!"

The next evening the Rev. John Graham preached from 2 Thess. i. 12, "That the name of our Lord Jesus Christ may be glorified in you, and ye in him, according to the grace of our God and the Lord Jesus Christ." The sermon is described as an excellent one, full of evangelical truth, and pervaded by the spirit of Christ—altogether in harmony with the ministrations statedly conducted in the building in after years.

On Tuesday, the 2nd of April, there was a public meeting of the Baptist brethren of London, Sir Samuel Morton Peto in the chair. Referring to the success which had attended Mr. Spurgeon's preaching, the chairman said that he believed the building itself was an evidence that the preacher's topic was Jesus only; because if ministers have recourse to what they deem intellectual or philosophical preaching, or any other than that of preaching Christ, we soon find, in the Baptist denomination, that empty pews show the result. The meeting was afterwards addressed by the pastor of the Tabernacle and the Revs. J. H. Hinton, A. C. Thomas, P. Dickerson, and Dr. Jabez Burns.

Another night there was a gathering of the various denominations for the purpose of hearing addresses on Christian union. The chair was occupied by Edward Ball, Esq., M.P., who, in the course of a long speech, said he had known Mr. Spurgeon, and worked with him in the cause of Christ, before his removal to London. He had witnessed his first efforts, he knew the village in which he first settled, and he could bear testimony to the wisdom of those men who thought his right sphere was not a mere village, but the great metropolis. The Rev. J. Hall then spoke for the Independents; Edward Corderoy, Esq., represented the Wesleyans; Rev. R. Bushell the United Free Methodists; and the pastor the Primitive Methodists, among whom, he said, he first found the Saviour. He explained the absence of other representatives by saying that they had not an Episcopalian, because the clergyman whom he had invited, though perfectly willing, was unable to come; nor had they a Presbyterian—the Presbyterian brother who was to have been there having telegraphed to say that he was taken ill yesterday.

The Rev. Octavius Winslow, D.D., preached on Thursday evening, 4th April, from the words, "It is finished;" and thus impressively closed his discourse:—"And now, from my heart, I ask the blessing of the triune God upon my beloved brother, the grand substance of whose ministry I believe, from my very soul, is to exalt the finished work of

Jesus. And I pray that this noble edifice, reared in the name and consecrated to the glory of the triune God, may for many years echo and re-echo with his voice of melody and of power, in expounding to you the glorious doctrines and precepts of Christ's one finished atonement. And God grant that none of you may be found rejecting, to your everlasting woe, the doctrine of the Cross. You may attempt to laugh it to scorn; you may make your excuses for its rejection; the hour is coming, ay, the hour is near, when death confronting you, the veil falling upon all earthly scenes, rising upon all eternal realities, then will you discover the unbelief and contumely that could trifle with the atonement, dispute it in life and in health, fail you in your solemn hour; and you will find yourself on the brink of eternity, without a plank, without a life-boat, without a star of hope to cheer the dark spirit's travel to the bar of God. Reject it; deny it at your peril; your blood be upon your own heads. And may God grant in his grace that ere long you who have believed in Him, confessed Him, and loved Him here on earth, may cluster around His throne, gaze upon His unclouded face, unite in the anthem of the blessed, and from those lips which once uttered that glorious sentence—'It is finished,' receive the 'Well done, good and faithful servant;' 'Come, ye blessed of my Father, inherit the kingdom prepared for you from the foundations of the world.' And to God the Father, God the Son, and God the Holy Ghost, we will all unite in one eternal ascription of praise. Amen."

A remarkable sermon by Mr. Spurgeon from the text, "For I will cleanse their blood that I have not cleansed," was preached on Sunday morning, April 7th, and the people were greatly impressed by it.

A sort of family gathering was held next night. The president was the Rev. John Spurgeon, the father of the minister. Among the speakers were former pastors

Rev. C. Room, Dr. J. Angus, and J. Smith; also deacons T. Olney, J. Low, and W. Olney.

The subject of Christian Baptism was specifically dealt with in a sermon preached on Tuesday evening, April 9th, by the Rev. Hugh Stowell Brown, from the words, " Buried with Him in baptism, wherein also ye are risen with Him, through the faith of the operation of God, who hath raised Him from the dead." The next evening a large number of believers of all denominations assembled to celebrate the Lord's Supper. Dr. Steane, Dr. James Hamilton, and Mr. Spurgeon presided at the tables. The deacons and elders of the neighbouring churches served the communicants; and Revs. J. Lafleur, of Canada, and J. Hitchens prayed. Every one present felt it to be a time of hallowed enjoyment. The offertory, amounting to nearly £100, was presented to the widow of a neighbouring Christian minister. The Sunday morning's sermon following, which was delivered by Mr. Spurgeon, was on "The Last Census;" and on the Sunday morning after that he preached on "The Missionaries' Charge and Charter"—a sermon on behalf of the Baptist Missionary Society. He pleaded earnestly that the best men only should be sent to the missionary field, and expressed a hope that some of his hearers would go. He said with great earnestness, " I would that the divine call would come to some gifted men. You who have, perhaps, some wealth of your own, what could be a better object in life than to devote yourself and your substance to the Redeemer's cause? You young men who have brilliant prospects before you, but who as yet have not the anxieties of a family to maintain, why, would it not be a noble thing to surrender your brilliant prospects that you may become a humble preacher of Christ? The greater the sacrifice, the more honour to yourself and the more acceptable to Him. I long that we may see young men out of the universities, and students in our grammar schools—that we may see our physicians, advocates, tradesmen, and educated mechanics, when God has touched their hearts, giving up all they have, that they may teach and preach Christ. We want Vanderkists; we want Judsons and Brainerds over again. It will never do to send out to the heathen men who are of no use at home. We cannot send men of third and tenth class abilities; we must send the highest and best. The bravest men must lead the van. O God, anoint thy servants, we beseech Thee; put the fire into their hearts that never can be quenched; make it so hot within their bones that they must die or preach, that they must lie down with broken hearts, or else be free to preach where Christ was never heard."

All through the month of April 1861 the opening services were continued. Other gatherings were held; among them a meeting for the statement and enforcement of Calvinistic doctrine, and one to hear a magnificent oration on "Nonconformity," by that popular leader of the people, Mr. Henry Vincent. After these services were over, the regular work of the tabernacle began in May, the whole building being free of debt, and the accounts showing that £31,332, 4s. 10d had been received, and the same amount expended. On the 6th of the month the pastor and friends who had signed the declaration in January now signed another testimony, acknowledging the goodness of God in that their expectations had been more than realised, both as to the amounts that had been received and the short time in which the work had been accomplished.

The building thus erected, paid for, and opened for the worship of God, is a vast and commodious structure, 146 feet long, 81 feet broad, and 62 feet high. There are 5500 sittings of all kinds. There is room for 6000 persons, who are frequently gathered there. There is a lecture-hall capable of holding 900; a school-room for 1000 children; there are six class-rooms, a kitchen, lavatory, and several

THE SCENE AT THE TABERNACLE.

other apartments below stairs. There is a ladies' room for working meetings, young men's class-rooms, and secretary's room on the ground floor; there are also vestries, for pastor, deacons, and elders, on the first floor, and several store-rooms on the second floor.

Yet the accommodation was not sufficient for the great and beneficent works carried on, and use had to be made of the adjoining places.

Every Sunday from the first there was a wonderful scene outside the Tabernacle before the commencement of the service. Crowds stood outside the gates waiting eagerly until they might enter. The seat-holders were allowed to gain an entrance by other doors up to within ten minutes of the time for the service to begin.

When at last the doors were opened there was a rush. People almost fought for places; and there was a clatter of feet and tongues, such as often was anything but a good preparation for that which was to follow.

But no sooner had Mr. Spurgeon lifted his hand and uttered the words, "Let us pray," than there was a great hush. It was the Sabbath indeed, and the enormous crowd felt itself in the Father's house; and as the beautiful voice of the preacher poured out the prayer that came from his heart, it seemed also to come from the hearts of the people. The six thousand were as one man, and one desire possessed the whole.

During the sermon no sound was heard but the sound of that one voice, which reached every ear. The people were afraid of losing a word, and so all eyes were on the face that seemed to shine upon them from the rostrum. And the words were always such as individuals needed, and such as they would remember. Happy were those who could hear Spurgeon every Sunday, and even twice a day! And scarcely less happy were those who heard him but seldom, for to such his words were so precious that they were never forgotten!

The *City Press*, in an article which appeared on September 2nd, 1891, thus recalls the early days of the ministry of the great preacher:—

"When Mr. Spurgeon first came to London he suddenly acquired that popularity which has not only never waned, but has gone on increasing from that day to the present time. At first, observant persons were much exercised in trying to account for such success; but probably there were few who thought that it would be lasting. When even the Surrey Gardens Music Hall was not half large enough to accommodate those who came, and when nearly 30,000 could be attracted to the Crystal Palace to hear him preach, the majority thought that the phenomenon would pass away like any other ephemeral fashion. Some shrewd people professed to have made the discovery that the public had made a mistake altogether, for the chief claim which such a preacher could put forth consisted in his assurance and vulgarity. The rocket might go up with a blaze, the stick— all there would soon be left—was destined to fall in darkness and smoke. People were like sheep, whether in following or in ceasing to follow, and this preacher, with his vast assurance, would soon find his level. Some who, on account of their religious profession, might have been expected the more ardently to second the preacher's efforts to reclaim the people, were amongst the most uncompromising opponents, and to such what was done or what was left undone by 'that Spurgeon' amounted to a very heinous crime indeed. His plain Saxon and his Calvinistic doctrines were apparently quite as objectionable as his round face and short figure. It was intolerable that such a youngster, who had, as it were, suddenly sprung upon the scenes, should attract and sway the multitude, when older men of education, and with unimpeachable notions of pulpit decorum, commanded a very ordinary following, if any following at all. What certain newspapers said about him it would be almost cruelty to their present editors in these times to reproduce. If the preacher had been a political adventurer, and the papers had appeared during the Reign of Terror in Paris, the language of some of them could hardly have been more violent. Such defenders as he had in the Press were men whose theological opinions were identical with his own. One of these was the late Mr. James Grant, of the *Morning Advertiser*, who was educated, we believe, for the Presbyterian Church; another was Dr. John Campbell, of the *British Banner*. Both of these were men of mark and a credit to their profession, and the support they accorded the preacher when so many were denouncing him was heartily appreciated."

CHAPTER VII.

THE PASTORS' COLLEGE.

THE philanthropic works of Mr. Spurgeon were as wonderful as his preaching services.

Reference has already been made to the Almshouses in connection with the New Park Street congregation. It will be remembered that these were founded by Dr. John Rippon. Mr. Spurgeon hoped that the old New Park Street property would still be used for Baptist purposes; but though a minister went there and did his best, it was too near the Tabernacle for any one to hope to fill it. We remember being present when the Tabernacle was so full that thousands were standing. Mr. Spurgeon told them that they would find comfortable sittings and hear the Gospel in Park Street if they would go, and added, "I am sure I would not stand all the evening to hear myself speak," but no one offered to leave the crowded place for the other.

It was evident that it was unwise for the Tabernacle Church to have the risk and expense of keeping up the New Park Street cause; and it was therefore decided to arrange with the Charity Commissioners for the sale of the property, the proceeds to go to new schools and new almshouses.

The foundation-stone of the new building was laid by the man who at the Tabernacle was only second to Mr. Spurgeon himself in consecration and usefulness—Mr. Thomas Olney, the senior deacon—on May 6th, 1867. Mr.

Spurgeon asked his congregation to contribute £1000 towards the building, and this was immediately done. One Sunday morning the pastor said that, in order to open the place free of debt, he would be glad if the people would contribute during the day £750 more, which were required to cover the extras. When night came it was found that the whole sum had been contributed.

The liberality of the Tabernacle people was almost as wonderful as the eloquence of their pastor. One day he announced that during the week he was going to lay the stone of a chapel somewhere in the country, and he would like to put upon the stone £100 as a little gift of sympathy from the friends of the Tabernacle; there would therefore be collections both morning and evening for that purpose.

At the evening service, however, he said that there would be no collection, as more than the sum he had asked for was contributed in the morning.

It will be readily understood that with such people to support him the pastor had not much difficulty with the almshouses and schools.

The building consists of two school-rooms, class-rooms, a schoolmaster's house, and seventeen alms-rooms. The occupants of the latter are women above the age of sixty who are members of the church, and they are chosen according to the years during which their names have remained on the church books, and the need of the applicants. Mr. Spurgeon succeeded in getting the money with which to endow the almshouses and place them once for all in a good position.

The school-rooms, which were intended for the week-day instruction of children, bore this inscription:—

"These buildings are connected with the ancient church now worshipping in the Metropolitan Tabernacle. Six of the almshouses, together with a school-room, were built and endowed under the pastorate of Dr John Rippon at New Park Street, Southwark. The present structures were completed March 1868.—C. H. and J. A. Spurgeon, Pastors."

One of the greatest works of Mr. Spurgeon's life was that in connection with the Pastors' College. "Spurgeon's students" are now known all the world over as very acceptable ministers of the gospel.

The originator of the College had the idea given to him in the first instance. Around the minister of the Tabernacle, himself a young man, it was natural that young men should gather; and there were many who after their conversion offered their services to Mr. Spurgeon for any department of Christian work in which their help would be acceptable.

There was one young man who from the first might be called his pastor's crown of rejoicing. He has been for years a most successful minister at Landport—the Rev. T. W. Medhurst.

Immediately after his conversion, under the preaching of Mr. Spurgeon, he set himself to do what he could. He commenced to distribute tracts and visit the sick, and he was a most earnest and successful Sunday-school teacher. The next thing he did was to attempt some open-air preaching; and in this he was greatly blessed of God, for many who listened to his voice as he preached at the street corner—a thing that was comparatively rare in those days—became converted, and began to live changed lives to the glory of God.

Mr. Spurgeon was delighted and thankful on account of this young man, and of course he did what he could to help him. He gave him much personal instruction, and he placed him under the tuition of a good Kentish minister, and it was he, Mr. Medhurst, who subsequently became the first student at the Pastors' College.

There was not in existence at that time the kind of

college which Mr. Spurgeon thought such men as those who grew up around him required. They were not men of wealth or education, and the ordinary college was beyond their means and attainments. He wanted men with the gift of preaching more than he wanted scholars. He believed that many a man of little learning but great piety might be blessed of God in work among the masses; and in 1856 the College was really formed.

But the real reason for its formation was stated by Mr. Spurgeon in a few notable sentences on the fourteenth anniversary of its establishment. They contain the true facts of the case as in a nutshell, and having regard to all that has happened since, it is important to use no other words than his own. "It must be frankly admitted," he said, "that my views of the Gospel and of the mode of training preachers were and are somewhat peculiar. I may have been uncharitable in my judgment, but I thought the Calvinism of the theology usually taught to be very doubtful, and the fervour of the generality of the students to be far behind their literary attainments. It seemed to me that the preachers of the grand old truths of the Gospel, ministers suitable for the masses, were more likely to be found in an institution where preaching and divinity would be the main objects, and not degrees and other insignia of human learning. I felt that without interfering with the laudable object of other colleges I could do good in my own way." And he therefore proceeded to do it, by establishing the Pastors' College.

Mr. Winsor and Mr. W. Olney, two of his deacons, promised to help him; and having secured his first student, he set to work to find the means of providing for him and the rest, when others should be added to the number. And for this he had not long to wait.

One of the first cares in connection with the College was to select a worthy and suitable tutor. The Rev.

George Rogers, minister of Albany Road Chapel, Camberwell, was at length appointed, and continued to fill the office of principal and theological tutor for many years, and indeed until he retired in consequence of his advanced age and its attendant infirmities. A number of young men followed the first student, and these were also received and placed under Mr. Rogers' care. Once every week they met at Mr. Spurgeon's house, and were privileged to enjoy the benefit of his shrewd and useful observations on preaching and practical church work. This was the origin of those weekly lectures given by himself, which have proved such a blessing to the students, and through them to the churches over which they have been called to preside.

There were many opinions in regard to the new College, and most of them were derogatory. Many thought it was not needed—that the existing Colleges provided all the ministerial training the Baptist denomination required. Some thought that the new institution would lead to jealousy and division in the ranks of the ministry. Others feared that a class of ill-trained men would be sent out to preside over the churches, who would lower the character of the Baptist ministry and of the denomination generally. Mr. Spurgeon did not trouble himself over-much in regard to these objections, for he was convinced in his own mind that the world was really in want of such men as he hoped to prepare for their special work and send out to labour. Without any disparagement of human learning and culture, and recognising the fact that in some cases superior literary attainments were desirable, he still felt that piety, prayerfulness, and zeal, with a fair share of education, were what, in a large number of cases, were most required.

Therefore the College was established, and now all the world is convinced that it was a right thing, and that it was greatly needed. Numbers of earnest young men have gone forth from it who have been very successful as preachers of the Gospel and pastors of churches. Some have gathered congregations of Baptist churches where none existed before; some have been the means of reviving decayed churches that were well-nigh dead. They have, as a rule, all proved themselves valuable acquisitions in the towns and villages where they have settled.

The one great design of the College has always been to train *preachers*. Poverty has not been allowed to shut any away from its doors, for there has been very little cost to the students themselves, even for the necessaries of life; but inability to speak so that the people would listen has been a very strong barrier to a man's entrance. The selection of candidates for admission is principally determined by evidences of eminent piety, of adaptation for public teaching, of great zeal for the salvation of souls, and of instances of actual usefulness, so far as, upon the best accredited testimony, can be ascertained. In the beginning the course of study was limited to two years, in some cases, where favourable openings for usefulness presented themselves, and suitable qualifications were possessed, even that brief term was shortened. Of late years there has been a tendency to lengthen the period of study—a tendency which is greatly for the advantage of the students, and of the churches to which they may minister in after years. Great stress is laid on extemporaneous speaking; it is encouraged and demanded in every way, and every facility is furnished for its improvement. An excellent library has been provided for the students, who can study the best books, both ancient and modern, and have besides the advantage of able guidance and counsel as to the books most likely to prove useful. They are also encouraged to provide libraries of their own, and are helped to acquire books easily and cheaply for their future use.

The first study of the young men who formed the nucleus of the Pastors' College was the house of their tutor, Mr. Rogers. But they used the class-rooms under the Tabernacle as early as the year 1861, and continued to work there until their new college was ready. They presented a busy scene. Whilst this ministerial education was given day by day, other plans of usefulness were prosecuted at the same place each evening. From the beginning, a certain number of young men were supplied with a sound elementary, commercial, and classical education, who were employed in business during the day. This arrangement proved invaluable to a host of young men. Nor were they slow to avail themselves of the advantages offered them, so that it presently became absolutely necessary that suitable buildings should speedily be provided in order to accommodate them. On 14th October 1873 the foundation-stone of the present College edifice was laid; and on 28th August 1874 the opening services were held with many manifestations of zeal and rejoicing. The entire cost, £15,000, was defrayed by the liberality of the Christian public. From one published report we gather that the nett result of nearly twenty-six years of tuition is as follows:—

Number of brethren educated in the College		620
,,	now pastors, missionaries, and evangelists	464
,,	without pastorates, but engaged in the Lord's work	28
,,	engaged in secular callings	18
,,	medical missionaries and students	7
,,	educated for other denominations	2
,,	dead	41
,,	names removed from the list	60

It has been Mr. Spurgeon's college in more senses than one. His people have desired above all things that the labourer, who was more than worthy of his hire, should have plenty of money; but he never cared for it, and he generously resolved to devote more than half the amount towards the College. There is a weekly offering every Lord's day at the Tabernacle for its support; this yields a large sum annually. In 1865 Mr. T. R. Phillips, one of the deacons of the church, generously gave a supper to the friends of the institution, after which a report of the work for the past year was read, and those present were asked to contribute as they felt disposed towards its support. At that meeting £350 were raised. Mr. Phillips gave a similar supper in the month of March every year after, and the contributions rose till, in March 1882, they reached the noble sum of £2071.

One of the pleasant and important functions in connection with this College supper was the annual statement made by the pastor, who then reported progress. In 1882 Mr. Spurgeon said he had intentionally decreased the number of students; and it is certain that he had some wise reason for doing so. He was also making a great point of missionary work, and some of the accepted men were under promise to take charge of, or establish, churches in some foreign field. Since the formation of the College six hundred and twenty men had been educated for the ministry, of whom four hundred and sixty-four are now engaged in the Baptist denomination as ministers, preachers, or evangelists, twenty-eight others, although without stated pastorates, being regularly engaged in Christian work. It was urged upon those sent out to build new chapels rather than trench on another man's foundation. They only received such as really felt themselves unable to do otherwise than enter the ministry, although they could certainly make more money in business. Many already had gone abroad in missionary work, while others were refused by the societies on account of the doctors declaring they were consumptive. He believed, however, they would go out somehow. He did not believe in the idea of only sending healthy men out, though it was doubtless right for the societies to adopt such. He was a very unhealthy person himself, yet he believed he should live to bury many healthy men; for many a creaking door kept on its hinges when many another gave way. He did not know what they would do to convert the world if they only sent out healthy men. Some of the students had gone over to other denominations; this, of course, was an astonishing thing. Those who thus changed were, as a rule, no particular gain to those who got them. He should like to see a very large number of church clergymen equal to Mr. Baptist Noel come over to the Baptist denomination, by being enlightened on the point of believers' baptism. Still, he preferred to have men who came straight out of the world, were convinced, and remained steadfastly abiding with them. Speaking of the many subscribers who had died during the year, and appealing for funds, he claimed that he put before them a thing which ran on its own wheels. He was looking for great things very speedily. Whatever censures or whatever praises were being given to the stirring movement of the Salvation Army, it was at any rate a very wonderful sign of the times. He remembered prophesying that God would one day set aside very much the regular ministry, and would send the Gospel to the people by the people of St. Giles and Whitechapel. The Lord called some of the very lowest of the land, and said, "Go and speak in My name," which they had done with great results. At the same time they must have men who did not murder the Queen's English, for the educated rising race could not be taken to those chapels where there was a very original grammar and pronunciation. They could help men at least to conceal their own ignorance, which was really all that Solomon could do.

Mr. Spurgeon was greatly encouraged not only by the young men who offered themselves, but by the readiness with which they were received into the churches and the usefulness which they manifested there. His story of the College is full of vivid interest. There were times when his faith was put to the test. From the sale of his sermons in America he was at first able to give £600 or £800 a year to the College; but this source of income was suddenly stopped after he had preached a sermon which was a severe denunciation of slavery. This was a trial to him. He was as determined as ever not to go into debt, and on one occasion he proposed to sell his horse and carriage and give the money to the College, but his friends dissuaded him from that. It was at this time that the weekly offering commenced, but at first it was not very productive.

On one occasion he was brought to the last pound when a letter from his banker informed him that a lady had paid in to his account £200 to be used for young men in the ministry. A little later another £100 was contributed in the same way by another donor. When the five hundredth weekly sermon had been published, Messrs. Passmore & Alabaster generously presented £500 to the College. Gradually the weekly offerings increased in value, until in the year 1869 the amount reached £1869—a curious coincidence in figures.

About £5000 a year is required by the College, and the sum actually spent there is only a small part of the necessities which have arisen through this effort to do good. New chapels have been required for the new men, and Spurgeon's sons in the faith always looked to him for help. In this work the founder of the College gratefully acknowledged the divine help. "The Lord found for me one of his stewards," he said, "who, on the condition that his name remains unknown, has hitherto, as the Lord has prospered him, supplied very princely amounts for the erection of places of worship, of which more than forty have been built or so greatly enlarged or renovated as to be virtually new structures."

It will be easily understood that money anxieties were not the only ones which came to Mr. Spurgeon from his college.

He had the heavy responsibility of deciding as to the men who were or were not suitable for the work of preaching. Now and then a mistake was made, and the heart of the master was greatly pained in consequence. He made careful inquiries; he asked the aid of college tutors and friends; he was himself no mean judge of character; but there have been, notwithstanding all the care thus exercised, two or three who have not proved themselves right men in right places. But these were solitary individuals only. There has been a great crowd of able, holy men trained for Christian service at the Pastors' College. "I devoutly bless God," said Spurgeon, "that He has sent to the College some of the holiest, soundest, and most self-denying preachers." In the year 1870 the Earl of Shaftesbury, speaking in Finsbury Chapel, said: "Nothing was adapted to meet the wants of the people but the gospel message brought home to their hearts, and he knew of none who had done better service in this evangelistic work than the pupils trained in Mr. Spurgeon's college. They had a singular faculty for addressing the population, and going to the very heart of the people."

Many of the students, before entering the College, had been members of the evening classes previously referred to. In this way the teachers became acquainted with the most promising young men there. The Tabernacle Church has always furnished the largest number; and it may be said that they had received a training before they knew it by listening to Mr. Spurgeon, for his strong personality influenced young men very greatly. Indeed it was almost always noticed at first that many of them tried to copy Mr. Spurgeon in pronunciation and manner. Some others did so unconsciously; they so loved and admired their master that they became like him. This has been less noticeable in the later than it was in the first years. But at no time could they have had a better pattern; for he showed them how to speak so as to interest and move the crowd.

Mr. Spurgeon had from the first very valuable helpers in his College. The Rev. George Rogers appeared to have been very specially endowed for the work of the tutor. Mr. Cubitt, of Thrapstone, threw into the services he rendered the College all his powers and zeal. The classical tutor, Mr. Gracey, a man of high ability and great consecration of spirit, won the esteem and gratitude of every student. Mr. Fergusson took the English elementary classes, and was not only able to find out what was in the men, but to impart knowledge so that it remained with them. Mr. Johnson and Mr. Selway also rendered always excellent service. But the greatest helper and comforter to Mr. Spurgeon was his own beloved brother, to whom he bore as long ago as the year 1870 this testimony: "I adore the goodness of God which sent me so dear and efficient a fellow-helper as my brother in the flesh and in the Lord, J. A. Spurgeon. His work has greatly relieved me of anxiety, and his superior educational qualifications have tended to raise the tone of the instruction given."

The statistics of the first ten years of the work of these men showed that they had baptised 20,676 persons, and that the gross increase to their churches was 30,677.

It goes without saying that the ministers from the Pastors' College are at the present time a great power in the land, for they hold some of the most eminent positions among Nonconformists, and many of them are men of culture and deep spirituality. They are, and will ever remain, absolutely loyal to Mr. Spurgeon. They have been tried, but have not been found wanting. They have loved him with no common love, and are enthusiastic in their praises of him, as indeed they always had reason to be. He held them together with a firm though gentle hand, and they were bound to him by ties that could not be broken.

He gave them of his best. He wrote nothing better than *Lectures to my Students*, which have been useful to every part of the Universal Church, but which were prepared with them alone in the author's mind.

Spurgeon cannot die while any of these men live, for they have been diligent learners of their master. And nothing could have been more blessedly helpful to these men, who in all parts of the world are bearing the burden and heat of the day, than was the Annual Conference held at the College. They were times of the most sacred spiritual refreshment and reconsecration. The communion service —who will ever forget that was once present? It was as if the heavens were opened above them, and they saw the very face of Christ.

But the greatest treat of these meetings was always the president's address. What a magnificent welcome greeted him whenever he appeared among his own men! And he was always at his best and happiest on these occasions; and the fire and energy of his talk was tempered by the tenderest, most father-like love. The sweet humility of his character revealed itself then. He was playful and serious, affectionate and dignified, a brother yet a king among them. The men came up to keep their yearly feast often tried and tired, but they went back heartened and encouraged, and always with renewed confidence in their leader, Charles Haddon Spurgeon.

Perhaps we cannot do better than give in this connection a part of Mr. Spurgeon's address at the last Conference at which he was present, in which he reviewed the work of the College. He said:—

"The Pastors' College has assisted in their studies for

the sacred ministry no less than 845 men. These were preachers before they applied to the institution; indeed, they had each one been preaching for two years at the least, and we believe they would have continued to do so. Thus the College has not increased the number of ministers, but we trust it has improved their quality. In some few cases the young brethren had received a high-class secular education; but they much needed Biblical instruction, and guidance as to the duties of the pulpit and the pastorate. But the mass of our men came to us with very deficient learning, or none at all; indeed, the College was originally instituted to help men of good natural parts who had not been able to acquire a sufficient education in their earlier days. We opened a door of hope for those who could not pass an examination in the standards of scholarship, but yet had been used of the Lord in the winning of souls. Although we have taken within our doors men of considerable early advantages, we hope we shall never be induced to shut out the order of men for whom our classes were first formed. When there is rich mental soil, whatever early neglect there may have been, the ground yields plentifully as soon as it is tilled; and in produce, the virgin soil frequently rivals that which has been cropped all along. Verily, 'there are last that shall be first:' men far behindhand in education feel their lack, and, by a desperate resolve, cause the republic of knowledge to suffer violence, and to be captured for the kingdom of heaven. We have no occasion to be ashamed of our students, nor of the marked advance which they have made in preparation for their life-work. We might all have done better; but we must praise the grace which has enabled us to do as well as we have.

"Since they have been out in the field, God has been gracious to our brethren, and made them to be successful winners of souls. There are great differences as to the measure of success; but so it ever has been. For the most part our brethren remain faithful and useful. The torrent of error is so strong that certain of them have been carried off their feet, and stand no more with us; but we are not discouraged, for we remember the firmness and growing graces of others against whom the floods cannot prevail. There remains a band of men whose hearts the Lord has touched, who are steadfast, unmovable. Had only one or two, such as we could mention, remained true to the old colours, we should have thought our labour well repaid; but there are with us many men valiant for the truth, and loyal to their heavenly King. To these, under God, we look for the maintenance and promulgation of the doctrines of the Gospel in years to come. They will 'hold the fort' till the Lord appears, or they will, ere they die, light up a candle in the dark places, which shall never be blown out."

In reference to this College the *Daily Telegraph* says:—
" Perhaps the most useful of Mr. Spurgeon's 'succursales' to that great Tabernacle, which will for ever be identified with his name and memory, is the Pastors' College hard by, which owed its existence to urgent necessity. Before the pastor of New Park Street Chapel had preached there for three months, many young men were converted by his burning words, and admitted to church fellowship. Aflame with zeal, some of these youths commenced to work for the good of others by open-air preaching and Bible readings in the homes of the poor. One of them, Mr. T. W. Medhurst, applied to Mr. Spurgeon to fit him better for the work, and was admitted by the pastor to lessons in the latter's own family. Gradually Mr. Medhurst's example was followed by others, for whom Mr. Spurgeon had no room in his modest home, which was then in Dover Road, Borough. In a short time Mr. Winsor, Mr. Olney, and a few other friends joined Mr. Spurgeon in putting down a small sum for purchasing books and hiring a room where the students

might assemble. Gradually the imperious demands for further instruction, in order to extend the kingdom of Christ, induced the large-hearted servant of God who has just expired to collect funds for the erection of his Pastors' College. To it Mr. Spurgeon contributed a large portion of his own income, and of the funds received from America for his sermons and writings, which there found a ready sale. Suddenly the fertilising stream of American bounty was dried up, as Mr. Spurgeon had estranged the sympathies of many Transatlantic readers by pleading the cause of the down-trodden slave. The great preacher named the financial difficulty in which he found himself to his affectionate congregation, and in a few days hundreds of pounds were placed in his hands. In 1874 the present buildings dedicated to the Pastors' College were completed, and its annual working expenses—about £7000—were supplied by the weekly offertory collected at the Tabernacle, by private subscription, and by collections in the churches of pastors who received their education within its walls. Since the College was first started nearly 1000 young men have been trained there for the work of their lives, and nearly 100,000 converts have become members of the Church through the labours of its students and graduates."

CHAPTER VIII.

THE WORK AT THE TABERNACLE.

WE take up the history of Mr. Spurgeon's labours in the year 1866, and find his life crowded with work. The year before he had visited Holland, and preached in most of the large towns. He was already well known there, for his sermons, translated into Dutch, had a large circulation. The Queen of the Netherlands expressed her desire to see him, and he had a long and most interesting interview with her.

Before passing on reference should be made to a very celebrated sermon which, during the years 1865-66, attained a circulation of 200,000. It was preached in June 1864, and its title was "Baptismal Regeneration." Few sermons, even of Spurgeon's, made such a stir as this. A great and indignant host rose against the preacher; and some pain came to him on account of the misunderstandings of those who ought to have known him better.

Few have been the utterances of any man which have aroused such strong feeling in the latter years, when happily good people have found something better to do than to denounce the religious opinions of each other. Of course the doctrine which Mr. Spurgeon attacked found many a doughty champion; and several good men and true wrote on the preacher's side. It is said that within two years, besides articles in newspapers, magazines, and reviews, more than one hundred separate pamphlets appeared for and against the dogma of regeneration by baptism, held by many in the Church of England. A collection of them, forming several good-sized volumes, are on the shelves of the Metropolitan College Library. One of the results of the controversy personal to Mr. Spurgeon was his entire withdrawal from the Evangelical Alliance. When the "Baptismal Regeneration" sermon was published, the Hon. and Rev. Baptist W. Noel wrote Mr. Spurgeon a brief remonstrance against certain expressions in the sermon. Then came a letter from Mr. James Davis, secretary of the Alliance, setting forth very strongly that Mr. Spurgeon had no alternative but either to retract the harsh language or withdraw from the Alliance. It was a great pity, and both parties afterwards must have regretted what then occurred, for Mr. Spurgeon withdrew from the Alliance, although, as is well known, he always had the utmost sympathy with the doctrines it inculcated.

The closing paragraph is a fine specimen of the preacher's boldness and earnestness:—" The time is come when those who follow God must follow God, and those who try to trim and dress themselves and find out a way which is pleasing to the flesh and gentle to carnal desires, must go their way. A great winnowing time is coming to God's saints, and we shall be clearer one of these days than we now are from union with those who are upholding Popery under the pretence of teaching Protestantism. We shall be clear, I say, of those who teach salvation by baptism, instead of salvation by the blood of our blessed Master, Jesus Christ. Oh, may the Lord gird up your loins! Believe me, it is no trifle. It may be that on this ground Armageddon shall be fought. Here shall come the great battle between Christ and his saints on the one hand, and the world, and forms, and ceremonies, on the other. If we are overcome here, there may be years of blood and persecution, and tossing to and fro between darkness and light; but if we are brave and bold, and flinch not here, but stand to God's truth, the future of England may be bright and glorious. Oh, for a truly reformed Church in England, and a godly race to maintain it! The world's future depends on it under God, for in proportion as truth is marred at home, truth is maimed abroad. Out of any system which teaches salvation by baptism must spring infidelity—an infidelity which the false Church already seems willing to nourish and foster beneath her wing. God save this favoured land from the brood of her own established religion. Brethren, stand fast in the liberty wherewith Christ has made you free, and be not afraid of any sudden fear nor calamity when it cometh, for he who trusteth to the Lord, mercy shall compass him about, and he who is faithful to God and Christ shall hear it said at the last, 'Well done, good and faithful servant, enter thou into the joy of the Lord.' May the Lord bless this word for Christ's sake!"

New Baptist chapels were being built in London at this time, and, as much money was needed to pay for them, a bazaar was held at the Tabernacle in January 1866, which produced more than £1700. Following this time of work came a time of prayer, for Mr. Spurgeon believed that without prayer there could be no power; and he therefore set apart the entire month of February for conference and supplication for the revival of the Lord's work in all departments of his church and congregation. One extract from his invitation to the various meetings of this season shows his sense of pastoral responsibility, and the earnestness with which he engaged in his work:—"We have need of renewed intercessions. It is by mighty prayer that the cause of God has been maintained in its vigour among us so long, and only by the same vehement pleading will the divine blessing be retained. He who worketh all our works in us first teacheth us to pray, and then grants us the desire of our hearts. With the view of raising the glow of our

INTERIOR OF THE METROPOLITAN TABERNACLE

fervour to a greater heat, and in the hope that the Lord Jesus will work through our humble means, we have arranged the following meetings, and hope to receive your most cordial co-operation in carrying them out so far as you feel that in any one or all of them you can be of service. May the Holy Spirit, without whom we can do nothing, assure our beloved church, and the great congregation among whom we labour, of His abiding presence among us, by giving gracious tokens of His power!"

Great success and blessing attended the whole of these gatherings. Among the results of the meetings, speedily realised, were the following:—Many of the children of the deacons, elders, and members of the church were aroused to a sense of their danger and need of salvation, and many of them who had long been halting between two opinions were led to decide for Christ. The ladies of the Tabernacle established a monthly meeting for prayer, especially for the conversion of their children. The number of inquirers on Wednesday evenings largely increased, and there was a general renewal of spiritual life.

The question was at this time often asked, "Will Spurgeon found a new sect and have it called after his name?" Those who asked the question usually answered it to their own satisfaction in the affirmative. A Mr. Tyler, a correspondent of the *New York Independent* in 1866, may be taken as a specimen of the class. "One word," he says, "about Spurgeonism in general. Silently, but rapidly, within the pale of this great Baptist sect in England, and covering all the land with its network of moral power, there is being formed a distinct body of Spurgeonite preachers—energetic young men trained in Spurgeon's college, imbued with Spurgeon's intense spirit, copying with an unconscious but ludicrous fidelity even the minutiæ of Spurgeon's manner of speech, proud of their connection with Spurgeon's name, and in constant communication with the 'head centre' in London.

More and more is Spurgeon separating himself from the general organisation of the religious world, and even of the Baptist denomination, and concentrating his work upon his immense church, his college, and the churches throughout the kingdom that have taken his pupils for pastors. If this goes on for another twenty years, Spurgeonism will be a vast organic and wondrously vitalised body; and, should circumstances warrant, this body may, as many intelligent Baptist ministers think, probably assume the name of its founder, and Spurgeon follow the example of Wesley, by founding a sect. He is certainly showing much of Wesley's executive and organising capacity."

This paragraph gave Mr. Spurgeon considerable pain. He declared that there was no word in the world so hateful to him as "Spurgeonism," and in strong language said that the work of forming a new sect he left to the devil. He preached no new gospel, and had no desire to separate himself from the religious world, but, on the contrary, he valued greatly the communion of saints, and did all that he could to promote it.

That which he said then he abided by twenty years later, when more than a few had come to think it a very desirable thing indeed that "the last of the Puritans" should promote a New Sect.

Mr. Spurgeon believed in fasting as well as in prayer, and in September a hundred and twenty students and ministers kept a holy day at the Tabernacle. It was such a season of blessing as few present had ever enjoyed before. Fasting was found to be a great help to prayer; and the devotions, being unbroken by the necessary distractions occasioned by taking refreshment, grew more and more fervent, till around the table of the Lord all hearts appeared to glow with love most vehement. The result was felt by those present in the increased power of their ministry, and in a larger measure of success attending their labours.

Before the year closed there was given to the preacher an opportunity of addressing a large meeting of the Society of Friends, on the "Life and Labours of George Fox."

But an unusual restriction was laid upon the preacher. Mr. Spurgeon would have liked permission to pour out his soul in prayer upon the spot, but it was intimated to him that silence would be preferable. This was not satisfactory to all. One of the most eminent ministers among the Friends published a letter afterwards, to the following effect:—" It was my privilege to attend C. H. Spurgeon's lecture on George Fox, at Devonshire House, on the 6th inst. It is almost superfluous to say how cordially I united with his powerful, truthful, and loving appeal to our Society. Indeed, his address altogether seemed to be an embodiment of what has been my own concern for years past, and which I have endeavoured, with far less ability, to impress upon my fellow-professors in religion. I cannot but view the whole thing as a message of mercy from the Almighty, and I am sure it will add greatly to our responsibility, as well as to our condemnation, if much fruit does not follow this renewed evidence of divine regard. I could really say in my heart, while listening to the earnest, simple pleading of this dear servant of Christ,

It is the truth, the very truth, and nothing but the truth;' so entirely did my feelings and my judgment go with it all.

"One thing caused me sorrow, however; I do not think our views and our practice on the subjects of prayer and of worship were correctly represented on this deeply interesting occasion. No doubt there was a jealousy in some minds lest these views should in any way be compromised, and I apprehend that these honest though groundless fears were the cause of their being, to a certain extent, misrepresented. Our worthy chairman told us, at the beginning and at the end, that it was to be a *silent* approach to the throne of grace. Now, if I know anything of Quaker principles, we have no more right to *enforce* silence than to *enforce* a vocal offering. Either way, I believe the work of the Spirit, upon or in the heart, should be left unfettered.

"I am sure the spirit of prayer was over the meeting at the beginning, and still more evident was the spirit of thanksgiving at the end; and I believe there was a call from the Lord for vocal utterance, which was prevented by human interference. Surely we might have safely trusted our dear brother, the lecturer, to follow his own convictions of duty in this matter; and I know that if he had not felt called upon to address the Almighty, there were other lips that would have been opened had liberty been granted; and I think such an end to such a meeting would have been altogether in accordance with gospel order, and with our own belief on the subject of divine worship.

"In conclusion, I venture to express a hope that, should we be favoured with another visit from one who is clearly prepared to appreciate and to approve our leading views of gospel truth, he may be left at liberty to do his Master's work in his own way, a condition to which he is fairly entitled, and which we claim for ourselves when similarly circumstanced.—J. G."

In the autumn of that year Mr. Spurgeon paid a short visit to Paris, returning, refreshed and happy, to spend Christmas at home. One of the first public engagements of 1867 was the delivery of an address to the Sunday-school teachers of South London, on "How to Raise the Dead." This address was most powerful and effective in its delivery, and in its published form has been extensively useful. The month of February was set apart, as in former years, for the purposes of special conference and devotion. Monday, the 18th, was a whole day of fasting and prayer, beginning at seven in the morning, and continuing without a pause or breaking up for meals, until nine at night—a day of prayer, in which the Holy Spirit was manifestly present all day. Throughout the day it was felt that the presence of the Lord God of Hosts overshadowed the place. The evening meeting in the Tabernacle was a most remarkable one. Heaven was besieged with impassioned prayers that souls might be converted and God be glorified. One after another fervent cries arose to God from those who were as if they would take no denial. And a great blessing followed the earnest prayers of God's people.

Mr. Spurgeon was ready for any work, as usual; and he had a happy time among the costermongers. A graphic sketch of his visit was afterwards published by "One who was there":—"On Tuesday, the 12th of March, Mr. Spurgeon preached a sermon to the street-vendors of Golden Lane and its vicinity, in the Evangelists' Tabernacle. Some of the dealers came with unwashed faces and uncombed hair, but the majority were dressed in their best clothes; and those who could not recognise them would hardly think that some were costermongers' wives. There were several in the fried fish line, two or three pickled whelks merchants, a number of cabbage and vegetable dealers, coke-sellers, wood-choppers, picture-dealers, and some representatives of street-sweepers. At seven o'clock Mr. Spurgeon ascended the platform, and opened with prayer. Then a hymn was heartily sung, and a chapter read and expounded. The preacher's prayer was frequently responded to; and when reference was made to the bodily aches and pains which so many suffered, and the poverty experienced by others, there were many deep sighs. The preacher's easy delivery, rapid flow of words, masculine thought, earnestness and directness, were thoroughly appreciated; and the little anecdotes, homely illustrations, and forcible hits were much enjoyed. One curious bit of criticism we heard from several. A coster's living depends largely upon his 'voice.' He therefore knows the value of good lungs, and is a connoisseur in voices. The preacher's voice was eulogised as 'wonderful,' 'stunning,' 'I never,' and other equally significant phrases. One coster had lost his voice, and probably he envied the preacher's gift. Another poor fellow—a follower of Joanna Southcott—retired from the hall, expressing great disappointment because no reference had been made to his own people—the Jews; and nothing had been said about the millennium, the teaching of which, he declared with much earnestness, always led the way to conversion."

The Tabernacle had now been in constant use for more than six years, and it needed a little renovation, since every part of it was for use and none for ornament. It was therefore judged advisable, at this time, to close it for some weeks for repairs. During the period thus occupied, Mr. Spurgeon preached for five Sabbaths, in the morning, at the Agricultural Hall, Islington. The first service was held on the 24th of March, and between eleven and twelve thousand persons were present. The preacher's delivery was slow, measured, and emphatic; and the attention was kept up throughout. At all the services the congregations were much larger than was anticipated; and on some occasions thousands were shut out. Many conversions followed, and neighbouring churches shared in the blessing. The result of this experiment was so satisfactory that others followed the example, and afterwards hundreds of gospel services were held in the Agricultural Hall.

The next thing to claim the attention of Mr. Spurgeon was the building of the orphan houses at Stockwell and in April he bought the land. In August he went to Hamburg, to attend the triennial conference of the German Baptists, and preach at the opening of the new Baptist chapel in that city. Home again next month, we find him on the 9th, surrounded by a party of about four thousand persons at Stockwell, presiding over the joyous proceedings connected with the laying of the foundation-stones of three of the houses for his Orphanage. So great and widespread was the interest awakened on the occasion, that the people in that southern suburb of London kept the day as a grand holiday. Mr. Spurgeon himself was in feeble health, not having fully recovered from an attack of rheumatism while at Hamburg, and it was arranged that Mrs. Hillyard, the foundress of the Orphanage, should have laid the stones; as that lady, however, was absent, he very appropriately performed the work. The united sums the collectors laid upon the stones amounted to £2200; and it was announced that in addition to the £20,000 given by Mrs. Hillyard, the money then in hand was £5500.

No one could endure, unless he had a constitution of iron, such a strain of anxiety and work as that to which the Tabernacle pastor was subjected; and Mr. Spurgeon's constitution was by no means an iron one. He was working at the rate of ten years in one, and was exhausting his powers at a fearful pace.

From this glad day at Stockwell he returned to his home, where his beloved wife was ill and suffering, to suffer himself from the over-strain. There was a pathetic article in the November number of his own magazine, *The Sword and Trowel*, which had by this time become well established, and which has always been Mr. Spurgeon's personal letter to his friends and the world. This article was called "On my Back," and it recorded the fact that he was feeling so weak and ill that he was obliged to cancel his engagements to preach in various parts of the country. He probably had at this time more requests for sermons than there were days of the year in which to preach them, for the hope of almost every church in difficulty was that Charles Haddon Spurgeon would give them a lift. It was therefore bad news for the country when the great preacher gravely assured all friends who were looking for him that the act of

God in laying him low exonerated him from all promises, and that he did not mean merely to say that he could not fulfil these now, but further, to declare that he never would be able to do so.

For it was borne in upon him now that the Tabernacle work itself was more than he could accomplish, and that he must positively decline to do anything outside his own large sphere. Even here he could not fill his place for a considerable period, and until he had spent a season in retirement and rest. He was racked with terrible rheumatic pains; but what he felt most was that he was a silent preacher, and therefore like an eagle bound. But in the article referred to there was a beautiful spirit of submission, and he closed by quoting the following quaint lines of Quarles:—

> "And were it for thy profit to obtain
> All sunshine? No vicissitudes of rain?
> Thinkest thou that thy laborious plough requires
> Not winter frosts, as well as summer fires?
> There must be both; sometimes these hearts of ours
> Must have the sweet, the seasonable showers
> Of tears; sometimes the frost of chill despair
> Makes our desired sunshine seem more fair;
> Weathers that most oppose to flesh and blood,
> Are such as help to make our harvests good;
> We may not choose, great God; it is thy task;
> We know not what to have, nor how to ask."

It was during this illness, and partly in consequence of it, that the Rev. James Archer Spurgeon, the only brother of the preacher, was appointed to help him in his work at the Tabernacle—an appointment which was the greatest possible comfort to the senior pastor, and a decided gain to the church. The Rev. J. A. Spurgeon has had the oversight, to a very great extent, of the philanthropic and business part of the work ever since, and he has most ably discharged it.

In the year 1868 Mr. Spurgeon preached the May Missionary Sermon to young men in connection with the London Missionary Society. It was delivered in Westminster Chapel, and was crowded with those who, listening earnestly, would not forget the preacher's words. Also, to the great joy of the Congregational Union Committee, he was able to give an annual address at the breakfast. It was as much a joy to Mr. Spurgeon as to the Congregationalists, because he believed it helped towards Christian union. He was at the same time careful in his utterances, for he had no sympathy with the idea of the absorption of the Baptist into the Congregational body.

In the *Sword and Trowel* for May 1868 there appeared a portrait of a man whose face and name were quite familiar to all frequenters of the Tabernacle—Mr. Olney, the senior deacon.

Every Sunday, when the young man went up into the pulpit, Mr. Olney used to accompany him and sit by his side. He was always at hand, therefore, if anything should be needed; and the presence of the old man must have been a support to the young minister, who could not have been all he was but for his highly nervous and sensitive temperament. "Father Olney," as he was affectionately called, did not live many years after the publication of his portrait. He became acquainted with Park Street Chapel during the pastorate of Dr. Rippon, and when the new chapel was built he was one of the trustees. He was chosen a deacon in 1838, and everything thereafter that touched the prosperity of the place was dear to his heart. No words can express the joy which he had in Mr. Spurgeon's ministry. It was really a beautiful sight to see him in the pulpit with the pastor; one knew that while one preached the other prayed, and so a double blessing was secured. He was a faithful friend to all, the poor as well as the rich; and he took under his fatherly, fostering care all the institutions connected with the Tabernacle, feeling almost as great an interest in them as the pastor himself.

In the month of June 1868 a pleasant thing occurred. The Baptist churches showed their appreciation of the services he had rendered them so generously and so long by presenting him with the sum of £1200 for his benevolent work—a sum that was afterwards increased to £1765. The following extract from the illuminated memorial which accompanied the gift will give some idea of the esteem in which he was held (and that esteem has been growing ever since) by his own denomination:—" Dear friend and brother,—We have much pleasure in presenting to you herewith a purse, containing £1200, the free-will offerings of a considerable number of individuals and churches of our denomination in the United Kingdom. We have a twofold object in this presentation. First, as a small token of the high esteem in which we hold you; secondly, to aid you in your noble effort to find a home for orphan boys. We have watched your past career with praise and prayer: praise to our covenant-keeping God, who has so richly endowed you with gifts for His service, inspired you with zeal in His cause, and blest you with Pentecostal success; prayer, that He would keep you blameless to the end, give you increasing love to and ever-growing success in His kingdom, and, finally, the crown of eternal life. We honour you for your work's sake, nor less for your generous love to all your brethren in the ministry, and to the churches over which they preside. To the blessed God, Father, Son, and Holy Spirit be all the glory!" On his birthday, the nineteenth of the month, he received the tenderest tokens of affection from his church.

Mrs. Spurgeon was dangerously ill in 1867, and had to undergo a very dangerous operation. Sir James Simpson, of Edinburgh, undertook the case, and the most skilful surgeons then living were with him. As usual the prayers of the Tabernacle were, however, relied upon as much as human skill, and God spared to the preacher the mother of his twin-sons to be his companion even to the end of the journey.

Mrs. Spurgeon was not able that year to open the great bazaar for the Orphanage, and it was therefore postponed for twelve months. Eventually she did open it, and the grand sum of £1400 was thereby secured for the orphans whom Mr. Spurgeon had taken into his loving care. A full account of this Orphanage will be found on another page.

Mr. Spurgeon occasionally lent his Tabernacle to other speakers who could fill it, and one of these was the Rev. E. P. Hammond, the children's preacher of America. He was in England conducting evangelistic services for the young in the autumn of 1867, and the great place of worship crammed with children was a sight to behold. Mr. Spurgeon had reason to believe in the possibility of the conversion of children,—what was he himself but a child when the great change came to him?—and he was exceedingly interested and sympathetic in regard to Mr. Hammond. Some people found fault with his methods, of course (there are hosts of lazy people with bitter tongues who can do nothing but find fault, and we ought not to grudge them that one occupation perhaps), and they expressed their surprise that Mr. Spurgeon should lend the Tabernacle to a man whose methods they thought were objectionable; but Mr. Spurgeon boldly defended him as "an earnest servant of God, and a prince of preachers to children."

Mr. Spurgeon's sermons had an enormous circulation in America, and whoever read them was anxious to see the writer of them. Great pressure was therefore brought to bear upon him in order to induce him to go over and deliver a set of lectures or sermons. If money could have helped his decision, very generous terms were offered; for he was asked to give twenty-five lectures in return for £5000. But the preacher was too busy at home; and towards the close of the year when this invitation was given, 1869, he was very ill with an attack of small-pox, which brought him low, and awakened much anxiety on his account. He was indeed frequently laid aside; and this fact makes the amount of work—literary work especially—besides all that was connected with the Tabernacle, simply marvellous. Even when he could not preach sermons he wrote them, and one that came from his sick bed at this time, on the text, "Unto you, therefore, which believe, He is precious," has comforted many thousands of sorrowful and afflicted ones in all parts of the world. During his illness one fact greatly rejoiced his heart: it was the liberality of his friends. His faith was heroic; and yet sometimes when he remembered the enormous sums of money for which he was responsible, he might well have been filled with anxiety, if not with despair. But during this dismal November, as again and again in his history, God moved generous hearts to new generosity; and he afterwards gratefully recorded how one friend called and left £500 for his Orphanage, and another sent in a letter £1000.

It was in 1870 that "Father Olney" died. "Never minister had better deacon, never church a better servant," said his pastor. And he missed him much. But he has always had a large band of helpers ready to serve him in every possible way. And the Tabernacle, the scene of so much heroic service for Christ, has given, and will ever give, plenty of opportunity for devoted men of all ages.

The great business of Mr. Spurgeon's life was to preach the Gospel, but he never held aloof from passing events, and his rousing words upon them must have often turned the scale in favour of righteousness and peace.

NATIONAL EDUCATION.

During this year, 1870, the great subject of National Education was before the country, and the question of School Boards was agitating the minds of men and women. Much more was made than need have been of what was called the Religious Difficulty. It appeared to many of the Liberals of the land that the only way to avert the difficulty was to exclude the Bible from the schools. Mr. Spurgeon strenuously opposed this, and declared that although he would not have denominational teaching, he would advocate the use of the Bible in any system of training that might be adopted. He expressed a hope that all Christians would unite to secure that the Bible be read in all schools set up by the State. " We must have no creeds, or catechisms, or denominative teaching; but there must be liberty for the children to read the word of God. We propose a conscience clause of a novel order, not one which allows exception from Bible reading to be claimed as a favour, but which makes the reading of it a privilege to be asked for by those who desire it."

In the course of the summer a large meeting was held in Exeter Hall, in advocacy of the Bible being daily read in elementary schools. The hall was crowded to excess by an audience of working-men; and the speakers, all working-men, delivered eloquent and effective speeches. Mr. Spurgeon took the chair on the occasion. When the resolution, that the Bible be permitted to be read in the national schools by those children whose parents wished it, was put to the meeting, it was carried amid a tumult of cheers, about twenty hands only being held up in opposition. The working-men of London were not prepared to withhold from their children the book of God.

At this time the Franco-German war was occupying the attention of Europe, and Mr. Spurgeon published his views on the war in the August number of his magazine. As an exposure of the sin and folly of war, the article is one of the most convincing ever penned. Many of the newspapers noticed it, while many reprinted large portions in their columns. The article was entitled "John Ploughman's Letter on the War." It was addressed to Napoleon, Emperor of the French, and William, King of Prussia, and opened thus:—"This comes hoping that you are getting better, or at least better tempered with one another."

"John Ploughman" did much to make the success of the *Sword and Trowel*. Its plain, terse language was liked by the people; and the stern truths, strongly though often plainly put, carried conviction with them to many thousands of hearts.

He could hit hard when he thought it was necessary; and perhaps his word-fightings made him some enemies, at least for a time. The following anecdote illustrates this:—

At the laying of the foundation-stone of a new chapel, Mr. Spurgeon had said, speaking of the small remuneration of pastors, that a very large proportion of the ministers of all denominations did not earn anything like so much as the men who were laying the stones of the building. The editor of the *National Church* took hold of the statement, and endeavoured to pervert it to his own purpose, by making the speaker say that, with few exceptions, Nonconformists in general pay their ministers a most miserable pittance; and then drawing the inference that the voluntary system was a failure. Replying to the perversion, Mr. Spurgeon said:—"This is not lying, but it is as like it as one pea is like another. When will men write with at least a decent show of honesty? We have never seen a prize-fight, but we always heard that the lowest bullies of the ring are accustomed to strike fairly, and we commend their example to the editor of the *National Church*."

Sometimes he was outspoken in mere playfulness, but even this was not allowed to go unchallenged. On one

THE METROPOLITAN TABERNACLE.

occasion there was a howl because of something he had said in favour of tobacco. He took no notice of most of the accusations made against himself, but he wrote a letter to the *Daily Telegraph* on this subject:—

"I demur altogether, and most positively, to the statement that to smoke tobacco is in itself a sin. It may become so, as any other indifferent action may, but as an action it is no sin. Together with hundreds of thousands of my fellow-Christians, I have smoked, and with them I am under the condemnation of living in habitual sin, if certain accusers are to be believed. As I would not knowingly live even in the smallest violation of the law of God, and sin is the transgression of the law, I will not own to sin when I am not conscious of it. There is growing up in society a Pharisaic system which adds to the commands of God the precepts of men; to that system I will not yield for an hour. The preservation of my liberty may bring upon me the upbraidings of many of the good, and the sneers of the self-righteous; but I shall endure both with serenity, so long as I feel clear in my conscience before God.

"The expression 'smoking to the glory of God' standing alone has an ill sound, and I do not justify it; but in the sense in which I employed it I still stand to it. No Christian should do anything in which he cannot glorify God—and this may be done, according to Scripture, in eating and drinking, and the common actions of life. When I have found intense pain relieved, a weary brain soothed, and calm, refreshing sleep obtained by a cigar, I have felt grateful to God and have blessed his name; this is what I meant, and by no means did I use sacred words triflingly. If through smoking I had wasted an hour of my time; if I had stinted my gifts to the poor; if I had rendered my mind less vigorous, I trust I should see my fault and turn from it; but he who charges me with these things shall have no answer but my forgiveness.

"I am told that my open avowal will lessen my influence, and my reply is that if I have gained any influence through being thought different from what I am, I have no wish to retain it. I will do nothing upon the sly, and nothing about which I have a doubt.

"I am most sorry that prominence has been given to what seems to me so small a matter—and the last thing in my thoughts would have been the mention of it from the pulpit; but I was placed in such a position that I must either by my silence plead guilty to living in sin, or else bring down upon my unfortunate self the fierce rebukes of the anti-tobacco advocates by speaking out honestly. I chose the latter; and although I am now the target for these worthy brethren, I would sooner endure their severest censures than sneakingly do what I could not justify, and earn immunity from their criticism by tamely submitting to be charged with sin in an action which my conscience allows."

CHAPTER IX.

SPURGEON AND HIS STUDENTS.

The work of training messengers of the Glad Tidings being very dear to the heart of the great preacher, to it he brought the whole-souled and insistent earnestness which characterised all he did—an earnestness born of a sure and certain belief in the truths he professed.

Penetrated with the firm conviction of the deep necessity of humanity for the Saviour of the World, Christ the Consoler, the Healer of its Wounds, its Light in Darkness, its Deliverer from Captivity, its only Life, he urged with all the force of his strong nature the call of his Divine Lord, "Come to Me," and strove to prepare a body of men for the ministry who should speak the Word with power.

To this end, in 1856, the Pastors' College was built close to the Metropolitan Tabernacle, and to it were welcomed such young recruits to the ranks of the ministry as had given practical evidence of power as "fishers of men," generally in a charge of two years' duration. The whole heart and mind of its founder were bent on carrying out the commands of his Lord, as he knew them, and being firmly persuaded of the truth of the doctrines as held by Calvinistic Baptists, he could teach none other, while he judged it inexpedient to allow the introduction of the jarring element of theological controversy where only harmonious and devout study were to be desired.

Accordingly the College was devoted solely to the better preparation of candidates for the Baptist ministry, that they might have time and means to become more closely acquainted with the Sacred Scriptures, and the meditations and experiences of devout minds of past and present times; to pursue courses of secular study which should strengthen their mental faculties, and enrich them with information; and also to develop as far as possible the power of ready speech; and all to the end that they might be well equipped for their sacred calling, and furnished with weapons true and effective with which to fight the battle of the Lord. No fees were exacted from the students, so that poverty was no bar to admission, and the end which the institution was to serve was held to be so important and necessary that its strong-hearted president was content to trust for its maintenance to the willing gifts of those who, acknowledging that their worldly store was but a trust put into their hands by Him to whom all things belong, would rejoice to be able to offer willingly of His own to the glory of God For himself, Mr. Spurgeon gave both money and labour, to the fullest extent of his power. He took quite a paternal interest in the young students, and his week-end lecture delivered to them was no dry and heavy discourse, which they might follow laboriously, albeit with a conscientious desire to profit by it; but the familiar and unrestrained utterances of one who loved them, who desired the best gifts for them, and who, out of the fulness of his own heart, gave forth instruction, exhortation, warning, and encouragement; impressing what he taught with homely and forcible illustrations, ready wit, and bright humour; rousing and sustaining the interest of his hearers, inspiring them with the faith, and love, and zeal which burned in his own soul; and winging his arrows of truth so that they flew straight to the mark.

As years went on many of those who had listened to him

within the College, and had passed out in succession to their appointed spheres of labour with the echo of his voice in their hearts, desired to possess themselves of the text of the lectures which had fired and inspired their youth, and in response to numerous requests Mr. Spurgeon published two volumes of selections from his lectures to students, which, while fulfilling the wish of those who had asked for them, he hoped would promote the welfare of the institution by making it widely known, and, as he trusted, by inspiring an interest in it which should be expressed in the form of practical help, while it was in his heart to extend the help of wise counsel, by means of the printed page, to other young preachers than those within reach of the spoken word.

The first volume contains thirteen lectures, the first of which takes as its theme "The Minister's Self-Watch." In it the Christian minister is considered as a special worker for God, his primary tools being *himself*—his body, soul, and spirit; and he is urged to pay most diligent heed to himself, that every power may be maintained at its highest point of efficiency, as a weapon whose perfection is of the utmost moment, and, alas! whose flaws may seriously lessen its usefulness or produce actual injury.

The aspirant to the office of a minister is assured of the necessity of the New Birth for himself before he can preach the Gospel of regeneration to others. This is the first essential qualification for his office, without which all others are of little value, for if the power of the Gospel of Jesus Christ be an unreality to himself, how barren of result must be the message he delivers! Dead to God himself, how should he have power to show others the way of life; and walking in chill ways apart from the Sun of Righteousness, what should kindle in his heart the constraining ardour that should draw the souls of his people with irresistible force to the feet of the Lord Christ? A picture is presented of such a pastor, maybe one whose silver speech has attracted large congregations, and in whose church those adjuncts of worship, the music of voice and instrument, are exquisitely attuned; and it is shown how easily the members of his flock may think themselves good Christians, mistaking their delight in the pleasant service for the inward worship of the heart; and then the lecturer vividly portrays the anguish of heart of the man, when in the world of spirits he is confronted with those who in their mortal life were given to his charge that he might show them the narrow way leading to life, and, meeting their accusing eyes, realises that he, their false shepherd, has guided them by easy paths into outer darkness.

But further: it is declared that it is not enough that a man should be a disciple of Jesus Christ; he must be strong in virtue and pre-eminent in piety, or he is unfit to undertake duties so sacred, and weighted with such solemn responsibilities as are inherent in the position of a leader of a Christian church. He must seek to live continually in the presence of God, the unfailing source of all perfection, from whom alone all grace and strength are derived; so only might he hope to walk worthy of his high calling, and maintain the fervour of love and zeal, without which his prayers, whether in private or in the congregation, would be poor indeed, and his preaching void of living force. He is bidden to remember that if his piety is weak, there will be a corresponding decline in the spiritual life of his people, especially among the weaker members of his flock, as many persons make the minister their standard of right life and action. The neophyte is plainly warned too, that instead of being removed from strong temptation, as some have supposed, he will be exposed to special perils and more insidious attacks than those occupying less prominent positions. He will not only have to combat temptations of the flesh, which he may at least easily recognise, and so guard against, but others more difficult to withstand, because they steal upon him unawares, or come disguised in garbs of seeming innocency. Especially must he be on the watch against drifting into a state in which his prayers and teachings become matters altogether outside himself, and are only regarded as duties belonging to his office. To give increased weight to these words of faithful warning the testimony of the saintly Baxter is added:—" Take heed to yourselves, because the tempter will make his first and sharpest onset upon you. If you will be the leaders against him, he will spare you no further than God restraineth him. He beareth you the greatest malice that are engaged to do him the greatest mischief. As he hateth Christ more than any of us, because He is the General of the Field, and the 'Captain of our salvation,' and doth more than all the world besides against the kingdom of darkness; so doth he note the leaders under Him more than the common soldiers, on the like account, in their proportion. He knows what a rout he may make among the rest if the leaders fall before their eyes. Take heed, therefore, brethren, for the enemy hath a special eye upon you. You shall have his most subtle insinuations, and incessant solicitations, and violent assaults. As wise and learned as you are, take heed to yourselves lest he overweight you. The devil is a greater scholar than you, and a nimbler disputant; he can transform himself into an angel of light to deceive. He will get within you and trip up your heels before you are aware; he will play the juggler with you undiscerned, and cheat you of your faith or innocency, and you shall not know that you have lost it; nay, he will make you believe it is multiplied or increased when it is lost. You shall see neither hook nor line, much less the subtle angler himself while he is offering you his bait. And his baits shall be so fitted to your temper and disposition that he will be sure to find advantages within you, and make your own principles and inclinations to betray you; and whenever he ruineth you, he will make you the instrument of your own ruin. Oh, what a conquest will he think he hath got, if he can make a minister lazy and unfaithful; if he can tempt a minister into covetousness or scandal! He will glory against the Church, and say, 'These are your holy preachers; you see what their preciseness is, and whither it will bring them.'"

Not only to *stand* against the onslaughts of the enemy of souls must a pastor seek to attain to great holiness, but because the man is reflected in his work, which is only worthy in proportion as he is so; and stress is laid on the importance of correspondence between the life and the doctrine; the man who instructs others as to their obligations must be careful to do as he exhorts his hearers, and leave undone nothing that he declares a duty, for the most persuasive words are powerless to win men to Christ in comparison with a holy and devout life. So too, in matters that might seem of small moment, he must order himself aright; must jealously guard his tongue against uttering light, unkind, or angry words; must owe no man anything, nor wound any by asperities of manner, and strive to obey the Apostle's injunction, to "Give no offence in anything."

Believing strongly that no man should seek to enter the ministry without a call from God, Mr. Spurgeon took as the subject for one of his lectures, "The Call to the Ministry." He first proved that it is in accordance with Holy Scripture that there should be overseers of the churches, and then went on to show how under the Old Dispensation no prophet was owned as such who had not been commissioned by God to speak in His name. It was not until his lips had been touched with a live coal from off the altar that Isaiah dared to respond, "Here am I, send me," when the voice of the Lord was heard saying, "Whom shall I send?" While the prophet Jeremiah answered with fear and trembling when he heard the words, "Before thou camest forth from the womb I sanctified thee, and I ordained thee to be a prophet unto the nations." "Ah, Lord God! behold I cannot speak, for I am a child." Then he received the command, "Thou shalt go to all that I shall send thee, and whatsoever I command thee thou shalt speak. Be not afraid of their faces, for I am with thee to deliver thee. Then," as the narrative continues, "the Lord put forth His hand and touched my mouth; and the Lord said unto me, Behold I have put my words in thy mouth." It was the mandate of the Most High that sent forth the prophet Ezekiel to the rebellious children of Israel. It is recorded, "And He said, Son of Man, stand upon thy feet and I will speak unto thee. And the spirit entered into me when He spake unto me, and set me upon my feet, that I heard him that spake unto me. And He said unto me, Son of Man, I send thee to the children of Israel. . . . I do send thee unto them; and thou shalt say unto them, Thus saith the Lord God."

As the prophets of the Old Law thus spoke only in direct obedience to the voice of God, so the Apostles, the messengers of the New Covenant, called themselves Ambassadors for Christ, and stewards of the mysteries of God. If they were ambassadors they must have been accredited by their Sovereign Lord, while no man can assume the office of steward unless he receives it from his Master. If a man should take upon himself this office without the assurance of his vocation, he must expect his labours to be barren of fruit, for he would be the successor of those prophets of whom it is written, "I sent them not, neither commanded them: therefore they shall not profit this people at all, saith the Lord."

With a great sense upon him of the obligation of each to await the Divine call, he entreated the young men before him to refrain from entering on an office of such extreme dignity, and upon which such solemn issues depended, without being assured of the special fitness attested by the choice of the Holy Spirit. He reminded them how frequently men err in the estimate of their powers and gifts, and quoted the lines—

> "Declare, ye sages, if ye find
> 'Mongst animals of every kind,
> Of each condition, sort, and size,
> From whales and elephants to flies,
> A creature that mistakes his plan,
> And errs so constantly as man!
>
> "Each kind pursues its proper good,
> And seeks enjoyment, rest, and food,
> As nature points, and never errs
> In what it chooses or prefers;
> Man only blunders, though possessed
> Of reason far above the rest.
>
> "Descend to instances and try.
> An ox will not attempt to fly,
> Or leave his pasture in the wood
> With fishes to explore the flood.
> Man only acts of every creature
> In opposition to his nature."

He then proceeded to indicate what they might consider evidences of a Divine commission. The first indication was an ardent, inextinguishable longing taking entire possession of them, and urging them to proclaim unweariedly Christ crucified, the Redeemer of the world: no careless, unconsidered wish, but one formed when their hearts were most deeply stirred by Divine love, laid often before God in prayer for the illumination of the Holy Spirit, and cherished even when its fulfilment would mean the renunciation of ease and worldly gain. If they were attracted by the prestige they hoped to gain from the ministerial office, or by illusive dreams of monetary advancement, or if any secular pursuit, even of the most exalted nature, would satisfy their hearts, they need not doubt that their work lay outside the ministry; but if, on the contrary, it was a necessity of their being to preach the Gospel, they might well believe they had in the desire a token of their mission.

But the glowing desire was not of itself sufficient. If God intended them to deliver His message, He would also bestow on them power, and wisdom, and freedom in speaking it; and though they need not conclude because their first efforts were halting that they had mistaken their vocation, yet unless they had in some measure the tongue of a ready speaker, even at first, it was not likely that they had been elected pastors and teachers.

Mr. Spurgeon approved generally of the custom prevalent in many country churches of requiring the young man who desires the charge of a church to preach before the congregation, as affording discipline of a wholesome, if sometimes painful character; and thought the general opinion of their fellow-students, with whom they were associated in close intimacy in various religious exercises, might assist them in coming to accurate conclusions as to their gift of utterance. And then he endorsed the words of John Newton, who considered one of the necessary evidences of a proper call to be "A correspondent opening in providence, by a gradual train of circumstances pointing out the means, the time, the place of actually entering upon the work. And until this coincidence arrives you must not expect to be always clear from hesitation in your own mind. The principal caution on this head is not to be too hasty in catching at first appearances. If it be the Lord's will to bring you into His ministry, He has already appointed your place and service, and though you know it not at present, you shall at a proper time. If you had the talents of an angel you could do no good with them till His hour is come, and till He leads you to the people whom He has determined to bless by your means."

The most convincing proof of their commission would be found in the conversion of sinners, and the building up of the people of God. However high their attainments, and however popular their preaching, if they were barren of fruit, they must be filled with fear lest they were in the wrong way; and though it was their part to work on even when the harvest of their toil was delayed, if they were indeed working at the command of their Master, they must not doubt that when they had planted and watered He would give increase.

In concluding his lecture, Mr. Spurgeon instanced types of young men aspiring to the pastorate whose disqualifications were openly manifest, selecting them from applicants for admission to the College whom his judgment could not approve, and to whom therefore he could not extend the aid they asked towards the accomplishment of their purpose. First, there was the man whose main object was evidently to achieve distinction, who believed himself possessed of superior ability, and who had chosen the ministry as affording suitable opportunities to exhibit the brilliancy of his talents. He would be entirely out of place as a Christian minister, whose glory must be only in the Cross of Christ. Then came one whose professions were admirable, but whose feet had slipped in the mire, and who could not stand against temptation, and whom contrition and humility should have kept in the background. Of another sort was the man who had nothing to say, but expended an immense, indeed a painful amount of force and fury in saying it. Others presented themselves who had physical defects rendering them unsuitable for the work of preaching, such as imperfectly formed organs of speech or weak lungs; while one, recommended for his piety, suffered from some unusual conformation of the jaw, which occasioned such contortions of the face in speaking, that the effect was irresistibly ludicrous, and could not fail to provoke constant laughter. A rather numerous class were the young men who accepted their failures in all other walks of life as an infallible indication that Divine Providence had intended them for pastoral duties. To these he pointed out that the qualities demanded of the overseer of a church would probably lead to success in business of a secular kind, and that incapacity for other labours was a sorry recommendation for the service of the Lord Jesus, which was worthy of the highest and best efforts of the most able men. One wonderful young man deigned to express a wish to enter the Pastors' College, who, according to his own estimate, possessed a most highly cultivated mind, extraordinary intellect, and preaching powers of a rare order; whom the wondering President felt compelled sadly to refuse, as he would tower so hopelessly above his brethren and instructors. There were still others, satisfactory in many respects, but who had not made up their minds as to the doctrines they held; whose principles apparently allowed them to accept any doctrine that might be convenient for them. With these Mr. Spurgeon could have no sympathy; he could not understand one professing to be ready to teach others who had not settled what were his own beliefs, and always refused to admit such to the College. Having held up before his hearers examples of unfitness for the sacred office, he showed them the ideal Christian minister in the words of St. Paul : " Giving no offence in anything, that the ministry be not blamed; but in all things approving yourselves as the ministers of God, in much patience, in affliction, in necessities, in distresses, in stripes, in imprisonments, in tumults, in labours, in watchings, in fastings; by pureness, by knowledge, by long-suffering, by kindness, by the Holy Ghost, by love unfeigned, by the word of truth, by the power of God, by the armour of righteousness on the right hand and on the left, by honour and dishonour, by evil report and good report; as deceivers, and yet true;

as unknown, and yet well known; as dying, and, behold, we live; as chastened, and not killed; as sorrowful, yet always rejoicing; as poor, yet making many rich; as having nothing, and yet possessing all things."

Prayer is taken as the subject of two lectures; the one treating of private, the other of public prayer. In that on private prayer, Mr. Spurgeon told his hearers that the minister must needs be pre-eminently a man of prayer. Throughout the day, amid all his occupations, devout aspirations and fervent petitions will rise to heaven, and in wakeful moments of the night his heart will seek God. To them as students he said, that the training they would receive in passing through the College would, after all, only afford them exterior helps; frequent communion with their Heavenly King would prove the sovereign power to mould their spiritual nature to highest perfection and fitness for service. In the preparation of their sermons, prayer would open to them fields of thought, and guide them in their choice of a subject, would illuminate the sacred text, and show its hidden meaning. Let them use in pondering its pages all the help afforded by the Commentaries of holy men, but above all let them beseech from the Author of Light irradiation of His own word. When they were about to stand before their people as ambassadors for Christ, fervent prayer would inflame them with love and zeal, so that their words would have power to rouse, to soften, and melt the hearts of their hearers. The love they learned from the contemplation of the crucified Son of God, and near communion with Him, would teach them how to speak with truest eloquence. After their pleadings and exhortations would it not be a natural impulse to a faithful preacher to fly to his Lord to express sometimes his hope and joy, at others to lament his want of fervour, and entreat that his poverty and weakness may not stay the work of the Holy Spirit, but that where he has failed to incline the hearts of men to their Maker, the Spirit of God might prevail.

Then the true pastor bears the needs of his flock on his heart, and carries them to the Great Shepherd, entreats the Great Physician for the sick, in body or soul, the Comforter for the sorrowful, Infinite love for the desolate, the fatherless and the widow, and Him who came to seek and save the lost, for the wanderer into a far country from the Father's house. Nor will his sympathies be limited to his own congregation; he will pray too for his country, and for all peoples and nations.

The more they considered the cost of the redemption of a soul, and realised its worth in the sight of God, the more they would be driven to prayer. In the biographies of some of the most successful preachers they would read how they laboured in prayer not only by day, but in the night, spending hour after hour in prayer and meditation. Mr. Spurgeon advocated retirement for seasons of special prayer, either alone or in company with devout men. So waiting on the Lord they would renew their strength, and contemplating His perfections, receive His image in their hearts and reflect it more truly than before.

Although Mr. Spurgeon was convinced that the use of a liturgy was not in accordance with the practice of the first Christians, he was willing to admit that extempore prayer was not always to edification,—not always even the expression of "sincere desire," and sometimes, if fervent in its spirit, couched in uncouth language painful to hear. He therefore offered some hints for the guidance of the students in public prayer. First, he insisted on the necessity of much private prayer, as the poverty and formality of so many prayers was due to a lack of devotion. The attitude of mind of suppliant man in approaching Him before whom the angels veil their faces should be that of deepest reverence and humility, nor should he dare to address the King of Heaven in the familiar tones of ordinary conversation. He bade them to beware of striving after effect in their prayers, making fine phrases " that they might receive glory of men," lest they merited and received the reward of the hypocrites; but rather let them seek the assistance of the Holy Spirit, that with their whole being they might come into the Divine presence, and so pray, as truly to present before God the desires and petitions of the congregation. He advised them as a rule to make short prayers—that is, in public—and to avoid using the stock phrases, made up often of misquotations from Scripture, whose repetitions are as wearying to the mind as the expressions themselves are foolish and inapt. He and they all professed to believe the Bible to be written in words inspired by the Holy Ghost; therefore it was incumbent upon them to use the utmost care to observe perfect accuracy in quoting Holy Scripture, lest they perverted the meaning of the word of God. Mr. Spurgeon thought it would be well not to observe a fixed order of conducting public worship, but to be guided in this by the direction of the Holy Spirit, and advised them to let prayer, and hymns, and sermon all follow the same line of thought.

Four lectures bear on the subject of sermons, Their Matter, The Choice of a Text, The Voice, and Attention. In treating of the first, Mr. Spurgeon laid it down as essential that the discourse must have some definite aim, and contain some truth which is to be declared, and pressed home. A mere array of high-sounding words arranged in flowery phrases and imposing periods is worthless; only when charged with the truths of the Gospel have they any weight. It is useless to rouse the emotions without directing them to right action. It is written in Hebrews viii. 10, " For this is the covenant that I will make with the house of Israel after those days, saith the Lord: I will put my laws into their mind, and write them in their hearts." A wise man commenting on this passage remarks, " Ministers are herein to imitate God, and to their best endeavour to instruct people in the mysteries of godliness, and to teach them what to believe and practise, and then to stir them up in act and deed to do what they are instructed to do. Their labour otherwise is like to be in vain. Neglect of this course is a main cause that men fall into so many errors as they do in these days." Mr. Spurgeon feared there was too much truth in the complaint that, after years of patient listening, it was still impossible to gather from the sermons of many preachers what were the doctrines held by them to be necessary of belief, and the obligations to be fulfilled. His next point, illustrated by telling similes, was that the sermon should really be an exposition of the text. If what they had to say had no relation to the passage of Scripture they had announced as their theme, or if they wished to range at will over any field of thought which suited their fancy, would it not be better to forego the aid of the text in starting on their ambitious career?

He charged them that while careful always to teach clearly the truths of their religion from the pulpit, not to give undue prominence to any one truth to the exclusion or overshadowing of others. Let them make the doctrines necessary to salvation their chief theme, and bring forward those attributes of God in Jesus Christ which would be most practically useful to men and women in the midst of the combat of life, with cares and fears and temptations pressing on every hand. Of what use were discourses directed to elucidating such points, as, Whether the healing properties of the Pool of Bethesda were actually the result of an angel's visit, or were produced by the physical agency of some spring, whose flow continued for short periods and then ceased awhile?

Supposing them to have gathered instructive matter in sufficient, though not superfluous quantity, their next care must be to arrange it duly. Let sound doctrine be the foundation, and the conclusions to be derived therefrom be built upon it, and truths of lesser significance give place to those of greater moment as the discourse proceeds, every thought being presented in its fitting place. And then they must not be content, unless, as life goes on, they are themselves advancing in power to see and teach the inner things of God; while their one absorbing aim, while life lasts, must be to proclaim Jesus Christ, the Hope of the World.

In choosing a text Mr. Spurgeon urged them never to omit to ask for Divine guidance. He owned that to him the selection of a theme was often a difficult matter, not because texts were few, but because so many subjects crowded upon his mind, each seeming to demand attention. He thought, however, that there were signs by which they might recognise the verse which contained the word appointed them to deliver. After devoutly considering verse after verse one would often specially strike the mind and arrest their thoughts, taking their whole imagination captive. Then let them accept this as given to them of the Lord. They would also find some indication of what was suitable if they thought over the probable needs of the people to whom they ministered, or pondered over the sins most prevalent among them. They should also call to mind the subjects they have already brought before their flock, so as to choose some fresh truth to exhibit. If, after making every effort of prayer and thought, no text suggested itself to their minds, still they need not despair.

He had learned from his own experience to have confidence in their Divine Master in such moments of perplexity. It had happened to him more than once to find the time draw near for him to speak, and still he had not been able to fix his mind on a text; but some apparently trifling circumstance had suggested a verse which had provided him with a fruitful theme for his discourse. One Sabbath evening during the singing of the hymn immediately before the sermon he turned to the text on which he had been meditating, when his eye was caught by another verse, which attracted him so powerfully that he knew not how to draw his thoughts from it. For a few moments he hesitated, but presently yielded to the strong influence that was upon him, feeling that the impulse might be from Heaven. He proceeded step by step, on the inspiration of the moment, but when he had finished the second division of his discourse the current of his thoughts seemed checked; he was at a loss, and there appeared to be nothing further to say. In his strait he looked to God for help, and it came in a very unexpected manner. From some cause the gas suddenly went out. The situation was one of great danger, for the place was thronged with people. He induced them to keep quietly in their seats, and addressed them in the darkness until the lamps were re-lighted on a topic suggested by the circumstance.

Shortly afterwards two persons were added to the number of church members, one of whom had been brought to Jesus by the part of the sermon preached on the importunate text that came to him unsought and would not be refused, while the words suggested by the extinction of the lights had been blessed to the other.

In his address on the Voice, Mr. Spurgeon gave some homely and practical hints on its management, urging that while their first and chief consideration must be the matter of their sermons, they would do well to give some attention to their mode of delivery. He ridiculed the artificial tones assumed so commonly in the pulpit, for falseness, odious always, was intolerable in the voice whose accents should be as true as the doctrines to be expressed. On this point a French writer remarks:—" Everywhere else, men speak:

they speak at the bar and the tribune; but they no longer speak in the pulpit, for there we only meet with a factitious and artificial language, and a false tone. This style of speaking is only tolerated in the church, because, unfortunately, it is so general there; elsewhere it would not be endured. What would be thought of a man who should converse in a similar way in a drawing-room? He would certainly provoke many a smile. . . . A man who has not a natural and true delivery should not be allowed to occupy the pulpit; from thence, at least, everything that is false should be summarily banished. . . . In these days of mistrust everything that is false should be set aside. . . . The instant you abandon the natural and the true you forego the right to be believed, as well as the right of being listened to."

Some men affected a pompous style of address, and rolled out their words with a majestic swell; others delivered them with a languid drawl; some appeared to consider that exhortations spoken through the nose instead of the mouth gained in impressiveness; others again conceived an unaccountable aversion for the letter *r*, and irreligiously substituted *w*, as more appropriate for pious uses. He wished them to understand that if these peculiarities were *natural* to them, no one would condemn them, but they were defects in which none need glory, much less were they worthy of imitation.

They should strive to acquire distinct utterance; neither mutter nor gabble their words, nor fall into the opposite error of painful deliberateness. Then it was not well in preaching on ordinary occasions to speak at the top of the voice. A sermon was not effective in proportion to the noise made in delivering it. In Elijah's experience, "The Lord was not in the wind." If they spoke so as to be heard at the far end of the room, be it large or small, they need not waste strength in sending the sound outside.

Nor was it advisable to maintain the same degree of force from beginning to end of the discourse. No rule could be given for their guidance in this matter. If they spoke only what they felt from the bottom of their hearts, the feelings that stirred themselves would teach them when to speak loudly or softly. He begged them to avoid speaking always in one unvarying tone, if they did not wish to lull their hearers to sleep, and also, because the habit would be injurious to themselves. An eminent physician says, when writing on "Diseases of the Throat and Lungs":—"From what was stated respecting the physiology of the vocal chords, it will be evident that continued speaking in one tone is much more fatiguing than frequent alterations in the pitch of the voice; because by the former, one muscle, or set of muscles, alone is strained, whilst by the latter different muscles are brought into action, and thus relieve one another. In the same way, a man raising his arm at right angles to his body becomes fatigued in five or ten minutes, because only one set of muscles has to bear the weight; but these same muscles can work the whole day if their action is alternated with that of others. Whenever, therefore, we hear a clergyman droning through the church service, and in the same manner and tone of voice reading, praying, and exhorting, we may be perfectly sure that he is giving ten times more labour to his vocal chords than is absolutely necessary."

All who have anything to say like to secure attentive listeners: he who has to speak the things of God, to put before his hearers life and death, that they may choose, must needs crave earnest regard to his words.

Mr. Spurgeon held that, as a rule, preachers must blame themselves principally if they failed to arouse the interest of their people. Sometimes bad ventilation was answerable for withheld attention; people would surely become drowsy in foul air, their remedy in such a case would be a good supply of oxygen. Instances were not unknown where officials walking hither and thither on various errands, such as arranging lights and windows more to their satisfaction, had caused unnecessary distraction. But apart from such causes, ministers often had to try their skill against the cares of the world, which press so insistently on many people that they can hardly escape them even in the House of God. They must see to it that their subject shall present greater attractions, so that it may engross their hearts, and raise them for a little above the earth. They must not clothe their thoughts in too many words; their language must be plain, and their manner animated. He strongly advised them not to read their sermons, but to speak without preparation would be still worse. Above all, the sermon should not be too long. A well-studied sermon would occupy less time in delivery than an ill-prepared one, and if the subject were one which deeply stirred the heart of the preacher, it would almost certainly enchain the attention of his hearers. Their greatest hope, however, would be derived from the assistance of God's gracious help; if the Spirit of God spoke through them, they need have no fear of wandering thoughts.

The results of the publication of the first volume of *Lectures* were extremely satisfactory. The sale was large and critics laudatory, but more acceptable still to its author were the assurances received from many ministers of the help they had found in its pages. The second volume was issued three years later, containing addresses on widely differing topics, but all aiming at assisting the young minister in his endeavour to become a worthy worker in the vineyard of God. The first points out their dependence on the Holy Spirit, and directs them to look to Him for knowledge and wisdom for their office as teachers, for inspiration in prayer, and for His quickening influence on the Word taught, and warns them too against forfeiting

His gracious help by the sins of pride and sloth, or by the grievous fault of permitting self-interest to dictate their professions of belief.

Among the series is a most interesting sketch on the "History of Open-air Preaching." It claims for the practice the authority of very ancient custom, to which the Old Testament records of the open-air preaching of Noah and Moses, Elijah and Jonah, and many other prophets, all witness; and shows that it is stamped with the approval of Our Blessed Lord, who Himself taught the people as they gathered round Him on the hillside, by sea and river, and in the streets of their cities. The Apostles followed the example of their Master, and after them succeeded a long line of famous open-air preachers. There were the preaching friars of the Middle Ages, later on the sturdy teachers of the doctrines of the Reformation, while in more modern times Whitefield and Wesley were notable examples of those who had obeyed their Lord's behest, "Go out into the highways and hedges and compel them to come in;" and who had thereby gained many souls to Jesus.

In remarking subsequently on the subject Mr. Spurgeon admitted that our English winters were not favourable to successful out-of-door speaking, and also that a building would ensure greater freedom from noise and interruption than could always be secured in the fields, but so many people could never be induced to enter the doors of church or chapel. *To these they must go,* for they were commanded to "Preach the gospel to every creature." Then he proceeded to give them some idea of the difficulties they would meet with in their attempts to address a street audience, the different kinds of opposition they might expect, with some useful hints as to how they might best overcome them.

In two amusing lectures on Posture, Action, and Gestures,

Mr. Spurgeon drew attention to some faults he was most anxious his students should avoid, or correct if they had fallen into them. The grotesque attitudes and absurd gestures of a preacher often proved real hindrances to the reception of truth by his hearers, for they occupied the attention of some at least of his congregation, to the exclusion of the subject-matter of the sermon.

He declared that pulpits, which hid the greater part of a man's body, were responsible to a great extent for the awkward movements of those who occupied them.

As the lecturer described some of the oddities of manner of which speakers had been guilty, his audience must have been convulsed with merriment, but his purpose was most serious. He hoped by ridiculing habits which were truly ridiculous to bring them into discredit, and at the same time strove to show them a better way. As models for imitation he instanced the attitude of St. Chrysostom, as he is generally depicted, and St. Paul preaching at Athens as represented by Raphael. These are the natural self-forgetful attitudes of men full of elevated and earnest purpose, surely the best safeguard against all affected and preposterous mannerisms.

Other lectures were "The Blind Eye and the Deaf Ear;" these treated possessions to be desired, shutting out sights and sounds best unseen and unheard; "Earnestness: its marring and maintenance," and "Conversion as our Aim," with which the series ends.

The two volumes were so universally appreciated by young ministers, that when requests for a grant from the Book Fund were received, they were often found to express a hope that the *Lectures* might be included in the list sent.

CHAPTER X.

WORK AND REST.

THE following conversation was overheard between two intelligent working-men, each waiting for a chance to "better himself" by a new engagement.

"I don't care much," said one, "whether I get it or not; the only thing is that it will mean a rise of two shillings a week for me, and where a man has a wife and family to keep that is a consideration."

"It is indeed," was the reply, "and that is why I am here. But no doubt more money will bring more work."

"It is sure to do that. I consider this is a very hard-working age. I do quite as much as I ought, what with my chapel, and Band of Hope, and Sunday Schools, besides my ten or twelve hours a day at my regular business; but I suppose I am not the hardest worked man of the age."

"No, you may be pretty sure of that. I wonder who is. It is certain that many of the public men we read of don't have a very easy time of it. There's Gladstone, for instance; a splendid worker he is."

"Yes; but my man works harder than Gladstone."

"Who is your man?"

"Spurgeon."

"Oh! you don't catch parsons hurting themselves with work, I know."

"Don't you, though? I believe that Spurgeon is really

killing himself by over-work. Look here! I cut this little bit out of the *Sword and Trowel*. It is a bit of Spurgeon's own. Shall I read it to you?"

"Yes, if it won't take too long."

"It won't take a minute. This is what he says—'The pastorate of a church of four thousand members, the direction of all its agencies, the care of many churches arising from the College work; the selection, education, and guidance in their settlements of the students; the oversight of the Orphanage, the editing of a magazine, the production of numerous volumes, the publication of a weekly sermon, an immense correspondence, a fair share in public and denominational action, and many other labours, besides the incessant preaching of the Word, give us a right to ask of our friends that we be not allowed to have an anxious thought about the funds needed for our enterprises.'"

"Yes, your parson certainly does work," acknowledged the man. "He doesn't get his bread and cheese for nothing. We will call him one of ourselves, one of the working-men of old England."

"You are right! I don't believe that there is any man in the whole world to beat him at work."

We agree with this man. But Mr. Spurgeon was all the time working at high-pressure; and the terrible pain that he had to suffer made the work doubly difficult.

And yet, how completely did the man possess his soul in peace! For one thing, Nature helped him as well as grace! The out-of-door life which he was able to live, and indeed compelled sometimes to live, made him greatly the richer. Spurgeon was a great lover of Nature, and constantly referred to it for simile, contrast, illustration, comfort, and warning. He said—"God seems to talk to me in every primrose and daisy, to smile at me from every star, to whisper to me in every breath of morning air, and to call aloud to me in every storm." He found instruction in all the works of the Almighty, even in those that are noxious and repulsive. Thorns and nettles were for him symbols of the small tribulations of life which are to be grasped firmly, or trodden under foot, by those who mean to conquer. Or they are evil thoughts that spring up in the hearts of those who are not filled with the love of God. Or they are the many evils of the world which every Christian is bound to try and uproot.

When he observed the action of the frost, how it hushed the songs of birds, silenced the babbling brooks, and is yet even in its hardness beneficent, as it destroys the insects which would injure the crops; how, when the work of the frost is accomplished, the thaw softens the ground, sets free the waters, and encourages the green leaves to burst from their coverings, he found a parallel in the dealings of God with men. He sends the frost of trouble and humiliation to destroy the insects of pride and selfishness that injure the character, and then the thaw of His love in their hearts, which softens them and gives to them the joy of springtime. Hailstones he compared to the conviction of sin, that comes to some with stinging and deafening force; and the soft snowflakes are that same feeling falling gently upon the hearts of others. He passed by the hedgerows and saw the roses growing among thorns, and the wild fruit on the brambles, and he thought of the sweetness that may often be extracted from troubles. Holy thoughts are like the birds whose singing fills the soul with melody, but unholy thoughts are as injurious to the mind as vipers to the body. Where snails have been one can tell by the track they leave. So our thoughts leave their mark upon our character, and for their number they resemble the leaves that are whirled about by the October winds.

Spurgeon also drew attention to the difference between our work and that of Nature. All that we do is done with great exertion and noise, but Nature works easily and silently. The earth, moon, and stars roll noiselessly in their orbits. The sun sends his effulgent rays to warm and enlighten the world without effort. The trees, grass, and flowers grow unseen and without sound while man sleeps. Black clouds gather in the sky, a warm wind blows on it, and it disperses almost imperceptibly. Rivers and streams are locked up by ice, but God sends a soft breeze, and the ice melts and the water is set free. And the lesson is this: If these mighty works are done so easily and swiftly, then ought God's children to trust him in all things, and believe in His power to help them.

Mr. Spurgeon took many of his illustrations from the operations of Nature in husbandry. The work of the farmer in different seasons, and the implements he uses, all had a spiritual meaning for him. The hearts of men are like fields intended for cultivation. They are not rock or desert upon which nothing will grow, but are like good soil capable of producing a crop of some kind. If we do not see that good seed is planted, rank weeds will spring up luxuriantly, for they do not require the hand of man to propagate them; the birds of the air and every wind that blows scatters the bad seed far and wide. And as wheat will never come to perfection without the care of the farmer, so the heart of man needs constant cultivation to ensure spiritual growth.

As the plough breaks up the clods of earth, and cuts and destroys the roots of the weeds, so a sense of sin breaks up the hard heart and constrains it to turn from evil, thus preparing it for the good seed of "The Word." It is of little use for the sower to throw seed into a field full of nettles, and it is just as futile to preach pardoning mercy to those who have not realised that they are sinners. Each season had for him a special charm. Youthful Christianity, fresh, bright, and full of the promise of a rich and fruitful maturity, was in his thought even as Nature's spring-time, with its

"FARM SERMONS."

bursting buds, springing flowers, and green blades of wheat, which fill the farmer's heart full of hope for the future.

As he walked in the hay-fields he mused upon the similarity of the life of man and grass. Frail at first, he grows in strength and stature day by day; as he reaches his prime he holds his head proudly, and bears himself bravely in the breeze. But the summer of his life passes, and he is bowed with age. The greenness of his youth is gone, and he becomes yellow and sere, and finally sinks in the dust. And even like grass, he is not always allowed to grow old, but is cut down in the full vigour of manhood. Walking in the harvest field suggested many thoughts to him. First, we all reap what we sow. If we sow wheat our fields will be covered with grain. If we sow tares our crop will be ruinous to us. And he thought of the final harvest of the world, when God's wheat shall be reaped and carried away by the angels. And of the joy of that great Harvest Home when the Lord's grain shall be garnered for evermore in Heaven.

Some of Mr. Spurgeon's sermons are exquisitely beautiful in his revelations of nature. One comes to the mind of the writer on the text, "Supposing Him to be the gardener," which is a good illustration of the use which he could make of such subjects; but for the tender touches of a loving hand that belongs to the true-hearted sympathiser with the wonderful world which God has made, we refer the reader to the exquisite volume, one of the later and most finished and beautiful of Mr. Spurgeon's works, called *Farm Sermons*. No library is complete without it.

Having such strong and deep affection for natural scenery, and such keen eyes to observe it all, Mr. Spurgeon must have enjoyed to the full the frequent respites which his affliction compelled him to have, and his holidays, spent in many beautiful spots in Italy, and especially in the South of France.

He never went away soon enough, nor stayed long enough, for his health's sake; but the bright sun and warm breezes from the Mediterranean gave him new life, and he always returned from Mentone ready for action.

One year was much like another for the amount of work which he had to do; every one brought him more than he could accomplish. It also brought him much to bear and much to enjoy.

At the annual meeting of the Tabernacle, in February 1873, his heart was made glad by the prosperity reported in all departments of the church. There had been added to the membership during the year 571, and it now stood, after all changes, at 4417. All the funds were in a better condition than at any previous anniversary, more money being raised in every section of Christian work. It was evident that the pastor's illness had not operated injuriously in any manifest degree. Pastor and people rejoiced together. New works of usefulness were being started. Among them an effort for the spiritual benefit of the blind was begun by a working-man, which has been productive of much good. In the month of March the annual supper connected with the College yielded the noble sum of £1900. The same month Mr. Spurgeon gave proof of his large-heartedness by making a collection at the Tabernacle towards the fund for building a new chapel for the church and congregation meeting at Surrey Chapel, under the care of the Rev. Newman Hall, and had the pleasure of sending Mr. Hall one hundred guineas.

The month of April was a happy month. On Good Friday there was a pleasant meeting at the Orphanage. The mothers and friends of the boys, as far as practicable, came to tea. The boys sang, and then Mr. Spurgeon gave them many wise and affectionate counsels; and afterwards comforted the widowed mothers, by reminding them of the faithfulness of God, and His care for all who trust in Him.

The Rev. Dr. Moffat, the venerable South African missionary, was present; and, after expressing his pleasure at all he saw, addressed the lads in a most interesting and affectionate manner. Two or three days after, a very remarkable gathering took place at the Tabernacle. About twelve hundred meat salesmen and master butchers sat down to a substantial supper to which they had been invited. After supper they were addressed by Mr. Spurgeon, who was in the chair, and Messrs. H. Varley and W. Cuff. The Butchers' Annual Festival has become a settled institution, and the improved moral tone of those employed in the markets is one of its good results. At the end of the month Mr. Spurgeon preached one of the annual sermons on behalf of the Wesleyan Missionary Society.

Mr. Spurgeon's sympathies have always been with the poor and oppressed, no matter what their colour or clime. When, therefore, the Jubilee Singers came over here from America in the summer of 1873, to raise funds on behalf of Fisk University, they received an early invitation to give one of their concerts at the Tabernacle. Of course the invitation was thankfully accepted, and a grand reception was given them. The spacious building was crowded, and hundreds had to be turned away for want of room. By this one concert the singers cleared upwards of £200 for their University buildings, while the success of the evening helped to prepare the way for their enthusiastic reception in other places.

On the 28th of August the Rev. George Rogers, the senior tutor of the College, celebrated his golden wedding, amid the hearty love and congratulations of his fellow-tutors and all the students. "Few such men," said Mr. Spurgeon, "are to be found, patriarchal in age but juvenile in spirit, full of wisdom and free to dispense it, living to do good, and doing it abundantly. Under God's blessing this eminent man has been the corner-stone of our College from its commencement, and at an advanced age remains so, being blessed with unabated energy, and enjoying the unbounded esteem and love of us all." A gold watch was presented to Mr. Rogers on the occasion, and a silver urn to his wife.

The President had the pleasure, on the 14th of October, of laying the first stone of the new buildings for the Pastors' College. The day was one of the brightest in his history. The people brought in their offerings from seven o'clock in the morning till ten at night. Chiefly by small sums the amount was made up to £1000, and the ministers and students brought in £300 more. The day was one of prayer among the students all day long, that the blessing of God might descend on the institution in future years, as it had been granted in years past. Thirty men went forth this year from the College to labour in the gospel ministry in various parts of the world.

He began the year 1874 by saying—" Our life is as full of toils, troubles, joys, and difficulties as ever it can hold, and is crowded with incidents." The Watch-Night Service at the Tabernacle, which closed the old year and introduced the new, was of such a remarkable character that a graphic description was given of it in the *Daily News*, and copied into several other papers. It was a service productive of the happiest results. On the 6th of January Mr. Spurgeon addressed two meetings—in the morning a crowded assembly gathered for prayer in the London Tavern; in the evening a similar meeting at the St. James's Hall. All too soon he was again compelled to forsake his work and hasten away to Mentone, to try to escape from bodily pains and mental weariness. During his absence he was much cheered by the tidings of a notable revival that had broken out in his church. Earnest brethren at home laboured the more zealously because of their pastor's absence. Special prayer-meetings were crowded; and conversions were numerous among young and old. There had been special efforts which were crowned with success, so that there was a time of the hopefulness of spring awaiting him. On his return, the pastor was made glad by the sights and sounds which greeted him on all hands. He and his people praised God together, and the joy of the Lord was their strength.

In March there was a second concert by the Jubilee Singers at the Tabernacle. The house was crowded to its utmost capacity, and the strange, sweet, weird music of the singers charmed all hearts. It was a marvellous success. Dr. Moffat was present, and as he stood forward, under the influence of deep excitement, to speak on the claims of Africa, his appearance was most striking and his earnestness contagious.

Monday, September 21st, was a red-letter day in Mr. Spurgeon's history, for on that day, in the presence of an immense multitude of friends, whose hearts were full of sympathy, he baptised his two sons on a profession of their faith in the Lord Jesus Christ.

The joy of the occasion was greatly increased by the presence for a few minutes of their mother at the service.

The two young men who thus consecrated their lives and talents to their father's God were the centre of much loving solicitude; but it may be questioned if the father's thoughts were not even more with the suffering wife than with their sons. Her affliction, borne as only a Christian lady could have borne it, debarred her from much ordinary joy; but her husband's deep love was manifested in a thousand ways.

It is not generally known, perhaps, that Mr. Spurgeon was a poet, though that there was much of poetry in his prose is well known. He was a hymn-writer too of very considerable power and popularity. But one of the sweetest things he ever wrote was addressed to his wife, and written when he was absent from her in Hull. This was the first stanza—

> " Over the space that parts us, my wife,
> I'll cast me a bridge of song;
> Our hearts shall meet, O joy of my life,
> On its arch, unseen, but strong."

CHAPTER XI.

A HELPMEET'S WORK.

A GREAT deal more than is perhaps generally realised depends upon the kind of wife a minister has, and in regard to the gentle and pious lady who was nearest and dearest to the great heart which took in so many, and who through long years of wedded life was the true heart-friend and intellectual comrade of Charles Haddon Spurgeon, we are quite sure that her loving companionship was to him both inspiration and solace in his grand work. Mrs. Spurgeon has been for many years an invalid, a great and constant sufferer, and at first sight it would seem that this would be an effectual bar to her usefulness. True, it made it impossible for her to lead, or indeed to take part at all, in any active church work at the Metropolitan Tabernacle; but Mrs. Spurgeon, with her heart full of wide sympathies and gentlest charity, could not be content to be an idler in the vineyard where her husband laboured so bravely. Her help in the enormous amount of secretarial work which the numerous branches of the Tabernacle involved, was invaluable, and Mr. Spurgeon again and again in his writings refers with gratitude to her loving ministry in this respect. It was while rendering this service that a thought, which must have been sent from God himself, was given to Mrs. Spurgeon—a thought from which has sprung one of the most acceptable ministries in this age of Christian help and service.

Mrs. Spurgeon had been reading her husband's book, of deservedly world-wide fame, *Lectures to my Students*, and as she read could not help wishing that counsel so wise and helpful might be placed within the reach of every minister in this country. With some the thought would have begun and ended with an idle wish, but the pastor of the Tabernacle and his wife were workers and not dreamers, and when Mrs. Spurgeon told her husband of her wish, his practical benevolence at once saw a way to its partial fulfilment. Money, in Mr. Spurgeon's hands, was never long idle, and they determined to "devote a few pounds" to the distribution of the book named among such ministers as would be most likely to benefit by the gift. It is interesting and touching to learn that Mrs. Spurgeon's contribution consisted of a number of crown pieces, which, from their comparative rarity, she had been saving as a curiosity for many years, and which were given willingly, nay, with the greatest joy and gladness, for the first hundred volumes to be distributed among Mr. Spurgeon's old college students. For a time Mrs. Spurgeon's bright idea was kept to the family circle and personal friends, for it was not by any means thought that it would grow to the dimensions that it afterwards did attain. Indeed, the family looked on the pet project with a good deal of the fond and tolerant amusement with which all a loved invalid's whims are regarded.

In July 1875 a note appeared in the *Sword and Trowel*, to the effect that Mrs. Spurgeon would have pleasure in presenting one hundred Baptist ministers with her husband's book, entitled *Lectures to my Students;* and so eagerly was this offer caught at by those for whom it was intended, that the kind donor doubled the number of volumes she had at first meant to give. In September of the same year Mr. Spurgeon wrote that his wife was daily responding to the urgent requests of ministers for this most helpful work.

MRS. SPURGEON.

She was enabled to do this through the kindness of some of the readers of the *Sword and Trowel*, who, approving her plan, sent donations to be expended in the purchase of books to carry it out. It was in this month that the "idea" received its name—a name which has been again and again blessed by ministers who have been benefited by its gifts—"Mrs. Spurgeon's Book Fund."

Perhaps it may appear strange to some that such a fund should be necessary. In thinking of the "minister," one naturally pictures a cosy, if not luxuriously-furnished study, lined with shelves replete with helpful books; but this picture is in a great many cases quite reversed by the reality. The spiritual labourer should be of all labourers the one most worthy of hire, but in many cases it is found that ministers attached to a small village cause receive a stipend so miserably low that the income of an ordinary tradesman is affluence in comparison to it. It is so much the harder for these men, because their training and education, while the best to fit them for their sacred calling, are not such as to enable them in a practical manner to face and fight the very stern realities which have to be overcome by the husband and head of the household. At the same time, in many cases ministers take up and follow some avocations in addition to their spiritual labours, which will enable them to bring grist to the household mill. All honour to these. The strain upon them is harder than can be realised by a great many, but their efforts are seen and accepted by the Lord of the vineyard, who in His own good time will give to them an exceeding great reward. The lot of the wives of these ministers, too, from a worldly point of view at any rate, is not to be envied. Many refined, intellectual ladies have, in order to make ends meet, to fill the place of general servant, seamstress, wife, and mother in their own person; and besides this, are expected to work in numberless ways among their husbands' church and congregation When a minister, his wife, and family have to live and keep up appearances upon salaries of £100, £90 £80, £70, and in some cases less than £60 a year, it will be seen that there is not much surplus money left for the purchase of the books which are to the minister as real a necessity as his tools are to a workman. This state of affairs is of course admitted on all hands to be decidedly wrong, and those to whom the principles of Nonconformity are dear deplore it as much as any. Many suggestions have been put forward for the alleviation of the burden which lies heavily upon so many— such as an amalgamated fund for pastors' salaries, or Union chapels for poor and scattered parishes; but the discussion of these plans does not rightly enter into a work of this kind. At present there *is* the need for a loving ministry such as Mrs. Spurgeon inaugurated, and while deploring the necessity for it, surely no true Christian could or would withhold his sympathy.

When it became known that the Fund was started many friends willingly sent money for so good an object, and Mrs. Spurgeon found that she was able to extend the help more widely than at first had seemed possible. As subscriptions increased she found that larger and more expensive volumes might be sent, notably the *Treasury of David*, that most valuable and scholarly work by the Rev. C. H. Spurgeon, of which we give a full description elsewhere, and which is acknowledged and used as a standard theological work by clergymen and ministers of all denominations. The work was not at this time complete, four volumes only having been published; but these were sent to as many recipients as the funds would allow, and were welcomed by the most gratifying and touching expressions of gratitude. From its inauguration, in August 1875, to the end of the next year, upwards of £1000 had been contributed. With this money more than five thousand volumes were purchased, three thousand one hundred and sixteen of which were the more important and costly of Mr. Spurgeon's works, while the remainder comprised a few of his minor productions, together with other theological works, new and second-hand, but all such as would be of real help to preachers in their study of the Bible. The number of ministers who benefited by these free gifts was seven hundred and ten, and the books were distributed in parcels of from four to eight volumes. When it is remembered that the whole of the management of this undertaking, including the duties of secretary, treasurer, and corresponding clerk depended upon Mrs. Spurgeon, assisted by such help as members of her family willingly gave, it will be admitted that the office was no sinecure. It is needless to state that the labour was entirely one of love on the part of Mrs. Spurgeon, and though sometimes her bodily weakness was so great that the work had perforce to be laid aside, and at other times was pursued while suffering intensely, she confessed at the end of the first year that the work had been its own delightful reward. The grateful letters sent by the recipients of the books, and telling of the help and joy her kind thought of them had given, gave her keenest pleasure; and in the quietness and monotony of her sick-room she had the delight of knowing that to her feeble hands had been allotted the blessed task of helping to gird on the armour of the Lord's warriors who were fighting His battle in all parts of the field. It is equally needless to state to those who have any conception of the beautiful character of Mrs. Spurgeon that her benefactions were made with all the grace and delicacy of which a Christian lady is capable.

It was in 1877, during the earlier days of its history, that Mrs. Spurgeon published a little book of explanation with regard to the Book Fund, describing its origin, its object, its sustenance, and its success. The first of these the reader is already acquainted with. In referring to the second we may say that the Fund, almost from its commencement, has benefited not only ministers of the Baptist denomination, but those of every denomination. This unsectarianism is one of its chief characteristics, and one most to be admired. Baptists, Independents, Methodists, Clergymen, Presbyterians, and others have all had to thank the Book Fund for welcome and valuable additions to their study book-shelves. That the necessity was much felt is proved by the great eagerness shown by ministers to obtain the offered help. Will it be believed that in some instances pastors are put to the utmost inconvenience and difficulty for want of a reliable Commentary? Others Mrs. Spurgeon vouches for who had absolutely never *seen* a new book for years except in a bookseller's window, until their hearts were made glad by a liberal grant of volumes through the instrumentality of the Book Fund. How is it possible for a man who has perhaps to preach four and five times a week, to keep his mind fresh and vigorous and to avoid his discourses becoming flat, stale, and unprofitable? It should be remembered that a village pastor is more dependent on books than those whose sphere of labour lies in a town. They are often so placed that intercourse with kindred spirits is an impossibility, or at any rate a luxury to be enjoyed only at long intervals. The intellect rusts for want of a suitable comrade to measure swords with, and the spirit flags in an unequal strife with life and its manifold difficulties. To those who have to do without, these good books must take the place of human companionship; to them they turn for inspiration and for consolation as to their own familiar friend, and when they are wanting the lot of a country minister must be poor indeed! The taking in of mental nourishment is as essentially necessary to such a man as is the keeping up of the strength of his body by material food necessary to the workman who earns his bread by the sweat of his brow. In thanking Mrs.

Spurgeon for well-timed help, many refer to the books as "bread to the hungry," and water to a weary traveller. Nor are these cases few and far between. Mrs. Spurgeon, after a year's constant correspondence with ministers of every denomination, was more than ever convinced that her Fund met a need that was most urgent and painful. The same story came from north, east, south, and west; not in complainings and jeremiads, but, read between the lines, in the thanks of overflowing hearts, whose very earnestness showed how overwhelmingly pressing had been their need of help. Surely to these Mrs. Spurgeon's Book Fund has truly been what her husband compared it to—"A fountain in the desert."

With regard to the sustenance of the Fund, its originator is able to state that she has never had to ask for a shilling. She contends that the work is God's, and since all the silver and the gold are His also, He will find the necessary funds for the carrying on of His own work. Such a faith cannot fail of its end, and this is proved by the fact that as the needs have arisen the money has always been forthcoming. From the receipt of the first donation of five shillings Mrs. Spurgeon had the faith to believe that her work had the smile of God upon it, and was pleasing to Him. "You will see," she prophesied to her sons, "the Lord will send me *hundreds of pounds* for this work." And though the "boys" laughed and joked and teased, as young men will, about the "hundreds of pounds," yet they became an accomplished fact; and, indeed, comparatively soon after the prophecy of their mother the hundreds grew into thousands, and the books were sent out almost daily in a steady flow to meet the constant demand.

At the same time Mrs. Spurgeon felt that she had still further cause for thankfulness in a matter that lay very near to her heart. The correspondence with ministers had in some instances brought to light the overwhelmingly sad fact that not only was the minister mentally famishing, but his family were wanting even the necessaries of life. How hard it would have been to the tender heart of Mrs. Spurgeon to know of these trials and to have had no means of lightening them may be guessed, but it was made providentially possible for her to minister to the bodily as well as the mental necessities of these servants of God. The thoughtfulness of one kind friend instituted a private *Pastors' Aid Society*, by placing in Mrs. Spurgeon's hands a sum of money to be distributed as she thought fit to necessitous cases, and to this sum her husband and other friends from time to time made additions.

One of the pleasantest tasks of the year 1877 was the presentation to every minister in the county of Argyle of the *Treasury of David* by a gentleman who entrusted Mrs. Spurgeon with the necessary money to carry out his wishes. Another very pleasing branch of the Book Fund "tree" was the presentation of the *Sword and Trowel* each month to sixty poor pastors who could not themselves afford to subscribe to the magazine by two friends upon whose hearts the wants of the ministers had taken hold. And yet another branch put itself out towards the end of the year, in the shape of a number of letters from ladies who were desirous of making Christmas a time of rejoicing to the families of poor pastors by the presentation of parcels of suitable clothing. These ladies wrote asking Mrs. Spurgeon for the names of some to whom the gift would be acceptable, and they could not have had a better adviser in this delicate matter, for Mrs. Spurgeon's warm, motherly heart kept a record of the particular family circumstances of each one of the many ministers with whom she had corresponded. She had no difficulty whatever in supplying her friends with the names of twenty-five families who would welcome their gifts; indeed, had there been sufficient parcels, there is no doubt that this number might have been doubled and trebled, for where there are little ones, even when means are sufficient, the mother's hands are always full of the sewing that the making of their little garments entails, and the relief that the receipt of a parcel of nicely-made clothing gives to her tired heart and head is known only to herself.

In this year books were sent to France, Spain, Sweden, Nova Scotia, Nebraska, Cape of Good Hope, Sydney, Adelaide, Bengal, Jamaica, and Barbadoes. Two Church of England missionaries, proceeding to India, were delighted to take out, for one of the works of their necessarily small library, *The Treasury of David;* while other missionaries of all denominations applied for and received the same helpful work, taking it with them to their far-distant scenes of labour in Damascus, China, the Punjaub, Ceylon, Delhi, Lagos, Timbuctoo, and many other places, where no doubt they have often profited by the help the books have given.

Such was one of the early year's work in connection with the Book Fund, and the years that have followed have been "like unto it," excepting that the sphere of the Fund's usefulness has been widened: more of God's people have had the privilege of ministering to the necessities of His servants, and more of His ambassadors have had their hearts cheered, their labours lightened, and their faith strengthened by the tokens of God's care of them through His people; while the loving spirit of the gentle lady who has brought the helper and the helped together has overflowed with gladness. Her "mouth has been filled with laughter, and her tongue with singing," and in spite of pain and weariness of the flesh she has constantly been able to say, "Bless the Lord, O my soul, and all that is within me, bless His holy name: Bless the Lord, O my soul, and forget not all His benefits."

Ministers, we have said, are not, as a class, well paid, and though of course in some cases the labourer is proved to be considered "worthy of his hire," in many more he is miserably underpaid. It became necessary, as time went on, to make a rule to the effect that no free grant of books could be made to a pastor whose total income from all sources exceeded £150 a year; but even this limit, it is sad to tell, left a wide field in which Mrs. Spurgeon could dispose of her gifts. For those whose incomes were over the sum named special terms were made, so that they might purchase Mr. Spurgeon's and other theological works at a much lower rate than through the ordinary channels.

It is to be noted that, in applying for grants of books, ministers nearly always ask for the works of Mr. Spurgeon, and not for those of any other author, although when she can do so, such as are likely to be of service, Mrs. Spurgeon adds to her parcels. *The Treasury of David* and volumes of Mr. Spurgeon's *Sermons* are the books most sought after, and these always form the larger proportion of the parcel. It is a testimony of the high esteem in which the great preacher's writings are held, that they should be so sought after by a class of men who, of all others, are best able to judge of their practical usefulness. It has been thought by some who do not properly understand the working of the Book Fund, that although it does all that it professes to do in the free distribution of the books, it is also a means of profit to author and publishers. We wish here emphatically to deny that there is any truth in this supposition. The works are supplied to Mrs. Spurgeon at cost price, and neither author nor publishers gain anything whatever by the transaction. None who know aught of the character of Mr. and Mrs. Spurgeon, and the upright and honourable business firm which brings out their productions, could give credence to any statement to the contrary. Mrs. Spurgeon refers again and again most gratefully to the kindness she

OTHER CONTRIBUTIONS.

experiences at Messrs. Passmore & Alabaster's hands in her constant dealings with them.

Sometimes friends, instead of contributing money, have sent parcels of books to Mrs. Spurgeon for distribution. While she is always glad to receive such as are really useful, she has been compelled from time to time to gently protest against the "cruel kindness" of some who have sent books of not the slightest value to those for whom they were intended. On one occasion, among a number of other worthless books, an old volume was sent bearing the following legend on its title-page:—"The Complete Housewife and Accomplished Gentlewoman's Companion, being a collection of upwards of seven hundred of the most approved receipts for Cookery, and above three hundred receipts of medicine. London, 1766." A great disappointment was experienced when a large packing-case of books, sent for the benefit of the "Clerical Library," and upon which, when delivered, Mrs. Spurgeon had to pay 9s. for its transit, was found to contain for the most part Unitarian works, books written against Believer's Baptism, and old hymn-books! It is much the better way for any really desirous of helping this good work to entrust money to Mrs. Spurgeon for the purchase of suitable books, unless they can send books of known excellence and practical use.

Some of Mrs. Spurgeon's friends, however, in thoughtful kindness, have supplied other necessaries to be placed among the books when she is sending off her parcels. A gentleman, who feels himself honoured in supplying Mrs. Spurgeon with an endless variety of note-paper and envelopes of the very best quality for her enormous correspondence, has also given her stationery, in most liberal quantities, from which she may select a good stock to place in the parcels of books for minister's use. That this addition is most welcome is proved by the grateful allusions to the gift contained in letters of thanks received by Mrs.

Spurgeon. Speaking of note-paper and envelopes reminds one of the very large number of letters which Mrs. Spurgeon has to receive and answer in connection with this work. In one month she has sometimes had upwards of seven hundred ! And when we remember that upon herself has devolved the responsibility of keeping abreast of this almost overwhelming mass of correspondence, we cannot help admiring the spirit of earnestness and activity, and above all of Christian love, which must have inspired those weak hands to such a gigantic task. During the year 1890 the receipts of the Book Fund amounted to considerably more than £1000, and 6867 volumes were distributed between 119 Baptists, 76 Independents, 109 Methodists, 122 clergymen, 7 Presbyterians, 48 missionaries, 1 Lutheran, and 2 Moravians. During fifteen years 122,129 volumes have in all been distributed. One lady supplies beautifully soft woollen shawls from Scotland, another dress lengths of nice material, and yet a third a number of good and tastefully-trimmed bonnets, fresh from the hands of the milliner, and we may imagine that these gifts rejoice the heart of the mother of a family in the same degree as the books do that of a father.

It is gratifying to learn that one of the indirect effects of Mrs. Spurgeon's efforts on behalf of poorly-paid ministers has been the determination on the part of some churches to pay such salaries to their pastors as shall make it quite unnecessary for them to receive outside help. May others make the same resolve, and that speedily !

Perhaps we cannot more fitly close this imperfect sketch of the work so dear to Mrs. Spurgeon's heart than by referring again to the bright, unwavering faith in which the work is conducted. So sure is Mrs. Spurgeon that she is doing the Lord's work, and that He will supply her with the necessary money, that she does not allow herself to feel any fret and worry with regard to ways and means. On one occasion when the quarterly bill for books became due, there was not nearly enough money in hand to meet it, which meant that the Book Fund would be, for the first time in its existence, in debt. But only an hour or two before the account was presented to Mrs. Spurgeon a friend sent a handsome donation to the Fund, which amply met the need and left a surplus over; and this and like experiences have occurred again and again in the history of the Fund. May the bright childlike trust never grow dim! In her recent sad loss, upon which we feel it almost sacrilege to touch, Mrs. Spurgeon has had need of a strength and hope which only the Divine Comforter can give to His own. May these be hers all along the rest of the journey until in God's own good time she too shall cross the dark river and enter into a sweet re-union with him who was for so many years the joy and strength and glory of her life, in the Father's home above!

CHAPTER XII.

YEARS OF GOOD.

EVERY year of a good man's life gives him fresh reason to sing of God's mercy. Certainly it was the case with Mr. Spurgeon. Something special seemed to mark every year, for his life was a very eventful one.

The year in which he baptised his two sons, and saw them at once begin to follow in his footsteps, had many smaller occasions for thankfulness; but the year 1875 was also a very auspicious one, although it brought him great sorrow and much pain. One reason for thankfulness was that the pastor of the Tabernacle had now been labouring among his people for twenty-one years; and another was that he was able to commemorate "Twenty Years of Published Sermons." This was a very gratifying fact to himself, and it was of considerable moment to the world. His congregation was, almost from the first, immense; but that which met at the Tabernacle, large as it always was, only made a very small part of it, for the printed sermons went everywhere, into all countries, and among all kinds and classes of homes.

Knowing this, it was little wonder that the gifted author of them felt his heart glow with gratitude as he wrote the leading article for his own magazine, *The Sword and Trowel*, for January 1875.

He acknowledged that "a penny pulpit of his own" had

C. H. SPURGEON.
(From Photo by J. Russell & Sons, London.)

been a boyhood's dream, and the realisation of it, though it made him feel more humble than proud, could not fail to be most gratifying.

He knew of several incidents in connection with the publication of his sermons that were very interesting. For one thing they were eagerly read by English sojourners in foreign lands, who were out of the reach of the sound of the Gospel which they loved. Spurgeon made a Sabbath of many a Sunday that would otherwise have had little of inspiration in it. To read the old message in the old tongue, made vivid and new by the thought and diction of the God-honoured preacher, was to link the wanderers with the home-land and their own people. And many a prayer of thanksgiving for this means of grace went up to God from desolate and unlikely places.

The sermons were read also in hundreds of pulpits, sometimes by men who acknowledged their indebtedness, but oftener by those who did not. But even under these circumstances they were frequently used by the Spirit of God to the conversion of those who heard them read; and though the author never knew a hundredth part of the good he had done, he may know some day—he knows now, perhaps—and so the thing will get righted at last. But even about this he would not be very anxious; God was glorified through him, and that was enough for Charles Haddon Spurgeon.

The sermons were spiritual food for poor men, but the rich were not forgotten.

There was a gentleman who so believed in the usefulness of these printed sermons that he himself distributed 250,000 of them; and he sent them to people of position, who would themselves be influenced, and be greatly able to influence others. Every member of both the House of Commons and the House of Lords received a bound copy of Spurgeon's sermons. A copy was sent to every student in the English universities; and there was a special edition beautifully bound, which was presented to and accepted by every king and queen in Europe.

As for the people who read them, their name was Legion. Mr. Spurgeon himself was assured that during the first twenty years alone they were read by millions.

The Tabernacle hosts felt that they would like to mark their gratitude for the twenty-one years of service which had been to them so great a source of blessing and help, by presenting him with a purse, in which they proposed to place £2000; but their minister refused to accept it, asking instead that it might be given to the College. They solaced themselves a little, however, by presenting him with a testimonial of beautifully written words, which sought to convey a small part of what they felt towards him. In the border of the testimonial were good portraits of the two brothers, Charles and James. This was presented at the annual meeting of the church, held in January.

But every winter brought such intense suffering to the heroic worker, that he must have found it difficult to be always cheerful. Gout and rheumatism did their best to quench the fire of zeal which burned within him. He had intended to get away from the fogs and cold winds of this winter in time to spare himself some of the pain; but before he could reach Mentone, with its blue skies and fragrant orange groves, he was again knocked down by his foe and kept prisoner. Even then his humour did not forsake him; for when speaking of his pain and disappointment he said that he had received many prescriptions for the gout, and would have been dead long ago if he had tried half of them.

He got away for a while in the early spring, but went back to his duties as soon as possible, and sooner than he ought.

At this time Messrs. Moody and Sankey were in London,

BRITISH AND FOREIGN BIBLE SOCIETY. 187

and there were several interchanges of friendship and help between them and the pastor of the Tabernacle. On one occasion Mr. Ira D. Sankey was present at the Tabernacle when Mr. Spurgeon was preaching, and before the service closed he sang the hymn which has since become well known to a mighty multitude—

"Ring the bells of heaven, there is joy to-day."

Mr. Spurgeon invited Mr. Moody to speak for him in the Tabernacle, and the American evangelist did so, and took part in several of the meetings connected with the church. Mr. Spurgeon also, on one occasion at least, preached for Mr. Moody one of his most powerful sermons, and it was listened to by not less than 10,000 persons.

At the May meeting of the British and Foreign Bible Society, held this year, as usual, in the Exeter Hall, Mr. Spurgeon gave a very interesting address. He spoke with deep fervour of the Bible and what it does for mankind, and how it grows upon the affections and influences the character of those who study it. He said that when the spirit of the sacred word was more earnestly received into the hearts of Christian people there would be more union among them.

In his address he related two very interesting incidents. He said that during a visit which he had lately paid to Italy, he and some friends were resting in the Colosseum at Rome, and feeling very happy they broke into song. The verse they sang was this—

"Jesus' tremendous name
   Has put our foes to flight;
Jesus, the meek and humble lamb,
   A lion is in fight."

Attracted by the sound, two strangers came towards them.

"May we join you?" said they. "What is it your are singing?"

They told them, and together they sang the next verse—

> "By all hell's hosts withstood,
> We all hell's host o'erthrow;
> And conquering them through Jesus' blood,
> We still to conquer go."

The song of triumph brought the hearts of the company into unison, and a pleasant interchange of Christian fellowship followed. One of the strangers was a clergyman of the Church of England, and the other an American.

The second incident was even more interesting.

Mr. Spurgeon said that a month ago he had hailed a cab and been driven home in it. When he paid the man he said, "It is a long time since I drove you last, sir."

"Did you ever drive me before?" asked Mr. Spurgeon; and added, "I do not recollect you."

"Oh, yes," said the man, "it is about fourteen years ago; but if you have forgotten me, perhaps you will remember this," and as he spoke he pulled a Testament from his pocket.

"What," said Mr. Spurgeon, "did I give you that?"

"Yes, sir; and you spoke to me about my soul, and nobody had ever done that before. I have never forgotten it."

"And haven't you worn the Testament out in all these years?"

"No, I wouldn't let it be worn out. I have had it bound."

Mr. Spurgeon thought that a good illustration of the fact that the gift of a New Testament is never made in vain.

It was in the summer of 1875 that Mrs. Bartlett died.

What happy Sunday afternoons were those which were spent in her class! Her addresses fitted in well with Mr. Spurgeon's sermons; and a day at the Tabernacle, which included the morning service, the afternoon class, the friendly tea together of many members of the class, and the evening service, with possibly the communion at the close (for at one time Mr. Spurgeon held a communion service every Sunday evening), was a perfect day.

Mrs. Bartlett was a very gifted woman, but her greatest gift was her loving heart of sympathy. Her class was one of the institutions of the Tabernacle, and certainly not the least in importance. Like so many others who have been especially useful in the Church, and like Mr. Spurgeon himself, she gave her heart to Christ while very young, and at once began to show her thanksgiving for His salvation in service. She did not go to London until after her marriage, but she settled at New Park Street then, more that she might be herself helped than with any idea of helping others. But in 1859 there was a class without a teacher. It was an important class, not because of its numbers, which had for some reason dwindled down to less than half-a-dozen, but because it was a senior class. Mr. Olney asked Mrs. Bartlett to take the class. She said she was afraid she could not, for she had a family to look after, and besides, as she was suffering from heart disease, she feared she was not strong enough. But she did not like to turn from the work thus offered her, and so she compromised the matter by promising to take it for a month. It increased every Sunday, and at the end of the month the new teacher had become too much interested in the work to wish to give it up; she therefore promised for another month, feeling that if this work had been given her by God, he would give her the strength to do it. So she went on with the duty, and the class grew, until there were fifty members at the time of the opening of the Tabernacle.

Everything had a new start then, Mrs. Bartlett's class among the other organisations. The young women of London found in her the friend whom they needed, and they began to love and trust her. She gave more and more time to them. Not only on Sunday did she meet them, but on two evenings in the week; and her Christian counsel and loving faithfulness were the means of the conversion of a host of women who are now filling important positions in homes of their own or business houses in all parts of England, and indeed in all parts of the world. Her home was always open to them, and her heart also. She was their friend as much as their teacher, and they honoured and trusted her, and thanked God for her.

It was no wonder that her class grew from one hundred to two hundred, and on to five or six hundred. The class was a great feeder of the church; sometimes more than a hundred a year from it were received into fellowship and baptised by Mr. Spurgeon.

Mrs. Bartlett trained them in all loving ministries. They had collections for the Pastors' College and the Orphanage, and, best of all, they had a fund for helping the poor of their own neighbourhood, which money was distributed by their own hands.

They mourned for their teacher as the widows mourned for Dorcas when she died, and to this day some of them can scarcely speak of her without tears.

For some time after her death there was a question as to who could worthily fill her place. But happily for the Tabernacle Church, Mrs. Bartlett's son, who had on several occasions taken the service for his mother, undertook the entire charge of the class after her removal.

Several notable events occurred in 1876 at the Tabernacle.

One of the first was a meeting to which all the open-air preachers of London were invited, and to which all who could came, glad to be inspired afresh for their arduous work by Mr. Spurgeon, than whom none was better fitted to address them.

Another was a friendly meeting between the students of the Regent's Park College and the students of the

Pastors' College. Dr. Angus accepted the invitation of Mr. Spurgeon, and took his men over in March. Their hosts were much gratified, and showed their guests every brotherly kindness and attention; and some excellent speeches were delivered to this united gathering of the future Baptist ministers of the country. A return visit of the Pastors' College students was made before the end of the year, and, beside others, two addresses were delivered by the two presidents—Dr. Angus taking as his subject, "Go," and Mr. Spurgeon, "Culture." Such friendly meetings were productive of much good feeling, and friendships were formed then that have stood the test of years.

Mr. Spurgeon was ill in April and May, breaking down after the Annual Conference of Pastors. He gave a striking address, taking as his subject, "*I believe in the Holy Ghost.*" He was himself at his best in the deliverance of it, and as cheery and encouraging as usual; but the excitement was followed by a period of deep depression. Readers of the *Sword and Trowel* will remember the pathetic article written during this illness under the suggestive heading, "Laid Aside—Why?"

He was better, however, when the time came for the celebration of his birthday on June 20th, when there was an enormous gathering at the Orphanage, and £500 were contributed toward the funds. Sir Henry Havelock presided at the evening meeting; and this was an especially joyous one, for five Spurgeons made speeches—Mr. Spurgeon's father, the Rev. John Spurgeon, his brother, the Rev. James Spurgeon, his two sons, Thomas and Charles, and the pastor himself. A few days later Mr. Spurgeon had the joy of baptising three persons who were the firstfruits of the ministry of his sons.

The fertile brain of the pastor of the Tabernacle devised a good thing on a certain Sunday in July He requested his own people to absent themselves on the evening of the

16th, that strangers might have a chance of all the best seats, and of hearing the preacher in comfort. The idea took splendidly. The strangers came in crowds, and the seat-holders did as they were asked, and absented themselves almost entirely. There was to be no collection, and the place was perfectly free to all comers. But it was not nearly large enough to hold those who pressed for admission. An open-air service was held for those who could not get in, and while Mr. Spurgeon was preaching several prayer-meetings for a special blessing on his words were held in different parts of the buildings. A great blessing followed this new departure, and the same plan was tried with equal success on several after occasions.

Mr. Spurgeon and his people believed in prayer. Once during this year sixty prayer-meetings were held at the same time in the houses of his friends. He wanted all to pray and all to work. In one of his letters he spoke of the "persevering, quiet believers who in secret implore the divine blessing, and then regularly give their aid to the continuous worship, service, and intercession of the church;" but he added, "we need also dashing spirits who will lead on in continually renewed efforts; thoughtful, practical men and women who will suggest and commence aggressive movements. We have such among us, but others need to be pressed into the service. One should canvass for the Sabbath School, another should break up fresh tract districts, and a third should commence a cottage service, and a fourth should preach in a court or alley which has not been as yet visited." The church could not be other than prosperous while prayer and service flourished in connection with it.

Early in 1877 Mr. Spurgeon went away to Mentone, but not until after the annual church meeting had been held, at which it was stated that the members now numbered 4938.

That year he addressed meetings composed of men in very different stations of life. First there was a gathering of working men in working clothes, to whom he talked "in workmen's language." A meat tea had been provided for these men by three friends. Later he held meetings for merchants and business men at the Cannon Street Hotel and the Friends' Meeting House in Bishopsgate, which had been readily lent to him. The meetings were held in the middle of the day, and at neither were there fewer than two thousand men. Two at least of these addresses are among the penny series published by Mr. Spurgeon's friends and publishers, Messrs. Passmore & Alabaster, under the titles of "The Claims of God" and "Faith in Christ."

"God's claim," he said, "is written in His law very succinctly, but there is a world in it—'Thou shalt love the Lord thy God with all thy heart, and with all thy soul, and with all thy mind, and with all thy strength; and thy neighbour as thyself.' You see it is a matter of the inner man, a spiritual claim which He lays upon us, but this is so wonderfully influential and comprehensive that it includes all kinds of active and passive service. Outward obedience and external religion, if they are genuine, always come out of love. Practical action towards God grows out of the heart-work which He first of all demands of us: that we should love Him is at once the source and the sum-total of all the service we can render to the Most High."

He used as an illustration a boy living in the father's house, coming to the table with his brothers and sisters, even joining in the festivities, but keeping his heart closed to his father. "You could not wish him away, and yet his presence there in such a spirit causes you the sharpest pain. 'Why have I not my boy's heart?' say you. 'What have I done to forfeit his love?' If you are conscious that you have behaved severely or ungenerously to him you rebuke yourself; but if, on surveying all your actions towards him, you can see nothing but love and kindness, it cuts you to the heart. Nothing that he can do, nothing that he can say, will at all content you until he gives you his love. And with God it is just the same."

The following extract is worth remembering:—" I think, in the service of our God, since there is no sharp line of division to be made between business and religion, when rightly viewed our religion becomes our business, and our business is a living part of our religion. It is mischievous to make a gulf in life between one set of actions and another, for life ought to be all of a piece. 'Whether ye eat or drink, do all to the glory of God.' Somebody found fault with us the other day for praying about politics. I know no politics that I shall not pray about. I know nothing among men that does not come under the broad heavens of my religion; even if it be something downright wrong, still may I pray *against* it. Religion should sit as queen both over politics and business. 'Oh, but,' they say, ' business is business.' I know it is, but business has no business to be such business as it often is. The greatest business of a business man should be to pay his debts to his God, and seek to live to His praise."

A day in the autumn of 1877 was spent entirely as a day of prayer by the Tabernacle church and its pastor. There were four gatherings : " the first for early risers, the second to sanctify the dinner-hour, the third to meet the convenience of people of leisure, and the fourth in the evening, to welcome the members of other churches."

The great sorrow of the year was the parting of the loving father and mother with their son, the Rev. Thomas Spurgeon, who had been ordered by his medical advisers to quit the country in search of health, and take a voyage to Australia. They all felt the parting very keenly; they were never so large a family that they could afford to miss one, and a sense of loneliness fell upon them. But they

THE FATHER'S SON.

might have known that his father's son would be heartily welcomed wherever he went. He was greeted by the Australians with the greatest warmth. More pulpits than he could occupy were offered him; the hospitable homes of the colony were at his service, and everywhere he met friends and work. He has found it difficult ever since to leave the sphere in which, excepting occasional visits to England, he has been engaged with great blessing and success for many years.

Mr. Spurgeon was too ill himself to be able to remain in England that winter. He had to go to Mentone in December, and remained there until the following March.

An enthusiastic welcome greeted his return. Two Tabernacles would not have been too large for the people. Heartily as he had been welcomed when returning from previous vacations, this seemed the warmest welcome of all. On Monday evening, 18th March, he met more than 400 new converts. Eighty-four persons had been added to the church on the previous Sabbath. The Butchers' Annual Festival was held on the 26th of the month, when 2100 of the London butchers and their wives were entertained in the rooms under the Tabernacle, and 600 of the masters and their wives and other friends had tea in the College Lecture Hall. After tea they all adjourned to the chapel, and as they were joined by the general public, the spacious building was rapidly filled. The chair was taken by the pastor, who addressed the men on their need of civility, morality, humanity, and true religion.

One of the most interesting meetings of the year was that of the Colporteurs, held on the 5th and 6th of May.

This association had now been in existence about a dozen years. It was formed, as everybody knows, for the purpose of meeting the sale of vicious literature by the distribution of good books. At first six men were engaged to try what could be done. Their packs were to be their passports to every door; their attempt to sell was to be an opportunity for preaching the Gospel, and the book itself a ready text. Like all other institutions started by Mr. Spurgeon, this also had been a great success. There were now eighty-six men fully employed as colporteurs, and eight gave part of their time as book-agents. During the year 1877 the men had distributed gratuitously 160,000 tracts, visited 500,000 families, and sold 84,147 books and 239,758 periodicals, for which they received £6651, 19s. 10d., that amount being £743, 18s. 1d. in excess of the previous year's receipts. The total subscriptions for the year amounted to £3702.

CHAPTER XIII.

THE STORY OF THE STOCKWELL ORPHANAGE.

THE sacred words of Christ, "To him that hath shall be given," are never more true than when they refer to Christian work and workers. It might have been thought that Mr. Spurgeon, with the pastorate of the largest Nonconformist church in the world, and all the multitudinous appendages to the same, with the Pastors' College, and with all his literary labour, had enough to do, and yet it was to him that the charge was given to take, house, feed, clothe, and educate some hundreds of otherwise helpless children. It is needless to state that Mr. Spurgeon had a deep sense of the need and importance of some provision being made for fatherless children who were left unprovided for, but until his duty was put very unmistakably before him he had not the slightest idea of founding an institution for this purpose.

It was in the autumn of 1866 that Mr. Spurgeon one morning received a letter which, used as he was to receiving communications of all descriptions through the post, must have surprised him not a little. The letter was from a lady, and its purport was that the writer wished to entrust to Mr. Spurgeon the sum of £20,000, to be used by him for the purpose of maintaining destitute orphan boys. She expressed her wish that, while recognising the necessity for training them to be good and intelligent citizens, the chief end should be the spiritual training of the boys, so that in after years they might, by the blessing of God, become Christian workers, either as ministers, missionaries, or in some other department of service.

The lady who wrote was Mrs. Hillyard, the widow of a clergyman. So astonished was Mr. Spurgeon at the liberality of her offer that at first he could not believe in it. It seemed too good to be true that, in these days of money-getting and self-seeking, a lady should be willing to devote a fortune to such an object. He, of course, complied with the lady's request for an interview, and found her in a house which was certainly not remarkable for its splendour. No signs of the owner being possessed of great wealth were visible, and Mr. Spurgeon felt more than ever that some mistake must have been make. "He had called," he said, "to confer with the lady about the *two hundred* pounds she wished to place in his hands." And upon the lady's answering that the money in question was many times that amount, Mr. Spurgeon made the characteristic reply that he thought a nought or two too many might have crept into her letter, and so thought it safer to err on the right side. All uncertainty about the matter was, however, soon set at rest by the securities for the £20,000 being placed in the possession of Mr. Spurgeon, and there and then he found himself pledged to the work of founding and superintending the erection of an Orphanage for fatherless boys.

It was characteristic of Mr. Spurgeon that he at once, and with his natural earnestness, set about the task committed to him. He had not gone out of his way to take up this work. Thoroughly as his large heart sympathised with the widow and the orphan, and fully desirous as he was to help to lessen their sorrow and their suffering, to do such a thing as erect a home for orphan boys had never entered into his plans. But when such means, without any seeking on his

STOCKWELL ORPHANAGE.

part, were placed in his hands, he concluded that it was God's will that he should do this work, and feeling sure of this, he set about it without a fear. To make plans and then ask for the Divine blessing was not the rule of Mr. Spurgeon's life, but rather to wait for Divine guidance, and then in full faith to expect the blessing of God upon His own work.

The first decision Mr. Spurgeon arrived at with reference to the prospective building was that its site should be within easy access to the Tabernacle, so that he might give personal oversight to the institution, and also that it might be within the ordinary compass of visitors to London. As may easily be imagined, it was a difficult matter to find such a site in so well-populated a district, but very fortunately, or rather, as the Committee of Management and its President properly considered, very providentially, a piece of land behind the houses in Clapham Road was just then offered for sale. The right of this was at once secured, and an article from the pen of Mr. Spurgeon appeared in the *Sword and Trowel*, making known the plan and asking for help, for it was necessary that, if a thoroughly good and useful institution were to be raised, a great deal more money must be forthcoming. The funds did not at first flow in so quickly as could have been desired, although numerous small sums were received which, while they did not greatly augment the Fund, yet much encouraged those who had the management of the plan. In June 1867 the committee had only about £600 in hand, but during the next three months the cause of the Orphanage prospered more abundantly, and it was thought advisable to commence operations.

Another point on which Mr. Spurgeon was thoroughly decided was that the Orphanage should be worked on what is now known as the cottage system. While admitting that it was a fine thing to rescue, provide for, and bring up orphans on any plan whatever, Mr. Spurgeon felt that to herd children together in one large barrack-like building, where they would have to live by rule, and in a sense lose their identity on account of being only units among so many, was attended by grave disadvantages. Of all others, those boys who have lost the loving yet firm control of a father are the ones who most need the quiet, refining, and gentle discipline of home life; and so it was decided that the boys who were to receive the benefits of the Stockwell Orphanage should live in separate families, so as to secure the personal oversight of each one by such as would have his best interests at heart.

The houses were built in a terrace, and number one has the name of the Silver Wedding House, from the fact that it was built by a lady (a member of the Metropolitan Tabernacle congregation) with money given to her by her husband to commemorate the twenty-fifth anniversary of their wedding.

The second home (the Merchant's House) was the gift of a wealthy city merchant, whose heart was touched by the appeal made on behalf of the fatherless, and who decided that he could not put his money out at better interest than by "lending it to the Lord," to be used for the housing of His little ones.

The third house in the terrace is called the Workmen's House. One of the deacons of the Metropolitan Tabernacle, who was a builder in a large way of business, undertook to provide everything necessary for the building if his workmen would give their time and labour. This was agreed to by the men, but it was afterwards found that the carrying out of their project would mean a breach of contract, so the money was subscribed instead.

It was on Monday, the 9th of September 1869, that the committee arranged a festival in connection with the laying of the memorial-stones of the three homes above named.

A very large company, numbering as many as four thousand persons, was present; and the fact that a great proportion of these were collectors testifies to the widespread interest that had been taken in the project. One of the most interesting items in the programme of that happy day was the paying over to the treasurer the sum of £2200. There was a good deal of excitement in the neighbourhood occasioned by this novel gathering, and the scene within the enclosure was most picturesque. The avenue that was to be was gay with bright dresses and happy faces, and on all hands were heard congratulations upon the fact that the good work was now in a fair way of being carried out. It had been arranged that the first of the memorial-stones should be laid by the good lady to whose loving, motherly thought the institution owed its existence, but through some mistake in the arrangements this was made impossible, and the duty devolved upon her commander-in-chief, Mr. Spurgeon. It will readily be believed that he performed the ceremony with all the happy adaptability to circumstances of which he was master. Earnest prayers were offered that the homes, through many future years and to hundreds of boys, might be a comfort and a blessing. The answers to these prayers have been graciously given ever since, are being given now, and we know that in the time to come

>"He who hath blessed will bless;
>He who hath fed will feed."

During the ceremony of the setting of each stone hymns were sung, to which verses had been added appropriately bearing upon the different homes, as for example—

>"Accept, O Lord, the grateful love
>Which yields this house to Thee,
>And on the *Silver Wedding House*
>Let blessings ever be."

The success which had attended the labours of the collectors was the cause of most enthusiastic congratulation. So energetically had they worked that the treasurer had now in hand £5500, besides the first £10,000 given by Mrs. Hillyard. Those who were privileged to share in the delights of this happy day went away well pleased with all they had seen and heard, and full of faith that the good work then inaugurated would, in the Lord's good time, be brought to a most satisfactory completion. The only cloud that threw a shadow over the proceedings (excepting a rain cloud which gave many of the visitors a wetting in the evening) was the evidently most delicate state of health of the beloved pastor. The greatest concern was expressed that the new work and responsibility, in addition to all the old which was upon him, might not prove too great a burden, and many private prayers that he might have special strength for special need were offered up for him that night by hearts that loved him.

The year 1867 was marked by two other happy events in connection with the Stockwell Orphanage. The one was the receiving by the committee of the handsome donation of £1000 from an anonymous donor; the other the first selection of seven boys for the Orphanage. The latter task did not give unalloyed happiness to those who had to discharge it. The number of boys to be elected was necessarily small in those early days, and, as may readily be believed, the number of applicants was painfully large. Many deserving cases had to be refused on account of its being quite out of the power of the trustees to give the desired boon. It had been intended to hold a monstre bazaar at the end of this year, the proceeds of which were to be entirely devoted to the Orphanage, but this had unfortunately to be postponed on account of the severe illness of Mrs. Spurgeon.

The fourth house in the terrace is a memorial building,

and was erected by the sons of the treasurer of Mr. Spurgeon's church to commemorate the memory of their departed mother. Surely such a monument is a more fitting remembrancer of a loved and loving mother than the finest marble monument or the most exquisite painted window that could be erected. The house is named "*Unity* House," that having been the Christian name of the lady.

The year 1868 was notable for the presentation of four more houses to the little colony which was so rapidly being evolved out of chaos. The origin of the first two of these is exceedingly interesting. Some friends, having observed with great sorrow the bodily weakness from which Mr. Spurgeon was suffering in the preceding autumn, felt that they would like to give him a token of their practical sympathy with him in the varied and arduous work to which he was committed, and which so told upon his health and strength. It is a proof that these persons thoroughly understood the spirit of Mr. Spurgeon, that they at once resolved to raise a fund for one or other of the institutions in connection with the Tabernacle. All the Nonconformist churches in England were asked to subscribe to this fund, and it was decided that the money so obtained should defray the cost of two Orphanage houses, which were given to the president on the understanding that destitute sons of deceased ministers should have the prior claim of election to these homes. The houses were called the Baptist Denomination Testimonial Houses, and the offering was one that gave the deepest joy to Mr. Spurgeon's heart. There is no one who is not the happier for a proof of sympathy from those who are one in faith with him, and Mr. Spurgeon was no exception to the rule. No personal gift to himself could have given him half the satisfaction that the help to the Orphanage did, and he "thanked God and took courage." It was on the 1st of June 1868 that the memorial-stones of the Baptist Denomination Testimonial Houses were laid by Messrs. Goodall and Aldis respectively, and the same day saw the commencement of the dining-hall, the foundation-stone of this building being laid by Mr. Olney.

Of the other two houses mentioned, the first was the gift of the students and friends of the Pastors' College, and the second that of the Sunday Schools of England. Mr. Spurgeon's thirty-fourth birthday—the 19th of June 1868—was the day chosen for the laying of the memorial-stones, and a very happy day it was to all concerned. Mrs. Spurgeon graced the gathering with her presence, and laid the corner-stone of the College House with her own hands, greatly to the delight of those present. The foundation, or rather the memorial-stone of the Sunday School House was very appropriately laid by the superintendent of the Metropolitan Sunday School (Mr. Olney), who was supported by a large number of the scholars in the school, all greatly pleased at being allowed to take part in the proceedings. Perhaps the most interesting item in the programme of this day, and certainly the most picturesque, was the presentation to Mrs. Spurgeon of twenty-six purses of money, for the use of the Orphanage, by as many dear little white-robed girls.

The Stockwell Orphanage is emphatically *unsectarian*. Though its President and the Committee of Management are members of the Baptist denomination, the question of sect has no weight whatever with them in choosing those who are to receive the benefits of the Home. This is of course as it should be. Persons of all shades of belief, and belonging to all sections of the community, willingly subscribe to support this noble institution, and it is only right that all classes should share in its benefits. Indeed, if any should have the prior claim, it should surely be those who have *not* had the advantage of early Christian training, because their need is infinitely the greater. The strongest passport to the favour of those who have the power of choosing the recipients is *urgent need*. The most necessitous cases are always entitled to the prior claim irrespective of class, sect, or locality, unless in the case of donors who are willing to give such a sum yearly as shall amply provide for the child they wish to benefit. The committee would naturally accept such a child, provided that the conditions upon which each one is taken into the home were fulfilled in his case. The committee have, however, respectfully declined to receive sums of money sent in the hope of furthering the chances of particular children, as to countenance this mode of procedure would mean in effect the placing of the Orphanage on an entirely different basis to the one at first decided upon.

As a matter of fact, of the 1513 children who at the close of last year had been received, 585 have been the children of parents professing the faith of the Church of England, 387 Baptists, 160 Congregational, 140 Wesleyan, 28 Presbyterian, 9 Brethren, 3 Roman Catholics, 2 Moravian, 2 Bible Christian, 2 Society of Friends, 1 Salvation Army, and 194 not specified. The greater number of these have been taken from the artisan class, although nearly all classes of the community have contributed children—ministers, missionaries, journalists, teachers, surgeons, solicitors, clerks, commercial travellers, railway and postal employés, soldiers, sailors, and those of many other callings. London has furnished 934 of the children who have thus been rescued from the sorrows and perils of unprotected orphanhood, and other places in England have sent 549, besides which there have been admissions from Wales, Scotland, and Ireland.

The great aim on the part of those who have the control of these children has been to bring them up "in the nurture and admonition of the Lord," and to send them out to take their place in life fully equipped for the battle, and with their sympathies thoroughly enlisted on the side of truth and righteousness. As a matter of fact, many embrace the Baptist religion; nor is this at all to be wondered at, since their best friends from early childhood have been of that persuasion.

As regards the system upon which the selection of children for the Orphanage was to be made, Mr. Spurgeon held very strong opinions on that subject, and his colleagues were thoroughly agreed with him as to the mode to be adopted. Perhaps the most common method of election to vacant places in institutions of this kind is that of election by subscribers' votes. Their supporters subscribe so many guineas, and receive in return so many votes, which at an annual or semi-annual election they may give to any case or cases they choose.

That there should be a canvass for votes given in this way is absolutely necessary, for unless the needs of the different candidates are brought under the notice of those who give the votes it is impossible for them to judge what will be the wisest way of disposing of them. The task of canvassing devolves of course upon the friends of the candidates—generally upon the widowed mother—and a most heart-breaking task it often turns out to be, taking her time and strength and money when she has the greatest need of all three, and then in the majority of cases ending in grievous disappointment. Some poor women have been known to spend as much as £50 in the effort to place a loved child in such an institution; and the *Daily News*, commenting on this evil, gave as an instance a case in which, from first to last, £60 was lost in canvassing for votes, etc. And in the end this fearful expenditure *was in vain!*

Far be it from us to condemn any methods chosen by any institution which has for its object the lessening of the care and woe in the world. In many cases the method of election by subscribers' votes appears to be the only one feasible, and it certainly has the advantage of simplicity in working. But the Home we are describing was at its commencement placed on an entirely different basis in this respect, and the results have justified this departure from ordinary methods.

The committee, fourteen in number, appoint visitors to inquire most searchingly into each applicant's case, and upon their reports the selection is made. It cannot be too emphatically repeated that the saddest cases—those of the greatest destitution and helplessness—receive always the first consideration and have the best chance of success. Of course this method of procedure is one entailing a great deal of trouble, and as a rule it takes a considerable time, for those who act in the matter freely *give* their services, and they have their daily avocations, besides the duties in connection with the Home. But when the selection is made and the children admitted, the managers have the satisfaction of knowing that they are relieving the most necessitous, and that the poor friends of the candidate have not had to suffer, either in time or pocket, for the gain of the little ones who have been taken into the Home. Perhaps it might be as well to mention here that boys who seek admission to Stockwell Orphanage must be between the ages of six and ten, and girls between seven and ten.

Now as to the dress worn by the little people. We are glad to be able to state that there is *no uniform* worn. Of course, among so many children it is impossible to avoid a certain similarity in dress, but in no case are any of the boys and girls dressed exactly alike. This plan is a very good one, inasmuch as it obviates the distressing sense of their difference to other children, which must be often brought home to the minds of many sensitive little ones.

True, the clothing worn in many cases is such as has been given by kind friends, and is not new; but it is always warm, comfortable, seemly, and, as far as may be, pretty. The advantage is more than ever felt when the time comes for the boys and girls to be sent out into the world. They at once take their places with those who are to be their companions without the degrading sense of inferiority which a garb distinctly "charity cut" would give them; and this is a blessing which cannot be understood by those who have never experienced the bitterness of facing the world with the feeling impressed upon them that they are different to those who are their compeers.

For many years the Stockwell Orphanage was open to boys only. The homes would accommodate two hundred and fifty, and needless to state they could always have been filled three times over. But in May 1879 Mr. Spurgeon received from Mrs. Hillyard a cheque for £50, with a proposal that they should at once set to work to extend their borders and double the number of their boarders by raising homes for as many orphan girls as there were boys in residence. At first Mr. Spurgeon hesitated—not because he did not feel the need of the proposed extension, but on account of the extra anxiety which such a scheme would entail upon himself and those who laboured with him. But on the occasion of the meeting held at the Tabernacle, May 19th, 1879 (when the sum of £6000 was presented to him in token of his people's loving gratitude on his completing twenty-five years of faithful service amongst them), he said that he had decided to follow what seemed to be the leading of Divine Providence in this matter, and there and then added £50 to the £50 given by Mrs. Hillyard, thus starting the subscription list for the *Girls'* Stockwell Orphanage.

Events justified faith and judgment. The adjoining property was just about that time offered for sale, so that

A REAL HOME.

it became possible for the two departments of the Home to come under the superintendence of the same management. Funds to the amount of £11,000 were forthcoming, and soon the handsome houses on the one side of the avenue were kept in countenance by as beautiful ones on the other; the noisy shouts of the boys at their play mingled with the happy laughter of the girls; and those whose loving thought had raised the Home felt amply repaid for all their care and anxiety as they saw their enormous family growing up healthy, happy, and good.

In addition to the buildings already named, there are the infirmary, recreation halls, and laundry, so that the whole institution forms a complete little town in itself; and many find life in it, under the firm and yet kind rule which is maintained, so happy and joyous a thing that they do not by any means wish to go out into the untrammelled freedom of the world.

What are the internal arrangements of the Orphanage? Any who wish can pay it a visit and judge for themselves, for it is at all times open to the inspection of friends. But for the benefit of those who cannot do this, we will describe, as far as possible, the daily home-life of the children. Each cottage will accommodate about thirty children, over whom a Christian matron acts as mother, and has complete control. Every house contains a kitchen, parlour, and bed-room for the use of the matron; while a beautiful day-room is provided for the use of each family, and two large and lofty dormitories, with bath-room attached. The furniture of the rooms is light and inexpensive, and it is extremely interesting to walk round the dormitories and see the eighteen little beds, covered with counterpanes, in the centre of which are marked the words, "Stockwell Orphanage." Each boy has a locker for clothes, etc., and at the head of each bed is hung an illuminated text and motto, besides a life-motto for each individual child. As far as the sanitary arrangements are concerned, everything that science and forethought could do has been done to secure the health and comfort of the inmates.

As far as compatible with order and good training, the children are allowed perfect liberty. After their hours of work and study they are allowed to play and amuse themselves exactly as they choose. Such as please can disport themselves in the gymnasium, cricket-ground, or swimming-bath; and there are also playgrounds for dry and recreation-rooms for wet weather. The education given is thorough and solid, such as will fit the children to fill useful positions in after-life. The master does not aim at teaching the lighter branches of study, nor at giving the children a classical education; French and German, Latin and Greek, may, if desirable, be acquired in after-life. In school all the children are thoroughly grounded in the three R's; the boys are taught shorthand and elementary science, while the girls become accomplished needlewomen.

A public testimony was borne to the Orphanage in 1878 which was of peculiar value. It appeared in a report made by order of the House of Commons, on the "Home and Cottage System of Training and Educating the Children of the Poor," by F. J. Mouat, Esq., M.D., Local Government Board Inspector, and Captain J. D. Bowly, R.E. It is as follows:—

"The Stockwell Orphanage, recently founded by the Rev. C. H. Spurgeon, is an institution of a higher order than the reformatories and pauper schools, and is not an industrial school properly so called. It is devoted to the education and training of fatherless boys, and is supported entirely by voluntary contributions in money or kind. The feature which caused us to visit it with reference to the present inquiry is, that it is based on the family system, there being eight separate houses, in each of which resides

MR. SPURGEON'S SCHOOL AND ALMSHOUSES.

a group of about thirty boys, under the special charge of a matron. Each house contains dormitories for the boys, and apartments for the matron, also a lavatory and the usual offices; but the meals are taken in a general dining-hall, and cooked in a general kitchen—an arrangement which doubtless conduces to economy, but which is to some extent a departure from the ideal family system.

"The boys' homes are arranged in a continuous terrace, each house being separated from the next by a party wall, as in an ordinary street; the schoolrooms are on a third floor over a portion of the terrace, and are commodious and airy. The standard of health is high; there is no general contagious disease in the school, and infectious fevers, when they occur, are easily prevented from spreading by early isolation in the convenient detached infirmary standing at the south-east end of the playground.

"The institution has been ten years at work, and the boys placed out in situations during that time have, as a rule, turned out well. In many respects this excellent school affords no ground of comparison with pauper institutions; but the point to be specially noted is, that the family system, even in the modified form here adopted, is stated to have been productive of undoubtedly good effects, not only as regards the formation of individual character, but also as conducing to a high standard of bodily health."

The domestic training of the children is by no means neglected. Each child has his or her own especial tasks to perform about the home; and the laying of meals, making of beds, sweeping and scrubbing of floors, cleaning of windows, and lighting of fires, becomes comparatively easy under the wise system of division of labour which obtains in the Orphanage. It may be mentioned here that the Stockwell children, on leaving, do not as a rule find it difficult to obtain situations; the training they have received is of such known excellence that no employer in want of a youth would hesitate to accept a boy from the Orphanage.

We cannot leave this part of our subject without a reference to the loved and respected manager and headmaster, Mr. Vernon J. Charlesworth. The Stockwell Orphanage has been his life-care and his life-work; and very much of its success has been the outcome of his untiring interest and unremitting toil. In the truest sense he has been the "guide, philosopher, and friend" of the boys; and many Christian men in responsible positions feel to-day that their life has been made what it is mainly through his influence and example. May God long spare him to occupy the post he has filled with such efficiency and grace!

A sad loss has now to be recorded. It has been Mr. Charlesworth's practice frequently to take the choir-boys of the Home to different parts of the country, to give concerts and promote meetings in order to make the institution and its needs better known. On January 13th, 1880, a meeting of this kind was being held in Bath. The boys' hearts had been made glad by the presentation of a new shilling each, which had been sent to them "with Mrs. Hillyard's love." Mrs. Hillyard was very ill at the time, and even while the meeting was proceeding she "fell asleep in Jesus." Her last words were, "My boys, my boys!" This touching event formed the subject of a poem by Marianne Farningham, which appeared in the *Christian World* about this time :—

A WOMAN'S LAST WORDS.

> The orphans' merry voices
> Were singing songs of love,
> Within our southern city,
> When a Christian passed above.

MRS. HILLYARD.

And the boys, who sang out sweetly,
In the keen delight of health,
Were trophies of her goodness
And triumphs of her wealth.

Not for herself, but others,
She used the gifts she had;
And what could one do better
Than make the orphan glad?
Her wealth was consecrated,
Her life was not her own;
And a great light filled the children
Who once were sad and lone.

Her tender heart had taken
The crowd of orphan boys
Into its own warm keeping,
And she lived to make their joys:
The good things God had given her
To brighten earth were theirs,
And the best of all their treasures
Were the woman's love and prayers.

Oh! earth might tempt with glitter,
And many voices call,
And fashion seek to keep her
Within its hold and thrall;
But she was true and steadfast
To the little ones bereft,
And they knew if they were fatherless,
A mother-heart was left.

The world was quite too busy
To note the work she did;
But there was One who watched her,
From whom it was not hid.
What matters earthly silence?
She has enough of fame,
For the men who once were orphans
Shall live to bless her name.

At length the enfolding shadows
Crept nearer to her heart,
And she knew it was the evening
When she and time must part.
She cared not for the leaving
Of earth with all its toys;
But all her heart's devotion
Was in that cry, "My boys!"

God heard! and for her guerdon
In His fair land of bliss,
Shall not the boys be given
She could not bear to miss?
And earth shall aye be richer
For the good men who shall come
To fill its places nobly
From the sheltered orphan home.

Oh, happy, honoured woman!
She has the well-earned rest
Of all the Master's servants
In the city of the blest;
And He will praise her gently
When she His face shall see—
"In blessing these my little ones
Thou didst it unto me."

God calls home His servants, but His work goes on. We cannot close this sketch without alluding briefly to the short but splendid career of one who as a lad was brought up in the Stockwell Orphanage. In several instances the boys, as they have grown up, have entered the Christian ministry, and in others they have become missionaries.

John Maynard was taken into the Stockwell Orphanage in 1869. From the first he was somewhat delicate in body, but his character developed year by year just as his best friends would have had it. When he left the Orphanage to take a situation in London, the whole of his spare time was spent in lodging-house mission-work, in which he was very successful.

Maynard had, however, an intense desire to become a missionary in foreign lands, and with this end in view he took a situation in Cape Colony, hoping that when on the spot a chance of serving God on the mission-field might offer. For some time this hope seemed destined to disappointment, but when he had been in his situation about two months an offer was made him by Mr. Batts, the Secretary of the South Africa Baptist Union (and formerly a student in the Pastors' College), that he should take charge of a small church just started in Graaff Reinet. With great diffidence, yet withal a feeling of deep thankfulness that God had thus made his way clear, John Maynard accepted the call. He stayed in Graaff Reinet for some time, and his ministry there was one of great power and usefulness. But John Maynard was a man who wished to be the best that he could for the Master's work, and after much prayer and heart-searching he wrote home to Mr. Spurgeon asking to be admitted as a student in the Pastors' College, in order that he might the more worthily and acceptably follow his high calling.

The rest of the story is soon told. He was admitted, passed successfully through his college career, and then the great desire of his life was realised. He was accepted by the Missionary Society for service on the Congo, that sphere in which so many of earth's noblest have laboured for a little while, and then fallen at noontide, victims of the cruel fever which Europeans seem quite unable to withstand. John Maynard went out full of love and enthusiasm, but only a few weeks was he allowed to labour, and then the Master called him to take his eternal rest, and one more name was added to the long list of Congo missionary martyrs. "As He will; all is well!" were among the last words he uttered on his truly happy deathbed. In the boys' department of the Orphanage is now a marble tablet, on which are the words—

<blockquote>
In Memory of
JOHN INGLES MAYNARD,
Of this Orphanage and of the Pastors' College.
From his youth he feared the Lord.
He went as a Missionary to Africa, and laboured for a short time at Underhill Station, Congo River; but fell asleep,
January 28th, 1886, in his 25th year.
</blockquote>

"Go ye into all the world, and preach the gospel to every creature."—Mark xvi. 15.

"Ye are my friends, if ye do whatsoever I command you."—John xv. 14.

The last and sorest loss the Orphanage has sustained is fresh in the minds of all. The loved guide and friend and father of the orphans has gone to his reward; his great heart is stilled for ever; his loving and wise counsel will be heard no more by the children who so dearly loved him. A giant worker is gone—*but the work remains.* May those be forthcoming who will worthily take it up and carry it on for Christ's sake, and for the sake of him to whom it was so dear!

CHAPTER XIV.

AFTER FIVE-AND-TWENTY YEARS

THE happy family at the Tabernacle took loving note of all anniversary days; and it was not likely that they would let such a date pass unnoticed as that which marked a quarter of a century of joyful fellowship between them and their beloved leader. Indeed there was a pretty memorial volume prepared by their publishers to keep the happy time always before the grateful people.

The first sermon in connection with the anniversary was preached in the morning of May 18th, 1879, by Mr. Spurgeon from Habakkuk iii. 2, "O Lord, I have heard thy speech, and was afraid: O Lord, revive thy work in the midst of the years, in the midst of the years make known; in wrath remember mercy." Mr. Spurgeon, after explaining that the name Habakkuk means the *embracer*, said—"In the text which I have selected this morning, with an eye to the celebration of the twenty-fifth year of our happy union as pastor and people, I see three points upon which I wish to dwell. The first is *The Prophet's Fear*, 'O Lord, I have heard thy speech and was afraid;' the second is *The Prophet's Prayer*, 'O Lord, revive thy work in the midst of the years;' and the third is *The Prophet's Plea*, 'In wrath remember mercy,' coupled with the rest of the chapter, in which he practically finds a plea for God's present working in the report of what he had done for Israel in the olden times."

In the evening the sermon was from the words, "Thou crownest the year with thy goodness," Psalm lxv. 11. The heads of the discourse were—1. The Divine Goodness adored; 2. The Encircling Blessing of the Divine Goodness is to be confessed; 3. The Crowning Blessing is confessed to be of God. A few of the closing words may be given:—
"Oh, if some hearts would yield themselves to the Saviour to-night, if some were converted to-night, what a crown that would be to finish up these years with! Testimonial, sirs? No testimonial can ever be given to the preacher which can equal a soul converted. These are the seeds of our ministry and the wages of our hire. . . May the Eternal Spirit lead many to give themselves thus to Jesus this night, and it will be the crowning joy of all the years!"

On the following day, Monday, several hundreds of the poorest members of the church were invited to tea, and in the evening the Tabernacle was filled with several thousands, who held a meeting of prayer and praise. Mr Spurgeon said the meeting was to be one of thanksgiving for twenty-five years of blessing. Mr. Olney offered the first praise-prayer, after the pastor had made a few affectionate remarks about him. "He is a link with the past," he said, "for he was here before my day. We are glad that he is raised up from the brink of the grave, and spared to us still. His number on the roll is five; and as he is far from being an old man, you will see that he has known the Lord from his youth. I was pleased to shake hands to-night with the oldest member. She has been in our fellowship some seventy-two or seventy-three years; and though she is weak and suffering, there is no happier spirit among all our thousands. I refer to our sister, Miss Fanny Gay."

Several persons offered praise—Mr. Thomas Spurgeon for the young believers who had been lately received into the church. Thanks on behalf of the Sunday School were offered by Mr. S. R Pearce, and Mr. V. J. Charlesworth for the blessings granted to the Orphanage, and Mr. E. J. Parker for the College, and evangelists, sang a hymn of thanksgiving.

Mr. Spurgeon's address was very characteristic. "An evil has come upon me," he said; "therefore at this period that I have to speak about myself. Last night I had a very difficult task. I felt that I must praise God for these twenty-five years of mercies, and I earnestly endeavoured to avoid all self-praise; but being personally mixed up with all this blessedness, I was compelled to become a fool in glorying. I did not like the task, and I felt glad when it was over; and I feel very much the same to-night, and yet I must speak to my Lord's praise, even though I be a fool. What He has done by our ministry on this spot is not gathered up in this place—no, not a thousandth part of it; nor is the influence that has gone forth with the sermons and other works confined to you, nor to a hundred times as many as you. No, there is scarcely a place on the face of the earth where our mother-tongue is spoken where the word of God, as sounded forth from this house, has not reached. In the bush of Australia and the backwoods of America, at the Cape of Good Hope and in the cities of India, I have at this moment hundreds of readers, among whom are many who have been led to Christ by the sermons."

Mr. Spurgeon's address was, naturally, a retrospect of his life and work in London, at New Park Street Chapel, at the Surrey Music Hall, and at the Tabernacle, and he told over again the marvellous story of how the money had come when he needed it. He referred to his difficulties. He said it was generally supposed that he preached without effort or trouble, but although he thankfully admitted that preaching was a source of great delight when he was once fully engaged in it, yet, as the deacons knew, for years he had never entered the pulpit without such a violent fit of trembling and distress, that sickness often came upon him.

He had often felt as if he would rather be flogged than face the crowd again. "I do feel more and more at home in speaking from the same spot to the same beloved people; but then the trial only takes another form, and while there is not so much fear just before preaching, there is far more labour and anxiety in striving to get the right subject, and to get one's soul into sympathy with it. To bring forth the right topics and make these interesting from year to year has caused me more effort than some might imagine. My happy task is one which taxes my physical, mental, and spiritual nature to the uttermost." But he had much consolation in the love of the people and the continued harmony of the church, and he felt that there was but one thing for them to do, and it was to go forward.

The next day there was a "Testimonial Meeting." The orphan boys were present, and they beautifully sang an anthem, "I was glad when they said unto me, Let us go into the house of the Lord." The Rev. W. Stott offered prayer. Mr. Carr, one of the deacons, read an interesting History of the Church during the past twenty-five years. It was a grateful retrospect and a graphic description.

Then the Rev. J. T. Wigner and Mr. William Higgs came forward as a deputation from the London Baptist Association, who brought the following letter from the committee:—

"TO THE REV. C. H. SPURGEON.

"DEAR FRIEND AND BROTHER,—The Committee of the London Baptist Association cannot deny themselves the pleasure of adding their congratulations to the many which will be offered to you on the present auspicious occasion. We do this on behalf of the one hundred and fifty churches in the Association, and we have requested our brethren, J. T. Wigner and W. Higgs, to express our feelings by word of mouth. Next to your own church, we venture to claim an interest in your continued health and ability for labour. We recognise in you one of the honoured fathers and founders of our Association. We rejoice in your long and abundant career of usefulness. We join our thanksgivings and prayers with those of the whole Church of Christ on your behalf. May you be long spared to preach the gospel which you love so much, and to be the leader in the manifold Christian agencies which you have so successfully originated, and in every season of weakness and depression may you be comforted with those consolations which you have learned so well to administer to others. We desire to express also our hearty congratulations to the church at the Tabernacle, with its elders and deacons, and to our beloved brother and colleague in the pastorate. Our Association is always made to feel itself at home at the Tabernacle, and we earnestly invoke upon its entire brotherhood the blessing of the great Head of the Church, our common Lord and Saviour.

"On behalf of the Committee,
"Yours faithfully and affectionately,
"WILLIAM BROCK, Vice-President.
"GROVE, HAMPSTEAD, *May* 20, 1879."

The Rev. Charles Stanford, D.D., delivered an eloquent address on the subject of "The Baptist Churches Twenty-five Years Ago and Now," at the end of which Mr. Spurgeon's favourite hymn,

"Grace, 'tis a charming sound,"

was sung to his favourite tune, "Cranbrook," and then Mr. William Olney presented the testimonial, the amount of which was £6233. The Rev. James A. Spurgeon presented a clock, saying, "This testimonial is given to him. He takes nothing, I know, for himself, but we do ask him to take this clock and the ornaments. May they be in his study until his golden wedding, and may they come here again at that jubilee, and we will look at them! I hope that the clock will enable him to maintain his constant habit of always being in time; and be always, if I may be allowed a pun, a striking token of your regard for him."

When Mr. Spurgeon rose to reply there was such a demonstration as living man has seldom had before; it was perfectly indescribable.

Mr. Spurgeon having received the money, gave £5000 of it to endow the Almshouses, and the rest for the Colportage and the Orphanage. The closing words of his address were these (the whole of what he said, and the other speakers said also, can be read in the memorial volume, *Spurgeon's Silver Wedding*[1]):—"This love to me is an amazement. I am the most astonished person among you. I do not comprehend it. It seems a romance to me. What I have done I shall do still—namely, love you with all my heart, and love my Lord as His grace enables me. I mean to go on preaching Jesus and his Gospel, and you may be sure that I shall not preach anything else, for it is with me Christ or nothing. I am sold up, and my stock-in-trade is gone, if Jesus Christ is gone. He is the sum of my ministry and my all in all.

"Now you will please to understand that I need all that you would mean if you were in my position, and I beg again to thank you most heartily, every one of you, especially the dear friends who read us the papers, and especially those who listened to them, and especially everybody."

The year 1880 was a great one in the history of Sunday Schools. It was the centenary of their commencement by Robert Raikes, and large numbers of people—deputations from all parts of the world—came over to London in June to celebrate it. One of the best of all the meetings was a

[1] Passmore & Alabaster.

Communion Service held at the Metropolitan Tabernacle, and presided over by Mr. Spurgeon. Thirty or forty of the foreign delegates and leading committee of the Sunday School Union were on the platform, and several thousand Sunday School teachers, who had come from everywhere to be present, were in the building.

It was a time which no one will forget. Mr. Spurgeon was very happy. "How glad I am to see you!" were his opening words. "I do most heartily feel communion with you, although members of different churches, because we trust, and we assume it to be so, that you are all members of the mystical body of Christ."

The opening hymn was—

"Come, let us sing the song of songs."

Dr. Dodd, of New York, offered the first prayer; he was followed by Mr. Spurgeon, and he by Mr. John Wanamaker, of Philadelphia, since Postmaster-General of the United States. Several minutes were spent in private prayer, after which Vice-Chancellor Blake, of Toronto, and the Hon. A. Vidal, of Sarnia, led the devotions, and Pasteur Paul Cook offered a prayer in French.

It may be said that Mr. Spurgeon was in his natural element at this meeting, and his address, delivered to a most sympathetic audience, was full of inspiration. We give a part of it, for which we are indebted to the memorial volume of the Centenary, published by the Sunday School Union (56 Old Bailey, London). He commenced by saying:—

"Beloved brethren and sisters, we are met together to-night, and the doors are shut, not for fear of the Jews, but that we may be in quiet, and be alone; and I hope that to-night Jesus will stand in the midst of us, and if He does we shall first be conscious of a Divine peace, for that is His benediction, 'Peace be unto you.' We shall then, doubtless, have a sight of His wounds as Thomas did, and I hope we shall cry in adoring recognition of Him, 'My Lord and my God.' And then will follow His breathing upon us, saying, ' Receive ye the Holy Ghost,' and then the renewed commission, 'As my Father hath sent Me, even so send I you.' Oh, that we might have a repetition of that visit! Jesus has never denied us a visit hitherto. No, He has often offered to visit us and we have refused Him. Remember it is not at the door of a sinner's heart that Jesus stands and knocks. According to the Scripture, it was at the door of His own Church that He stood and knocked, the Church of Laodicea Let it not be so with us to-night, but when He knocks let us hasten to let Him in, and before He knocks let us set wide the door, and go and seek our Beloved, and entreat Him to come now and manifest Himself to us, as He doth not unto the world.

" Our theme to-night is Jesus, and nothing else but Jesus. Dear brethren and sisters, you have nothing else to teach that I know of. I almost wish that you were as ignorant as I am, for I know nothing else, and when I get to the end of the Gospel I am spun out. I know no more, and have no wish to know more; I determine not to know, I am a know-nothing. I determine not to know anything among you save Jesus Christ and Him crucified. So our subject is Christ, and we begin with this. You are all in Christ, that is assumed by your coming here, for none others were invited; and if there are any out of Christ, they certainly have no right at this table, and they will be doing sin if they come. If thou believest with all thine heart thou mayest, but not else. But you are so, you are in Christ, and you are in Christ altogether. All there is about you that is worth being is in Him. Are you saved? You are saved in Christ Jesus. Are you justified? You are justified in Christ Jesus. Are you sanctified? He is made of God unto you sanctification. Have you any wisdom? He is made of

God unto you wisdom. Do you not feel it? Oh, I trust we not only say it, but in our very hearts are conscious of it.

"Now, then, as teachers, being such to begin with, we must always do our work for Christ, and I am sure there is no way of doing it well except we keep continually before our mind's eye that it is work done for Him. He is our blessed Master, and we love Him so, His work is so dear to us, that we can do anything for Christ; we cannot always say that we would for His Church, although His Church is so fair in His eyes, that she ought to be fair in ours. We don't always see her good points; we begin to get a little weary of her sometimes, generally because of our pride of heart, but we never get weary of Him. We can do anything for Him.

"You, dear friends, that give up your Sunday, which other Christians think should be altogether a day of rest; you that have learned to rest on the wing, and find your sweeter rest in service, you, I am sure, would not do this except you did it for Him. Your wages are found in the fact that you are serving Him. This is your reward, and you have never asked any other, except to be permitted to do this for Him, even to feed His lambs. You go about such work as this cheerfully when you do it for Him. You would not feel happy in doing it for the superintendent, nor for your fellow-teachers, nor for the Church, nor altogether and alone for the children, but oh, your feet are quickened because you run for Him.

> "'Tis love that makes our willing feet
> In swift obedience move.'

For Christ's sake you do it carefully, for you feel if it be done for Him it ought to be well done. If you are going to teach for the school you ought to have some respect for your teachers, and do it well, but if it is teaching for Jesus Christ it ought to be first-class teaching.

"The best teachers ought to be those who teach Jesus for Jesus' sake, and if there is a way and art of teaching, you and I ought to know it, for we ought not to bring our Master second-rate stuff. If you sat at the loom you should weave the best that could be woven for the King Jesus. There is a nobility about the work done for such an one as He. Even though it be but the loosing of the latchets of His shoes, or the spreading of a mantle along the way He is to ride, anything for Jesus should be done with all the heart, and soul, and strength. And in proportion as you feel you are doing it for Jesus, you do it cheerfully, and you do it carefully at the same time. Have you got dispirited? Is your heart cast down? Have you got a little weary?

"Have you heard what they say about Sunday Schools, and have you been somewhat affected by the hard remarks that are made, and been tempted to say, 'Well, let them do it better if they can, I have had enough of it.' Oh, it is for Jesus. You were not working for these fault-finders, you were doing it for Jesus. You wanted to please Him.

"If my servant is at work in the garden, or the field, and is doing what I pay him for, and I tell him that I am perfectly satisfied with him, if some passer-by looks over the hedge and finds fault, he smiles, for he says, 'I shall not go to him for my wages on Saturday night.' Do it for Jesus, and you will be looking forward to His verdict, 'Well done, good and faithful servant.' Do it for Jesus. Do it personally, as unto Jesus. That breaking of the alabaster box is an extravagant action; that pouring out of the precious myrrh to fill the room is an extravagant waste until it is done for Jesus; and then for Jesus self-sacrifice is prudence, and to die is but to save your life. He that lives altogether for Christ has in the best sense lived for himself; and he that shall never live for himself at all, but, self-forgetting, shall give himself wholly up to his Master, shall have taken the road to procure for himself the highest degree of happiness and immortality. Do it all for Jesus then.

"And then, brothers and sisters, as it is in Jesus, and for Jesus, so let it always be in the Spirit of Jesus. We must teach with the abilities which God hath given us, endowed with the Spirit of God. What can we do unless God be with us? What can we not do when He is at our right hand? Stop awhile with that lesson which you have studied till you have baptised it in the Spirit of Christ. Stop awhile, though it be the 'old, old story of Jesus and His love' that thou hast told so often. Thou wilt tell it too often, and it will get to be a mere routine tale without life and power, unless thou stop to gird thyself anew with the eternal Spirit. Oh, do it all in the Spirit of Jesus, or not at all, for every conversion that a man makes another man will unmake, and all soul work done of unaided human wit will be undone. 'Every plant which My heavenly Father hath not planted shall be rooted up.' Plant not, therefore, without the Father, and work not without the Spirit, lest, like the builder on the sand, all that thou hast built shall vanish in a night.

"Let us always work for Jesus with Jesus. Let us keep in His company. It is thought by some that we can only see Jesus now and then, but that was not our Lord's opinion, for He said, 'Abide in Me.' I think that some believers fancy it is quite impossible to keep an unbroken walk with God. But even in those dark times, before the revelation of our Master, Enoch walked with God by the hundred years together. Why should not we, during the short span of life, enjoy unbroken communion with the Lord Jesus Christ? Let us aim at it. Oh, that is the way to make a preacher or teacher get a sight of Christ—to come down from the cloud with the gold reflected on his brow. How can we get these sights of Christ? They come to us in divers ways by the Spirit of God; sometimes by the realisation of faith. Oh, have we not seen the Lord sometimes when our faith has been so practical and real, when, though eyesight could not introduce us to the Saviour, we have been as certain of His presence as though we did behold Him?

"Then sometimes He will draw you near to Him, then He will seem to wrap you in His crimson vest and tell you of His name, and your heart will be exceedingly glad. Do you not often get these near approaches of Christ when you read His Word? For what are the Scriptures after all but revelations of Jesus? Here I behold my Saviour's face almost in every page, and the ordinances too, for are they not windows of agate, and gates of carbuncles, through which we see and approach the Master? I trust it may be so to-night, that in these emblems before us you may find His real presence; for we do believe in His real presence, not corporeally or after any superstitious sort, but of His real presence. It is all the more real because it is not carnal, and to spiritual minds all the more true because it is altogether spiritual. So, brethren, in our hearts will we approach Him. We came here to see, we came here to have fellowship one with another, but most of all with Him. O my God, grant this may be a festival night; may His banner over us be love!

"We must have some holy days and holidays, and bonfire nights, and let this be one of them, one of the most glorious days we have ever had, because we got nearest to Christ, and, secondly, nearest to our hearts' joy.

"But you teachers have other things besides these. Beside faith and love, and ordinances, and His Word, you may have very sweet fellowship with Christ in your work. Your work is so Christlike you ought not to be without Christ in it. First, you should have deep sympathy with Christ, and fellowship with Him, in the love you have for your children. Oh, how Jesus loved and loves! He is all love, and He loves the little ones. Look at them, if you can, through Jesus Christ's eyes; seem to say, I love them for his sake

He said, 'Suffer the little children to come unto Me, and forbid them not; for of such is the kingdom of God.' I would not only suffer them to come, but aid them to come as best I can. The more you love, the nearer you will be to Christ. There is never a man, there is never a woman, that loves, but that he is doing what Christ is doing, moving in the same groove with Christ.

"So when you are in communication with Him, you will have closer fellowship still; when you are toiling for your little ones, hard at work, in spare moments getting your lesson ready, wearing yourselves out, denying yourselves almost necessary rest—why, you know then what Jesus had to do for you; how He laboured for you; how He spent and was spent for you; and so you get to see Jesus and have fellowship with Him. And, still better, when it comes to being grieved over your children, when you are disappointed, when heart-break steals over you, when the hot tear stands in the eye, then will Jesus be very near you. You will begin to know how you disappointed Him, how you grieved Him. You will keep near to Him, and begin to weep over your own faults while you are bemoaning the faults of the little ones, and then you will say, I must have that boy brought to Jesus, and your heart swells, and your love seems pent up as though you must die if you do not bring that child to Christ.

"Oh, then, you must have fellowship with Jesus: for there is a happy time, by-and-by, when you hear the first note of repentance; when you trace the first token of faith; when you have some hope that your child has taken Christ into confidence; when you are able to entice the little one to the church; when you can sit in your seat in the house of God and see half-a-dozen all brought to Jesus through you: then you will have sympathy with Jesus in that joy which was set before Him, for which He endured the cross, despising the shame. May you have very much of this joy, this next akin to the joy of heaven, the joy of having done good in bringing souls to Christ!

"Dear brothers and sisters, that is all I shall trouble you with just now, but may you get into actual abiding in Him and with Him who is your All in all; and I am sure you will go to your classes to see the desert turned into a garden, and the wilderness blossoming like the rose. Don't you sometimes get away from Jesus, after forgetting that you are doing it for Him? Come back, then, to-night: the Lord is willing that you should. You recollect how He spake to Laodicea. He said, 'Thou art neither cold nor hot; . . . I will spue thee out of My mouth:' but He afterwards said, 'Behold, I stand at the door, and knock.' His coming back to His Church would restore her to her place, and cause Him to delight in her.

"He stands at thy door, brother, now, knocking to come back. Thou needst not stay to make thyself better that He may come. Let us tell saints the same as we tell sinners: He is willing to come now, to come, as it were, with the fulness of delight. 'If any man hear My voice, and open the door, I will come in to him, and will sup with him, and he with Me.' 'Well, I have no supper for Thee.' He brings it Himself. He comes to sup with us, and He brings the viands—the outward tokens of them, at any rate—

> 'His dearest flesh He makes my food;
> And bids me drink His richest blood.'

"He has brought the feast; we have but to bring the appetite; and the Lord be with you till the day break, and the shadows flee away. May the well-Beloved turn in and tarry with every one of us, and to His name be the glory. Amen."

Mr. Olney and Mr. Tresidder offered prayer, and the whole service was most impressive.

One incident, which only Mr. Spurgeon would have

thought of and carried through, was exceedingly thrilling. He proposed that the whole assembly should join hands, and form an unbroken chain extending from the floor to the platform, and from the platform to the galleries, and that then the congregation should sing—

> " E'er since by faith I saw the stream
> Thy flowing wounds supply,
> Redeeming love has been my theme,
> And shall be till I die."

At first the people were slow to understand and to obey; then there was some difficulty about the joining together of those above with those below: some had to stand on the stairs, and for strangers to take each other's hands was scarcely in accordance with the usual custom of English folk; but Mr. Spurgeon uttered a cheery word, and prevented the thing from becoming ridiculous, and there were few dry eyes when the singing had reached the last verse—

> " Then in a nobler, sweeter song
> I'll sing Thy power to save,
> When this poor lisping, stammering tongue
> Is silent in the grave."

Mr. Spurgeon was always a great friend to the Sunday School Union, and this service was only one, though certainly it was not the least that he rendered them.

The next year, 1881, he preached another remarkable sermon for the Baptist Union. The meetings were held at Portsmouth, and he had no doubt all the more joy in being there because of his attachment to, and joy in, his first student, Mr. Medhurst. Of all the services of that Conference none was appreciated more sincerely than Mr. Spurgeon's sermon. It was delivered in an immense place, the large Music Hall, which was densely packed. The text was, "Without Me, ye can do nothing." It was a text after his own heart, and his words were stirring and forcible. One part of it was full of tender comfort—"I pick up my text and hold it to my ears, as many a child has held a shell, and within the shell the child hears the rolling of the sea with its convolutions, so within my text I hear a sweet, sweet song. Put it up to your ears and try it—'Without Me, ye can do nothing.' Lord, what is there that I want to do without Thee? Lord, Thou hast tied and tethered me to Thyself by this blessed text, which is so sweetly bitter, so intensely precious to my heart when I come to get into its depths; what could I want to do without Thee? Suppose there were something I could do without Thee, then there would be a little crown for my head, but now I can do nothing without Thee; then there is one great crown for Thy brow, and Thou shalt have all the glory. I am so glad for the Church that she can do nothing without Christ, because, suppose there was something she could do without Him, suppose it was Sunday-school teaching, then the dear little children would never have Jesus Christ in the room; or if it were street preaching, then we should keep Christ in the chapels and never have Him at the street corners, and that part of our work which the Church could do without Christ would be a kind of Bluebeard chamber, locked up for the Master, and I know not what mischief would soon be discovered there. O God, we thank Thee that we can do nothing without Christ, for of all things I should dread success apart from Christ. To win, if there were such winning, a name and fame for the Church of God in which Christ had no finger, were but to exalt her with a damnable exaltation that were a curse to the world and to herself. No, let it stand, 'Without Me, ye can do nothing.' Then, as we have a great deal to do, we shall draw out of the text a reason for going to Christ, an argument for being permitted to come. We shall here have a reason for knocking, and knocking again, at that blessed door. I held my text up to my ear once more, and as I listened I began to laugh. I could not help it, and I laugh again now as I remember it. 'Without Me, ye can do nothing.' I laughed the laugh of Abraham in his faith, for I thought, Well, if Christ's friends can do nothing without Him, then His enemies cannot. If His apostles cannot do anything, then depend upon it His opponents can do less. He is not with them; and therefore as He is not with them, they can do nothing—just nothing at all. Let them howl on—let them rave on—let them rage on—they can do nothing."

The discourse closed with a note of sarcastic and triumphant defiance:—" I have read very constantly that the old-fashioned gospel has nearly died out. I was reading the other day that those of us who believe in the old evangelical doctrine—and especially the Calvinistic doctrine—have got to be so miserably few that we are of no account,—that, in fact, we do not exist at all; that though there may be one or two persons who still believe it, we may be reckoned to be dead, and they dance over our graves, and say the gospel is gone. Dear brethren, they tell us that if it is not quite gone it is very nearly gone. Then put on your nightcaps. You who believe in evangelical doctrine, go home and go to bed, your mission is all over, advanced thought has done away with you entirely; and if it has not quite done so, there are men coming, great men, men of thought and men of culture, who are going, once for all, to sweep you away with the besom of destruction. Wonderful, is it not? very wonderful! and I will tell you how I thought of it. One afternoon—a very hot afternoon—away in New England, in one of the old Puritanical chapels, chapels which were built, you know, as if they were intended to withstand seven earthquakes at once, all the pillars immensely strong—enormous pillars—the roof not very lofty but very substantial, and the only thing about the chapel which you could commend—for it was uglier than any other portion—on that afternoon the minister was prophesying on dry bones, and very dry they were; some were asleep, and others were being edified, and just in the middle of this delightful service up rose a lunatic in the midst of the congregation, denounced the minister, and said he would there and then pull the chapel down about their ears; so getting up to one of the pillars this new-born Samson proceeded to carry out his threat; the good women began to faint, the men were all up, there was a rush to the aisles, and nobody knows how many might have been killed, when an old deacon, sitting under the pulpit, calmed all the tumult in a moment; he said, 'Let him try.' That is exactly what I say, 'Amen.' They shall never succeed, for God is not with them; and if He be not with them, how can they prosper?"

CHAPTER XV.

SPURGEON'S PHILOSOPHY.

SPURGEON was essentially a matter-of-fact man, and possessed a large fund of sound common sense; nowhere is it displayed more fully than in the two books, *John Ploughman's Talk* and *John Ploughman's Pictures*. He has a word there for all the common failings of mankind, which are to him as the "little foxes that spoil the vines."

His first words of rebuke are for the idle, for whom he, as a busy man, seems to have had a great antipathy. He said that it was hardly worth while to try and improve them, for there is not enough good grain to pay for the trouble of threshing it out. He was of Carlyle's opinion, that harsh measures should be taken to force them to work, and would even go as far as Solomon, and say, "Who will not work, neither shall he eat," for, as they are of no use, and only a burden to their neighbours, the world would be better without them. He reminded us of the punishment meted out to the drones in a hive of bees, and believed that mankind might imitate the example of these little insects with benefit to the community. Some say, "Better do nothing than mischief," but this our moralist denies, believing that idleness is the most fatal vice a man can have. Dr. Watts' little hymn is truer than most people think, and it is in the lazy man's heart that the eggs of the most deadly reptiles of sin are hatched. He saw no use for idlers except to make the grass grow in the churchyard, when they die. He had a word to say to the workpeople who never work with a will, but go through their tasks as if leaden weights were attached to their hands, looking at the clock at short intervals to see if it is not time to leave off. On the first stroke of twelve down go their tools and off go their aprons, and they leave the shop, having accomplished about half as much work as they ought to have done. And then they grumble because the master does not give them as much wages as he does those men who work with all their heart. If every one were of Spurgeon's opinion these dawdlers would be employed by nobody, for he declared that he would sooner throw his money away than be irritated by seeing these people pretend to work. He did not forget to administer a rebuke to those among the rich who do absolutely nothing which is of service to their fellow-creatures, but exhaust themselves in a wearying round of vain pleasures with the object of killing time. His expressions with regard to these people were somewhat socialistic; he thought it a disgrace for them to be squandering in luxury money which they never earned. He would have every one work for their bread. He mourned over the fact that even in Christ's church these lazy people are to be found, bringing reproach on the name of Him they profess to follow. He exhorted them to throw off their lethargy, and, like their Master, work untiringly until He called them to their eternal rest.

Next Spurgeon let his arrows fly at the religious grumblers, for whom nothing is right, except it chime in with their own preconceived opinions. They believe that upon religious questions none can instruct them; that they have sounded the depths of God's purposes towards his creatures; that they know exactly how far His mercy and loving-kindness extend, and when the vials of His wrath will be poured out on an erring world. Having made themselves acquainted, as they think, with the high truths of Heaven, and knowing perfectly those things which angels desire to look into, they feel that their mission is to criticise and correct all with whom they come in contact. They go to church and listen to the sermon, and if the minister's ideas are not in conformity with what they think is right, they shake their heads and say that he is unsound. If there is nothing in the matter to object to, they grumble at the manner of the preacher. Either he wants energy or is too noisy, speaks too fast for reverence or is so slow that he sends people to sleep, is too high-flown or uses language that is too common. The poor man can do nothing right for them. It is these fault-finders who discourage and depress young ministers, and make them feel inclined to give up their work.

But Spurgeon bade them not despair, but persevere in speaking the truth in plain terms that every one can understand, and if they honestly do their very best, they may expect God's blessing in spite of the critics. He regretted to find that these grumblers are so busy picking flaws in their neighbours that they have no time to cultivate either manners or morals, so that their daily walk and conversation does not always bring credit to the cause which they profess to have at heart.

He begged them to turn their attention to their own shortcomings, and try to improve themselves before they attempt to correct others.

Spurgeon next gave a word of advice to those amiable people who are the servants of any one who chooses to demand service of them.

He reminded them that if they turn themselves into beasts of burden, every one will try to load them, and that there are always plenty of people about who will take advantage of good nature. But he did not desire that they should go to the other extreme, and become surly and disobliging. He advocated the happy medium. Our character should not be like lead, that yields easily to pressure, nor like iron that cannot be bent without breaking; but it should be like finely-tempered steel, that is both strong and pliant.

Spurgeon agreed with Solomon that there is a time for everything; a time to please others and a time to refuse to do so, and that last time begins when any one wishes us to act contrary to the dictates of our conscience.

Then we must make it patent to our friends that we have a will of our own, powerful enough to enable us to do what we think right in the teeth of all opposition. And if we have commenced treading the downward road, let not the jeers of boon companions, nor the fear of displeasing them, prevent us retracing our steps, for if we give way to the sneers of these professed friends, they will accompany us to the door of ruin, getting out of us as much as they can on the way; but, arrived there, they will bid us good-bye, and wonder how we could be such fools as to go so far.

Our philosopher acknowledged that gentleness is a Christian virtue, but maintained that it may be carried too far, and that it is necessary to let our enemies know that we recognise the injustice of their conduct towards us, although we do not seek to be revenged on them. He cited in support of this Paul's words in answer to the keeper of the prison when he told him that the magistrates had sent word that he and Silas might go free, "They have beaten us openly uncondemned, being Romans, and cast us into prison; now they cast us out privily; nay, verily, but let them come themselves and fetch us out." Paul felt that they had treated unjustly himself and Silas, and he was not going to screen the magistrates by slinking away unobserved, as if he had been guilty of some bad action.

No, he wished to give his oppressors a fright, which would perhaps deter them from repeating the offence in future.

After gentleness comes patience, a virtue which is not cultivated half enough in the opinion of Mr. Spurgeon, who gave it a high place in his estimation, and even preferred it to cleverness, thinking that in the long run it brings most happiness. The impatient man is never content; his tribulations and sufferings seem to him interminable, and he feels that it would be better to curse God and die than to support them any longer. He looks round on his neighbours and thinks that nobody's troubles are so bad, no sufferings so great, no difficulties so unconquerable as his. But such should not be the spirit of the children of God. The followers of Jesus should be as patient as their Master. They should let patience have her perfect work, and the reward will come in after days.

Hope is twin-sister to patience, and if cultivated would make many lives happier. Hope sustains the soul in the midst of the heaviest trials. It was the blessing that Pandora carried at the bottom of her box full of evils. Even the unreasoning hope of those who look at everything through rose-coloured spectacles, and see good fortune approaching them at every turn, is better than constant complaining.

The misfortune is that sometimes this hopefulness prevents people from buckling to work themselves. They think it is hardly worth while for them to begin, as in a little while perhaps some rich relative will die and leave them a fortune, or some friend of theirs will offer them a good situation. They are like Mr. Micawber, always waiting for something to "turn up." So that hope, which should be a blessing, is by their folly turned into a curse.

No man has a right to hope for more than reason and the Bible promise. Some hope for things that are contrary to nature. They take their sons into the public-house, and then hope they will grow up temperate men.

A man marries a girl who has only her good looks and fine clothes to recommend her, who is never content at home, but must be always gadding about seeking pleasure, and who is perfectly ignorant of all the details of household management, and hopes she will turn out a thrifty housewife. These hopes are just as sensible as placing a cask of lighted paraffin in a powder magazine, and hoping the gunpowder will not explode. And the speaker had a solemn word for those who say they hope to go to heaven, and yet have spent all their lives in serving Satan. He warned them that their hope has nothing to rest on, for only those who believe on the Lord Jesus Christ can inherit eternal life.

His next words were addressed to those who do not know the value of money, and consequently spend it as fast as they can. A man toils all his life, scraping and saving to accumulate a fortune, and then dies, leaving all his wealth to his son. As the old man did no good with his money, because he hoarded it, so nobody benefits by it when it belongs to his heir, because *he* squanders it in riotous living. Lightly come, lightly go! We never value that which has cost us nothing to obtain. There are plenty of ways in which fools can get rid of their money. If they wish to go to ruin by express, they try gambling or horse-racing, or invest their wealth in bubble companies, thus delivering themselves an easy prey to those who make it their business to fleece silly sheep. And it is not only the rich who waste their substance. How many poor men, as soon as they receive their wages, walk off to some public-house to fill the landlord's coffers, instead of using their earnings to make their homes and families more comfortable! How many people will purchase things they do not need, simply because they are cheap, forgetting that an unneces sary article is dear at any price! Those who wish to get on in the world should spend as little as possible, and make sure they get their money's worth.

Another, who has about as much chance of success as a spendthrift, is the loiterer, the man who is always too late. He runs into the station just as the train is steaming out, and lays the blame on the clocks. When he was a boy he always arrived at school just as the door was locked, and if he was invited to a country expedition, he presented himself at the starting place just in time to see the last van disappearing in the distance. These are the folk who like to take things easily. They see no use in wearing themselves out with anxiety. "Care killed the cat, and the less you worry the longer you will live," is one of their favourite sayings. But one may ask if it is worth while for these people to live at all, for they are of use to no one, unless as an example to the young. Better a short and useful life than a long and lazy one. A lost opportunity never returns, so we had better be on the alert to seize it as it flies, and then we shall never complain of bad luck.

Besides being always on the look-out for opportunities of usefulness, we have to keep our eyes open to guard against the many snares that beset our path, and the traps that are set everywhere to catch the unwary. Now, as John Ploughman says, some people are not so sharp as others, and are therefore more easily caught, so he gave them a few words of warning, hoping they may preserve some unsuspicious traveller from the net of the fowler. "Beware," he says, "of the man who too openly vaunts his piety, for it is too often like the tea displayed in the grocer's window. Passers-by see all there is of it—that is, the thin layer on the top; underneath is nothing but a deal board."

Shun flatterers; all they want is to use you for their own purposes. When you have served their turn, they will only laugh at your credulity. Do not judge a man by his words, but by his deeds; it is easy to talk, but those who waste their time in chattering seldom have the inclination to act. Avoid courts of law, or you will be in the position of the two dogs who quarrelled for a bone. While they were occupied in fighting another dog appeared and bore away the prize.

Never refuse work because you think it beneath you; keep at it until you find something else, for anything is better than idleness.

Trust not in men, for they may fail you, but seek wisdom at the hands of the Lord.

John Ploughman seems to have been very fond of his home, and sings its praise with no uncertain voice. Everything belonging to it was sweet to him, and he could not think how men could leave their homes and go to a publichouse to spend their evenings. Of course he allowed that everything should be made pleasant and attractive by the wife, but he mourned the fact that men who have no reason for doing so will desert the society of wife and children for the boon companions of the pot-house. There they sit and muddle their brains with beer, and spend the money that should make the home and its inmates comfortable.

Ploughman is the sworn enemy of the beer-shop, and everything else that takes a man from home. He preaches a little homily to the husband, who should be the mainstay of the home, and not the dread of all its occupants, as too many are. He should treat his wife with kindness and consideration, and then the children, following his example, are likely to grow up to honour their parents.

The influence of the father is needed in the bringing up of the family, and happy is that household where the father dedicates his leisure to cultivating his children, entering into their amusements, sharing their joys, and sympathising with their sorrows. Where there are big boys in a family the father's firm hand is needed to hold the reins, or the team will be liable to kick over the traces. Some boys and girls rarely see their father. He is absent all day at business, and in the evenings goes out for pleasure. But this is not as it should be. The ideal family needs both father and mother. Each have their separate influence, although each is exerted for the same purpose—the bringing up of their children to be honest, upright, God-fearing citizens.

But although the husband can do a great deal to make the home happy, the wife can do still more. Home is her sphere. She rules supreme there, and if she be wise she may counteract to a great extent the influence of bad companions. A clean house, a bright fireside, and a well-cooked meal are very attractive to a tired and hungry man, and the wife can see that these await her husband's return. And she can serve him with smiles and gentle words, which will be an additional attraction.

But John mourns over the undoubted fact that some homes are made unhappy by the wife. She does it sometimes by neglecting her work to gossip with the neighbours, or by running into debt for finery, and sometimes the cleanest and thriftiest of women makes the house unbearable by her temper. If a woman is constantly scolding and finding fault she must not be surprised if her husband does not stop to listen.

But Ploughman does not believe that it is often the fault of the wife if the home is miserable, because, says he, "It is not the woman, as a rule, who spends the money at the beer-shop, it is not she who gets drunk and reels home and knocks everybody down who crosses her. She does not sit warm and snug by the roaring fire of the 'Pig and Whistle' while her husband and children cower over a few dying embers at home." He wishes to know if we can wonder that a wife's tongue gets somewhat sharp when her drunken husband demands a good meal, and yet has never given her the money to buy either the food itself or the coal with which to make a fire to cook it. He waxes righteously indignant against these exacting fellows, and thinks they would be all the better for a taste of the lash.

He has no patience with men who speak ill of women, as in his opinion they are quite as good as their husbands, if not better. He is astonished at the many old rhymes that have been strung together derogatory to women, but thinks it only shows the worthlessness of the men who made or perpetuated them. He finds much to praise in the fact that women have not retaliated in the same way, as it is certain they have had much more reason to complain than the sterner sex. He believes that if a man treats his wife with consideration and kindness he will find his reward in her love and respect. They talk of women's tongues, but let them listen to the noisy chatter of men who have been drowning all the sense they possess in cans of ale, and they will find it quite as foolish as any woman's gossip.

He closes the chapter with his own experience of married life, which he declares to be far happier than that of a single man, and adds that he who seeks a wife from the Lord, and in whose home the presence of Jesus abides, will never be disappointed in his hopes of bliss.

John Ploughman had some excellent words for those who were beginning life. When the young folks are fairly started in housekeeping, he tells them that if they wish to get on they must work, for there is nothing for the idle but poverty. Lazy folk often look at their more prosperous neighbours and say, "Ah! they have had good luck." They are mistaken. The good fairy that has aided them has been nothing but industry. They have toiled while the grumblers were in bed or taking their pleasure, and they find their reward in increased prosperity. But earning money alone will not secure a competence. It is necessary to be careful in the spending thereof. The wise man spends little. His desires are few. Those whose wants are less than their incomes need not be afraid of dying in the workhouse.

Ploughman is an ardent advocate of temperance, and he adjures every one to begin their saving with the beer-money. He feels that if the amount squandered in liquor were saved there would be no poor people in England. He warns men against making money by any but honest means, for it is better to be poor than to risk one's soul in amassing wealth. Also in the long run fair dealing will be found to pay best.

Deny yourself in youth so you will be able to make provision for age, and your declining years may be your happiest and best. Many people make themselves trouble by running into debt. They spend more than they earn, and buy things they have not the money to pay for. It is a humiliating thing to be dunned for debt, but what numbers of people have to submit to it because of their own folly. A man ought to shun debt as he would a pest-house, but many are so used to it that they feel it no disgrace.

John Ploughman declared that there are three things that he has earnestly striven to avoid since he married, and the first one is debt, for he considers that to be a kind of dishonesty, as one is eating other people's food and wearing other people's clothes. He is very severe on those who live beyond their income, insisting that such a course is mean in the extreme; besides which, he does not see how men who are constantly in debt can be truthful, as they are always promising to settle their accounts, yet never do it. Therefore if borrowing leads to falsehood, who will not say that it ought to be avoided?

His scorn is great for those who drive about in carriages, and whose names are to be seen at the head of subscription lists; who give right royally to public charities where their names will be published, but who have not common justice enough to pay their tradespeople. To him it is a scandal that such folk should be at large. His motto is—the less you owe the sooner you can pay.

He closes his remarks by saying that he supposes it is of no use to preach to these offenders, as they will take no notice, so he will leave off, for he objects to labour at impossible tasks. There is so much to be done in the world, that it is waste of time to attempt that which can never be accomplished.

In Ploughman's journey through life he has observed, like many others, the tendency of the world to kick a man when he is down. There is "nothing succeeds like success," and, on the contrary, nothing is so fatal as failure. How many men have proved this to be true. While they prospered their friends were numerous, and they heard on all sides nothing but praise. But when, for some reason or other, perhaps by no fault of their own, adversity visits them, where are their so-called friends then?

Are they by their side helping and cheering them? No, they pass by on the other side with scornful looks; and if they deign to say anything, wonder why their fallen friends had not more sense than to be gulled by so-and-so.

Almost every one has a word of blame for the unsuccessful man, and some even lend a hand to keep him down when he has once fallen. Some who have been jealous of his previous success rejoice that he is brought low. Even those whom he has helped in days gone by forget his benefits, and the poor man can only find friends and counsellors in the usurer and man of law. These will stick to him till every penny is gone, then they too will bid him adieu.

But the moralist acknowledges that there are some magnanimous souls who prove themselves real friends in the time of adversity; unfortunately, they are only too rare.

Happily, there is one Friend who never fails, and

Ploughman bids the sufferer turn to Him for help, and he will find his confidence justified.

There is an excellent chapter on "Trying," which all young folk should read.

In these days when men are grumbling incessantly, and saying they can't get on; when politicians, for their own selfish ends, are encouraging them in their discontent, and blaming the Government (whichever party is in power) for men's poverty, it is refreshing to find somebody who has courage enough to say that, as a rule, it is a man's own fault if he does not prosper.

There are so few people who buckle to work as if they really meant it. The thoughts of the young nowadays are bent on pleasure, and duty takes the second place.

No young man who has health and a fair share of common sense need fail in life. All he has to do is to work hard and deny himself a little, and prosperity is sure to come. So says John Ploughman, and it is to be hoped that all young men will make his personal acquaintance without loss of time.[1]

[1] *John Ploughman's Talk.* Passmore & Alabaster. Price One Shilling, boards.

CHAPTER XVI.

TO THE JUBILEE YEAR.

FREQUENT illnesses, although they did not lessen the usefulness of the pastor, made it absolutely necessary that as the years passed he should live a more quiet life than formerly. And he passed the time in two delightful places—in his own beautiful home at Westwood, and at lovely Mentone.

Westwood, on Beulah Hill, Upper Norwood, where the last years of Mr. Spurgeon's too short life were passed, is a pleasant house standing in its own grounds. It has a lawn and an arbour, some fine trees and shrubs, and is altogether an ideal English residence. Mr. Spurgeon enjoyed it to the full, and so did many other people by his hospitality, especially the students of the College, who were many times invited to spend a happy day there with their beloved master.

Mr. Spurgeon's study was originally a billiard-room; it is comfortable and light, and in it some of the best work of its owner was done; for there he laboured with his beloved "Armour-Bearer," Mr. J. W. Harrald, as long as he could work at all.

There too were held some very happy family gatherings, the more notable perhaps being that of the Golden Wedding Day of the pastor's father and mother, which was celebrated there on May 14th, 1883. Mr. Spurgeon's father and mother, brother and sisters, one of his sons, and his

WESTWOOD HOUSE, RESIDENCE OF MR. SPURGEON.

wife, were all present, with other relatives and friends, to the number of forty. They mourned the absence of the Rev. Thomas Spurgeon, who was in Australia; but there were many reasons for tender thanksgiving, and the host especially recorded with joy that they were all serving Christ publicly. "Our own dear departed grandfather, so long an honoured soul-winner, used to rejoice in five of us as ministers of Christ, but now we are seven."

It was indeed reason for joy to the father that his two sons, the one honoured and blessed as the pastor of an important church at Greenwich, and the other a successful minister in Australia, were following in his steps.

Through the gates of Westwood what illustrious persons have passed! And as to the letters, they could unfold many an interesting story if they were allowed to speak. Mr. Stephenson tells of one from the widow of General Garfield, in which she says that one of her most beautiful memories is of a happy Sunday morning when she sat beside her husband in the Metropolitan Tabernacle and listened to Mr. Spurgeon.

At Mentone the pastor found another home in the Hotel Beau Rivage, where he stayed when driven away from England by its cold winds and fogs. Many people chose that of all the towns on the Riviera in which to sojourn when they knew that he was there, because they hoped to be able to listen to some of his addresses. The drivers used to point him out to the occupants of their vehicles; and one of them said to a friend of the writer's, "See! there is the Pope of England."

And a very good Pope too!

Mr. Spurgeon's popularity remained with him up to the very last.

It was scarcely more easy during his latest year of preaching than his first to get into the Tabernacle and find a comfortable seat without a ticket. There was ever a crowd outside waiting for the doors to be opened, and in 1891, as during the years that preceded it, visitors to London heard Mr. Spurgeon as one of the greatest treats that could be enjoyed.

The love of his people never waxed dim. We have given an account of their rejoicings when he had been with them twenty-five years, but the book would not be complete without re-telling their affectionate rejoicings when, in 1884, he commemorated his jubilee.

It was on an evening in May that the great jubilee celebration was first discussed, in a friendly gathering at the house of one of the deacons. Pastor J. A. Spurgeon presided, and after several speeches had been made the meeting terminated, £1000 having in the interim been promised as the nucleus of the great Testimonial Fund.

The outcome of this little gathering was seen on the evenings of June 18th and 19th, when crowded meetings were held in the Tabernacle that were most deeply interesting, and that will never be forgotten by those who were privileged to attend them. The first was a "domestic" meeting, at which only the members of the church and congregation were expected to be present; the second was a grand public meeting, and was presided over by the Earl of Shaftesbury. At both the meetings the veneration and love that was felt by all classes of the community for Mr. Spurgeon found expression in such eulogistic speeches as might well have made a lesser man vain. But Mr. Spurgeon was too good, too great, too truly humble a man to be "spoilt by kindness," and all the appreciative remarks that were made, and the numberless kind messages, from all parts of the world, that were received by him, only seemed to make his heart overflow with gratitude to his Heavenly Father, from whom comes every good and every perfect gift.

Mr. Spurgeon himself presided over the meeting held on

TABERNACLE SOCIETIES. 251

June 18th, which was interesting from the fact of its *representativeness*. One of the first items of all the pleasant items in the programme was the reading out by Mr. J. W. Harrald (Mr. Spurgeon's secretary) the names of the different societies present or represented, which list we subjoin:—

The Almshouses; the Pastors' College; the Pastors' College Society of Evangelists; the Stockwell Orphanage; the Colportage Association; Mrs. Spurgeon's Book Fund, and Pastors' Aid Fund; the Pastors' College Evening Classes; the Evangelists' Association; the Country Mission; the Ladies' Benevolent Society; the Ladies' Maternal Society; the Poor Ministers' Clothing Society; the Loan Tract Society; Spurgeon's Sermons' Tract Society; the Evangelists' Training Class; the Orphanage Working Meeting; the Colportage Working Meeting; the Flower Mission; the Gospel Temperance Society; the Band of Hope; the United Christian Brothers' Benefit Society; the Christian Sisters' Benefit Society; the Young Christians' Association; the Mission to Foreign Seamen; the Mission to Policemen; the Coffee-House Mission; the Metropolitan Tabernacle Sunday School; Mr. Wigney's Bible Class; Mr. Hoyland's Bible Class; Miss Swain's Bible Class; Miss Hobbs's Bible Class; Miss Hooper's Bible Class; Mr. Bowker's Bible Class for Adults of both Sexes; Mr. Dunn's Bible Class for Men; Mrs. Allison's Bible Class for Young Women; Mr. Bartlett's Bible Class for Young Women; Golden Lane and Hoxton Mission (Mr. Orsman's); Ebury Mission and Schools, Pimlico; Green Walk Mission and Schools, Haddon Hall; Richmond Street Mission and Schools; Flint Street Mission and Schools; North Street, Kennington, Mission and Schools; Little George Street Mission, Bermondsey; Snow's Fields Mission, Bermondsey; the Almshouses Missions; the Almshouses Sunday Schools; the Almshouses Day Schools; the Townsend Street Mission;

the Townley Street Mission; the Deacon Street Mission; the Blenheim Grove Mission, Peckham; the Surrey Gardens Mission; the Vinegar Yard Mission, Old Street; the Horse Shoe Wharf Mission and Schools; the Upper Ground Street Mission; the Thomas Street Mission, Horselydown; the Boundary Row Sunday School, Camberwell; the Great Hunter Street Sunday School, Dover Road; the Carter Street Sunday School, Walworth; the Pleasant Row Sunday Schools, Kennington; the Westmoreland Road Sunday Schools, Walworth; the Lansdowne Place Sunday School; Miss Emery's Banner Class, Brandon Street; Miss Miller's Mothers' Meeting; Miss Ivimey's Mothers' Meeting; Miss Francies' Mothers' Meeting.

When it is remembered that all of these have grown out as offshoots from the parent church it will be seen what a great and complete organisation the Metropolitan Tabernacle is, and how clear-sighted and of what wise judgment it was necessary the head of such a church should be possessed. Large as the number of church members has always been, there must with so many outlets of service have been plenty for all to do, and it is good that the rich feast provided by Mr. Spurgeon week by week should be handed on by his hearers, so as to give nourishment, not only to those who heard him, but through them to others.

The first speaker at this home meeting was Mr. Spurgeon's dear friend, Mr. D. L. Moody. In referring to his wonderful evangelistic mission work in England, Mr. Spurgeon made a free quotation of the Scotch song, "Bonnie Charlie"—

"Bonnie Moody's gaein' awa',
 Will ye no come back again?
Better loved ye canna be,
 Will ye no come back again?"

In the course of his speech Mr. Moody referred to a

former visit to England paid by him in 1867, and said that on that occasion the first public building in England he entered was the Metropolitan Tabernacle. "I was told," said he, "that I could not get in without a ticket, but I made up my mind to get in somehow, and I succeeded. I well remember seating myself in this gallery. I remember the very seat, and I should like to take it back to America with me. As your dear pastor walked down to the platform my eyes just feasted upon him, and my heart's desire for years was at last accomplished. It happened to be the year you preached in the Agricultural Hall. I followed you up there, and you sent me back to America a better man. Then I went to try and preach myself, though at the time I little thought I should be able to do so."

The next business done was the reading of the list of other bodies of Christians who had sent messages of congratulation and friendship. They were a long list, and included some from all parts of the world. Then came the great event of the evening—the reading of the address to Mr. Spurgeon from the church and congregation by one of the deacons, Mr. B. W. Carr. It commenced thus:—

"To the Rev. C. H. Spurgeon, Pastor of the Metropolitan Tabernacle.—With a united voice of thanksgiving to our ever blessed God on your behalf; with a cordial acknowledgment of the good services you have rendered to the universal Church of our Lord Jesus Christ; and with a profound sense of the high character and wide reputation you have established among your fellow-Christians, we beg to offer you our sincere congratulations on this the fiftieth anniversary of your birthday.

"Accept our assurance that no language but the language of personal affection could fitly express the esteem in which you are held by ourselves and by the numerous constituency we represent. Were it possible for the lips of all those who love you as a brother, and those who revere you as a father in Christ, to sound in your ears the sentiments of their hearts, the music of their chorus at this glad hour would be like the noise of many waters.

"As our minister you are known to the utmost ends of the earth. Richly endowed by the Spirit of God with wisdom and discretion, your conduct as our ruling elder has silenced contention and promoted harmony. The three hundred souls you found in fellowship at New Park Street Chapel have multiplied to a fellowship of nearly six thousand in this Tabernacle. And under your watchful oversight the family group has increased without any breach of order.

"You came to us in the freshness of your youth.... The fair prospect of your spring-time has not suffered from any blight. Your natural abilities never betrayed you into indolent habits. The talents you possessed gave stimulus to your diligence. A little prosperity did not elate you, or a measure of success prompt the desire to settle down in some quiet resting-place. You spread your sails to catch the breeze. The ascendency you began to acquire over the popular mind, instead of making you vainglorious, filled you with awe, and increased the rigour of that discipline you have always exercised over yourself. These were happy auguries of your good speed."

The address referred in very graceful terms to the incidents and labours of the pastor, and especially to that which he had done for the widow and fatherless, and declared that hundreds and thousands of pious individuals owed him thanks for being their faithful steward and kind executor. It concluded thus :—

"On your head we now devoutly invoke those blessings which we believe the Almighty is abundantly willing to bestow. May your steps in the future be ordered of the Lord as they have been in the past! May a generation yet unborn witness that your old age is luxuriant and fruitful as your youth! May your life on earth wind up like the holy Psalter that you so much love! Be it yours to anchor at last in David's Psalm of Praise, prolific as it was of other Psalms, into which no groan or sigh could intrude. So may you rest in the Lord with a vision of the everlasting kingdom dawning on your eyes, and Hallelujah after Hallelujah resounding in your ears."

The address was followed by a short speech from the Rev. John Spurgeon, the great preacher's father, who spoke tenderly yet humorously of "that boy" who sat on the platform beside him. He confessed with joy that he had had the privilege of preaching forty-five years, and alluded to the fact that his boys were both preachers, as also were his boy's boys.

The next speaker was Mr. Spurgeon's brother, Pastor James A. Spurgeon, whose speech was full of love for his brother, and full from the beginning to the end of the true humility that marks a Christian gentleman.

Mr. Spurgeon's son Charles next addressed the meeting, alluding in feeling terms to his twin-brother, then upon the sea, whom he wished at home that night that he might speak to the love and filial reverence they bore their father. "I have gone into my father's study and sat at his feet to learn many a time," said he in the course of his speech, "but I never had the cheek to open my mouth before him. When he said, 'Charlie, what are you going to preach from?' I wished I could get to the other side of the door as quickly as possible, for I was afraid if I told him the text he would want to know what the divisions were, and would probably say that the middle one was wrong."

Rev. Archibald Brown, in a most feeling speech, alluded to the great help he had received from Mr. Spurgeon during their almost life-long friendship, and spoke as an old "College man" for the students past and present—"On behalf of every man connected with the College, believe me when I say that as a preacher we admire you, as a man of God we love you, and as our President we revere you. The entire College owes everything to you, and deeply and sincerely we thank God for the past, we congratulate you on to-night's meeting, and wish you many blessed returns of to-morrow."

Mr. H. H. Driver then presented an address from the students to Mr. Spurgeon. It was most beautifully engrossed, and was altogether a real work of art. At the bottom of the scroll was a portrait of the Tabernacle in miniature, with Mr. Spurgeon's true life-motto—"We preach Christ and Him crucified," and on the reverse were representations of the entrance to the Orphanage, and the famous *Sword and Trowel.* There is also a Bible grasped by a hand, and above the seven volumes of Mr. Spurgeon's greatest work, *The Treasury of David.*

The Sunday School's offering was the next presented to the pastor, and it took the form of a little book, on the cover of which was engraved "Pastor's Jubilee Testimonial Fund, June 19th, 1884. The offering of the Metropolitan Tabernacle Sunday School to their beloved Pastor, Charles Haddon Spurgeon." Inside was an alphabetical list of teachers and scholars, and Mr. S. R. Pearce, in presenting the book, also handed to Mr. Spurgeon a cheque for £63, that being the sum contributed by the scholars.

Mr. W. J. Orsman, who has done noble work among the costermongers of Hoxton, next spoke, giving some account of his labours there, and addressing to Mr. Spurgeon most loving and filial good wishes. He was followed by the Rev. W. L. Lang, F.R.G.S., who presented an address on behalf of the Baptist ministers of France.

The last speaker was Mr. William Olney, jun., who, in the absence of his father, the senior deacon, who was unable to be present, having started on a long sea voyage by order of his medical adviser, was called upon to tell the meeting something of what the Church was doing in various ways for the sake of humanity and for God's glory. One sentence from his telling speech must be quoted, for it gives the key to Mr. Spurgeon's marvellous power. "Our pastor has a double influence. He has a repellent influence and an attractive influence. He first of all puts pins into the cushion and drives us away, and makes us feel we cannot stay in the congregation while souls are perishing outside, and then he so preaches Christ that we are compelled to come back, even though the pins prick again. So we are continually kept going to and fro, first getting a sip from the brook, and then carrying the water to those perishing of thirst."

This meeting was the "home gathering"; the one held on the next night was a public meeting, and was at least equal in interest to that of the night before. The good Earl of Shaftesbury presided over it with his ever-ready grace and tact. On entering, Mr. Spurgeon met with a most enthusiastic reception; round after round of applause greeted him, handkerchiefs waved, and men shouted, and what must have been a dearer proof to him than all beside, every face lightened up with joy and love at the sight of him, and as he took his place on that his fiftieth birthday every heart wordlessly, but none the less plainly, wished him "Many happy returns of the day."

After prayer, the first business of the evening was the reading of the list of the various societies there represented, together with the large number of congratulatory addresses, telegrams, and letters which had been received, after which the Earl of Shaftesbury, who on rising met with the warmest reception, said:—

"This is the fiftieth birthday of our admirable, our invaluable friend, Charles Haddon Spurgeon. It is right, it is indispensable, it is necessary that he should have the testimony of his congregation, and he has it. But it is also necessary, right, and equally indispensable that he should have the testimony of outsiders like myself to show what we think of the man, and what we think of his career as a devoted servant of our blessed Lord, and a conscientious and faithful labourer for the advancement of His kingdom. . .

"What a powerful administrative mind our friend possesses is shown by that list which has been read of the various societies and associations constructed by his genius and superintended by his care. These are more than enough to occupy the minds and hearts of some fifty ordinary men. Why, it seems to be the whole world in a nutshell! Mark what he has done by his missions, and his schools, and his various institutions. I remember when Mr. Spurgeon occupied Exeter Hall during the construction of this magnificent edifice. A nobler edifice I never saw. Filled as it is to-night, I confess that it completely overawes me. In his early days he adopted a mode of preaching which was, to my mind, most effective, most touching, and most instructive. It was that of taking a chapter of the Bible and going through the paragraphs and verses in succession. When I heard him I invariably said, 'This is a man after one's own heart; preach where he will he cannot fail to touch the hearts, to arouse the intellects, and to stir to the depths the consciences of those that listen to his exhortations.'

. . . . . .

"The great force of our friend consists in the doctrine that he has invariably preached. He has ever preached 'Jesus Christ and Him crucified' as the mainstay of his ministrations, the solution of life's problem, the help of every one in this world, and the hope of every one for the life to come. This it is that has given him a deep, strong, and permanent force over his congregation. It holds together such mighty masses as I now see before me. This it is which brings them now, with heartfelt reverence and deep gratitude, to give thanks to Almighty God that this good man has been allowed to live to the present day, and which leads them to express to him the gratitude and reverence that they bear to him for his long and blessed services."

The Earl of Shaftesbury then called upon Canon Wilberforce, who, in a telling speech, referred to the marvellous influence for good which Mr. Spurgeon had been and still was in our country:—

"It would be simply impertinent in me to stand here and say words of praise of such a man as your pastor. We are not here to glorify him: we are here to glorify the living God who has made him what he is, and who has used him in such a wonderful manner to draw souls to Himself during all these years. We thank God for the life that he has been enabled to lead, and if you want a testimonial to his power and to his present position, look round at this Tabernacle. Just see these throbbing hearts pouring themselves out in love towards him, many of them full of gratitude for the spiritual blessings that they have received from God through his means. I suppose that there is hardly an individual man—I am not exaggerating when I say it—whose sphere of influence is so widely extended. Independently of the thousands that he speaks to here in this Tabernacle, there is, as we know, the weekly sermon, which is translated into about seven modern languages, and which goes all over the world to bring solace and comfort to the hearts of men; for he does preach the love of God: he does tell us that God's heart is yearning over us, and that he would draw us to Himself by the attractive power of the Lord Jesus Christ.

．　．　．　．　．　．　．

"And to-day is the Jubilee of him whom you love. What is the meaning of Jubilee? Does it not mean the setting free of captives? Are there still any that are bound by the shackles of sin in this congregation? Would you make the preacher a birthday present? Would you keep Jubilee as it ought to be kept? Now, in the name of Jesus, rise up and walk. Shake those shackles of sin from you. Be free upon this his Jubilee. May the Lord spare your beloved pastor to you many years, that he may have more souls for his hire, and in the end, when the education of this life is over, may every single individual of this mighty mass meeting be over there in the blessed rest which the Lord has gone to prepare for them that love him! I ask it for you through Jesus Christ, our Lord."

The Revs. Dr. Todd and J. P. Chown next had the pleasure of presenting to Mr. Spurgeon the address of the London Baptist Association.

At this point of the proceedings the chairman had to leave, pleading that his health was not so robust as it had been. As the noble and liberal-souled old gentleman rose to go the whole assembly cheered him with great heartiness. His place was taken by the pastor, and after the audience had sung a hymn they had the pleasure of listening to the Rev. O. P. Gifford, pastor of a Baptist church in Boston, who handed to Mr. Spurgeon an address from his brother ministers in Boston. This gentleman pointed his speech with a very amusing anecdote:—

"It is said that, in the States, a schoolboy was once asked, 'Who is the Prime Minister of England?' and he replied, 'Charles H. Spurgeon.' 'A little child shall lead them,'" said the speaker, "in speaking the truth. Your political Prime Ministers change ever and again. Thank God, your Gospel Prime Minister has held on his way these many years."

Sir William McArthur, M.P., next spoke. He said:—
"It is a remarkable fact that God, in His providence, raises up men in particular crises in the history of every country. He raised up Luther; He raised up Wycliffe; He raised up

Wesley; He raised up Whitefield. Coming down to later times, the names of illustrious men survive in the affections of the people; and, sir, I believe that at this particular time in the history of this country God has raised you up to occupy a sphere of far-reaching influence.

. . . .

"I think that one great secret of your success in the ministry has been your humility. It is no mean virtue for a man placed in your position to be always modest, and to be simple and unaffected, as you have ever manifested yourself to every one with whom you have come into contact. I believe that the truth is you have been humble before God, and you have attributed to Him all the praise and glory."

Revs. W. Williams, of Upton Chapel, Lambeth, and Dr. Parker, Chairman of the Congregational Union, next addressed the meeting. The latter referred to the change that had come over the spirit of the age. Mr. Spurgeon as a young man had been the subject of ridicule and abuse, but, though he had not changed, the people had changed their minds about him, and he was now cited as a model of pulpit eloquence. Dr. Parker concluded by saying:—"I wish, along with all my other brethren, to live and to work with Mr. Spurgeon in terms of mutual confidence and brotherly affection; and I wish that we may be one in every high aspiration—one in every gracious prayer. I want the hostile world to see no break nor flaw between us. I am speaking now of the whole denominationalism of the evangelical churches; and I believe that, when that union and solidarity are really effected, they will constitute an argument which the most hostile critics of Christianity will find it impossible to answer."

At the close of Dr. Parker's speech came the most important and interesting event of the evening. After the address from the church had been again read, and some verses of the "Jubilee Hymn," composed by Mr. Vernon J. Charlesworth, had been sung, Mr. T. H. Olney, one of the deacons, in happy terms presented the pastor with a cheque for £4500 in the name of all his people. He was followed by Mr. W. C. Murrell, who remarked that the cheque for £4500 was presented "on account," and who thanked each individual who had helped in the good cause.

The pastor, on rising to reply, was for some minutes unable to be heard for the storm of cheering and applause with which he was greeted. He said:—"My dear friends, am I really expected to make a speech after this display of your loving-kindness? It is not merely the waving of handkerchiefs, and the crying of 'Hurrah'; it is what I have been hearing the last two days. It has been enough to melt a heart of stone."

Referring to the magnificent gift he had received, he said:—"You will remember that some years ago you were so good as to give me £6000 and more as a testimonial; and I went away that night with a very light heart, because I handed the whole of it over to you back again for the work of the Almshouses, and some other works. That is exactly what I proposed to do to-night—just the same thing over again, only I am not permitted to do it. A very large number of the donors said that they would not give anything if my Jubilee day was made a pretext for assisting the societies. They put it as strongly as that; they had given the time before, with a view of giving something to me, and they would not a second time give unless they did give to me. At the start I proposed four objects to be helped, and I asked the donors to allot their money to one or other of those four as they pleased. In pursuance of that request there has been an allotment made. Judge how very little that idea seemed to take with our friends! Having it before them, and having it pressed upon them by myself, they have allotted £81, 9s. 6d. to the Almshouses, £31 to the Colportage, £74 to the Orphanage, and £43 to my son's chapel at Auckland, and there is a pound or two—perhaps three—allotted to societies, and that is all; and all the rest is evidently left by the will of the friends totally free. Well, it must be so, and I accept the money for myself so far as that is the expressed desire; only if I give it now to any charitable enterprises in any proportion you give me full liberty to do as I like with it. You will not suppose that I am not having it, because I do not know how I can better have it than by being allowed to give it away. I cannot be debarred from this gratification. I will go the length of saying that I will take some portion of this for myself. But first of all there will be £1000 needed to pay for the house at the back, and furniture and all sorts of things; and I shall pay to the church treasurer £1000 for that object. Then I want to give something to St. Thomas's Hospital. Then I want to give to the church £200, to make up what is given to the Almshouses to £200, and also to give to the deacons £100, which they may keep to lend to persons who can use a loan well. I want also to give to the Baptist Fund for the relief of poor ministers £50, on the behalf of my son Charles, to make him a member of it. I should like to give £100 to the fund for augmenting the salaries of our poor brethren. I should like to make up the amount for Colportage work to £200. I should like to give £250 to the tabernacle at Auckland. I should like to give at least £100 to my wife's Book Fund for poor ministers. I have a little list here, but if I were to read any more, friends might object that I was doing contrary to their wish.

"Now I thank everybody who has given £100, and everybody who has given a penny. God bless you, and return it to you in every way!

"The Lord bless you! The Lord bless you! The

Lord bless you yet more and more, you and your children!"

After the Rev. J. P. Chown had offered up prayer, the singing of the Doxology brought the meeting to a conclusion.

CHAPTER XVII.

SPURGEON AS A COMMENTATOR.

AT the close of the year 1869 the first volume of the *Treasury of David*, Mr. Spurgeon's greatest literary work, was issued from the press.

Searching the Scriptures diligently, he had found in the Book of Psalms an inexhaustible storehouse of delight and profit, and thought he could in no way better express his own thankfulness for their priceless contents than by offering, for the participation of others, the treasures he had himself gained from them.

In the preface to this volume he acknowledges with humility his consciousness of many imperfections, but rejoices and blesses God, by whose gracious help alone he has been able to accomplish anything of worth, and sends it forth confidently, believing that what had been written in dependence on Divine guidance could not fail of usefulness.

The comments accompanying the text are original, although, Mr. Spurgeon says, a few suggestions were gathered from various authors. To further elucidate and illustrate the Psalm under consideration, he gives, in addition to his own exposition, many quotations from writers of acknowledged authority. In the course of the work will be found contributions from writings of saints and martyrs and divines through all ages of the Church's history, and extracts from poets and philosophers of ancient and modern times. The authors quoted are very numerous, and represent many shades of religious thought; therefore the writer's name is appended after each quotation, that the opinions expressed in it may be referred only to himself; for, while Mr. Spurgeon desired to concentrate upon the study of the Sacred Book all the light that could be gathered from the devout meditations of many diverse minds, they sometimes implied beliefs not in accordance with his own. The comprehensive collection of appropriate extracts with which the work is enriched cost much time and pains, but it was a labour of love, and in it he was indefatigably assisted by Mr. John L. Keys. Books without number, at the British Museum and elsewhere, were turned over and closely scanned. Sometimes the most patient sifting would reveal but little suitable matter; at other times their labour was plentifully rewarded.

Mr. Spurgeon completed his exegesis of each Psalm by some suggestions intended solely for the use of lay-preachers, who, possessing but inconsiderable store of knowledge, could yet give but scant time to the preparation of a sermon.

With the exception of his own comments, this first volume was the fruit of a period when bodily weakness debarred him from preaching. Compelled for a time to forego the happiness of bearing witness for his Master by word of mouth, he strove to glorify Him by his writings.

The volume contains twenty-six Psalms. In each case the title is first considered, and the divisions into which the composition naturally falls. Then follows an exhaustive exposition of each verse, and at the end of the Psalm a goodly number of explanatory notes on each verse, these being quotations from different authors. Besides the suggestions for lay-preachers referred to above, there is also a

MR. SPURGEON'S STUDY.

list of works bearing on the Psalm in question, as guides to the further study of the subject.

The note on the title of Psalm I. instructs the reader to consider this song of David as an introduction to the rest. It thus indicates the purposes of the book—to set forth the blessedness of the righteous, and the doom which awaits the wicked.

The first three verses describe the conditions that constitute the joy of a good man, the occupations that engross him, and the bliss that is promised to him. The Psalm declares:—"*Blessed is the man that walketh not in the counsel of the ungodly, nor standeth in the way of sinners, nor sitteth in the seat of the scornful. But his delight is in the law of the Lord; and in His law doth he meditate day and night.*"

The commentator shows how accurately the steps in the downward path of sin are here marked out. One who walks carelessly with those who leave God out of their lives soon becomes familiarised with sin, so that vice ceases to be shocking to him, and if he follow the same path, he finally loses his sense of God's Being, and eternity, heaven, and hell become to him words empty of meaning. At first, not careful to avoid contact with sin, he presently willingly remains amongst those who openly set God's laws at defiance; and at last, unless Divine mercy interposes, becomes even as they, and, as it were, takes his seat as a teacher of evil.

The man of God is delineated as one with whom the "counsels" that rule the conduct of such as mind only earthly things have no weight. He seeks a higher law by which to walk, even the "law of the Lord," which is "perfect"; and guides his way according to the "statutes of the Lord," which are "right," and rejoice the heart; and His commandments, which are pure, and enlighten the eyes. In this law he *delights*, musing upon it by day and night, finding in God's word strength for the day, and thoughts of peace in the night; songs of praise for his gladness, and assurances of help and deliverance in the dark hour of trouble. "The law of his God is in his heart; none of his steps shall slide." This is the man who is *blessed*. The word is used, as is stated in the exposition, in a plural sense, and implies that joys are multiplied upon the righteous man.

In the remarks upon verse 3, "*And he shall be like a tree planted by the rivers of water that bringeth forth his fruit in his season; his leaf also shall not wither; and whatsoever he doeth shall prosper*," emphasis is placed on the word *planted*, as indicating God's proprietorship and care, and therefore implying safety in the dread day spoken of by our Lord, Matthew xv. 13, "Every plant which my Heavenly Father hath not planted shall be rooted up." The *rivers of water* are considered as figures of forgiveness, the promises of God, the gracious influence of the spirit, and fellowship with Christ, whose supplies shall never fail; while the seasonable fruit represents virtues proper to each hour and circumstance of life. The simile of the never-withering leaves appears to be taken as applying to the profession by words of a man's religion. When our Lord cursed the fig-tree that bore leaves only, he said, "Let no fruit grow on thee henceforth *for ever*." "And," the evangelist continues, "presently the fig-tree withered away." Our Lord thus taught his disciples that the power to bear fruit is life; for the mandate which deprived the tree for ever of that power was practically a sentence of death passed on it. The image of a tree bearing fruit in his season, and whose leaves are always fresh and green, seems to picture a man drinking so deeply of the rivers of God as to *abound* in life, manifesting itself richly in spirit and deed, and also endowing his words with the beauty and power of life.

The last clause of the verse promises prosperity upon his

work. Mr. Spurgeon lays stress upon the sureness of the promise, even when success is not apparent. Failures and reverses are not necessarily evils; but always

> "Ill that He blesses is our good,
> And unblest good is ill,
> And all is right that seems most wrong
> If it be His sweet will."

"*The ungodly are not so; but are like the chaff which the wind driveth away.*" The Vulgate and Septuagint version, "Not so the ungodly, not so," is here quoted as a more emphatic rendering of the original, making the denial to the wicked of the good man's blessings doubly strong, and the phrase, "They are like the chaff," is noted as aptly describing their character as essentially worthless and destitute of life. "*Therefore the ungodly shall not stand in the judgment.*" These words prophesy the confusion of face which shall fall upon them in the last great day of assay. "*Nor sinners in the congregation of the righteous.*" The contrast is here shown between the Church on earth and the august assembly of Heaven. Here the tares and wheat grow together, and the godly are ever grieved and disquieted by the works of evildoers; but there is the "congregation of the righteous," in which none shall stand but the pure in heart. "*For the Lord knoweth the way of the righteous.*" The more exact translation is given as, "The Lord *is knowing* the way of the righteous," expressing God's continued oversight of the path His people tread; whether it leads through cloud or sunshine, he takes account of their steps. "*The way of the ungodly shall perish.*" His remembrance shall be clean blotted out, or shall remain only as a thing of loathing.

Following the expositions, whose purport has thus been generally indicated, are explanatory notes on the Psalm as a whole from three authors—Thomas Watson, A.D. 1660; Sir Richard Baker, A.D. 1640; and John Fry, A.D. 1842.

The extract given below is from the writings of Adam Clarke (1844), and is one of eight selections illustrating verse 1: "*That walketh not in the counsel of the ungodly.*" Mark certain circumstances of their differing characters and conduct. 1. The *ungodly man* has his *counsel;* 2. The *sinner* has his *way;* 3. The *scorner* has his *seat.* The *ungodly man* is unconcerned about religion; he is neither zealous for his own salvation nor for that of others; and he counsels and advises those with whom he converses to adopt his plan, and not trouble themselves about praying, reading, repentance, etc., etc. "There is no need for such things; live an honest life, make no fuss about religion, and you will fare well enough at last." Now, "Blessed is the man who walks not in this man's counsel," who does not come into his measures, nor act according to his plan.

The *sinner* has his particular *way* of transgressing: one is a *drunkard*, another *dishonest*, another *unclean*. Few are given to every species of vice. There are many *covetous* men who abhor *drunkenness*, many *drunkards* who abhor *covetousness;* and so of others. *Each has his easily besetting sin;* therefore, says the prophet, "Let the wicked forsake *his way.*" Now, blessed is he who stands not in such a man's *way.*

The *scorner* has brought, in reference to himself, all religion and moral feeling to an end. He has *sat down*—is utterly confirmed in impiety, and makes a mock at sin. His conscience is seared, and he is a believer in all unbelief. Now, "Blessed is the man who sits not down in his *seat.*"

No less than ten quotations refer to verse 2. One by Joseph Caryl, 1647, thus comments on the phrase, "*In his law doth he meditate.*" "In the plainest text there is a world of holiness and spirituality; and if we in prayer and dependence upon God did sit down and study it, we should behold much more than appears to us. It may be, at once reading or looking, we see little or nothing; as Elijah's servant went once, and saw nothing; therefore he was commanded to look seven times. 'What now?' says the prophet. 'I see a cloud rising, like a man's hand;' and by-and-by the whole surface of the heavens was covered with clouds. So you may look lightly upon a Scripture and see nothing; *meditate often upon it*, and there you shall see a light, like the light of the sun."

Out of many notes on verse 3 a quaint saying of John Trapp, of the seventeenth century, is given:—" Outward prosperity, if it follow close walking with God, is very sweet; as the cipher, where it follows a figure, adds to the number, though it be nothing in itself." Another quotation on verse 5, from the same writer, reads—" The Irish air will sooner brook a toad or snake than heaven a sinner."

On verse 4, where the ungodly are compared to *chaff*, Sir Richard Baker says—" Here, by the way, we may let the wicked know they have a thanks to give they think little of; that they may thank the godly for all the good days they live upon the earth, seeing it is for their sakes and not for their own that they enjoy them. For as the chaff, while it is united and keeps close to the wheat, enjoys some privileges for the wheat's sake, and is laid up carefully in the barn; but as soon as it is divided and parted from the wheat, it is cast out and scattered by the wind; so the wicked, whilst the godly are in company and live amongst them, partake for their sake of some blessedness promised to the godly; but if the godly forsake them or be taken from them, then either a deluge of water comes suddenly upon them, as it did upon the old world when Noah left it; or a deluge of fire, as it did upon Sodom when Lot left it and went out of the city."

The first volume of this unique work met with a very hearty welcome, not only for the sake of the admirable expositions of the famous preacher of the Tabernacle, but for the wonderful assemblage of illustrative matter, drawn from sources so varied, which his researches had brought to light. It is easy to imagine with what delight the book would be hailed by many a preacher and Biblical student possessed of only a small library and out of reach of any extensive collection of theological works. The book was a library in itself as regarded the subject of which it treated.

Mr. Spurgeon foresaw that the entire work would comprehend years of patient investigation, but his whole mind was bent on completing the delightful task he had begun, if he might thereby glorify God; so in submission to His will, praying and hoping for Divine permission and assistance, and cheered by the manifest appreciation of what he had already accomplished, he laboured on with unabated ardour, and in less than twelve months after the publication of the first part a second volume was ready for the press. Like the first, it contained twenty-six Psalms, and its arrangement was precisely similar to that followed in the earlier volume. A few changes had been advocated from some quarters, but by far the larger number of those he wished to help regarded those same points where alteration had been suggested as special excellencies; therefore the old order was still adhered to. Quotations from the old Latin writers are introduced more freely in the second volume than in the first, and in the preface Mr. Spurgeon draws special attention to their works, as comparatively unknown to his readers, but furnishing abundant and reliable aid in interpreting the Holy Scriptures He again, however, disclaims all responsibility for the opinions contained in the extracts quoted from any author.

Here too he gives expression to his ever-growing belief, that only those who have themselves meditated profoundly on the inspired songs of David can have any adequate conception of the wealth they contain. To the loving and reverent student the Holy Spirit reveals ever new and

A HOLY PLACE 273

infinite depths of beauty and awe. He tells us that, as he pondered over some of the Psalms contained in this book, holy fear fell upon him, and he shrank from the attempt to explain, in words that seemed all too poor and feeble, themes so sublime. He hesitated long before beginning the exposition of the 51st Psalm, restrained by a sense of insufficiency, and seeming to hear a voice which said, "Draw not nigh hither, put off thy shoes from off thy feet." He speaks of it as a Psalm that should sink into the heart, and move it to tears and prayer—as burdened with the sighs of a heart broken by contrition, and yet bearing a Divine impress, as though the God against whom David had sinned, and from whom alone the grace of true repentance comes, had given him words for his sorrow.

The exposition, explanatory notes, and also suggestions for sermons on this Psalm are very full. Among many striking notes may be mentioned one from Frederick William Robertson on verse 1, and a pathetic enlargement of verse 11 from Fra Thomé de Jesu. "*Cast me not away from Thy presence*, Lord, though I, alas! have cast Thee from me, yet cast me not away: hide not Thy face from me, although I so often have refused to look at Thee; leave me not without help, to perish in my sins, though I have aforetime left Thee." Other extracts are from Thomas Chalmers, the Right Rev. A. P. Forbes, Bishop of Brechin, Adam Clarke, St. Ambrose, who lived in the fourth century, Thomas Fuller, the poet Cowper, Dr. Pusey, John Calvin, Christopher Wordsworth, with several from the writings of Sir Richard Baker, one of which, on verses 16 and 17, is given below. *For thou desirest not sacrifice; else would I give it: thou delightest not in burnt-offering. The sacrifices of God are a broken spirit: a broken and a contrite heart, O God, thou wilt not despise.* "And now I was thinking what were fit to offer to God for all his loving-kindness he has showed me; and I thought upon sacrifices, for they have sometimes been pleasing to Him, and He hath oftentimes smelt a sweet odour from them; but I considered that sacrifices were but shadows of things to come, and are not now in that grace they have been; for *old things are past, and new are now come:* the shadows are gone, the substances are come in place. The bullocks that are to be sacrificed now are our hearts; it were easier for me to give Him bullocks for sacrifice, than to give Him my heart. But why should I offer Him that He cares not for? my heart, I know, He cares for; and if it be broken, and offered up by penitence and contrition, it is the only sacrifice that now He delights in. But can we think God to be so indifferent that He will accept for a broken heart? Is a thing that is broken good for anything? Can we drink in a broken glass? Or can we lean upon a broken staff? But though other things may be the worse for breaking, yet a heart is never at the best till it be broken; for till it be broken we cannot see what is in it; till it be broken, it cannot send forth its sweetest odour; and therefore, though God loves a whole heart in affection, yet He loves a broken heart in sacrifice. And no marvel, indeed, seeing it is He himself that breaks it; for as nothing by goat's blood can break the adamant, so nothing but the blood of our scapegoat, Jesus Christ, is able to break our adamantine hearts. Therefore, accept, O God, my broken heart, which I offer Thee with a whole heart; seeing Thou canst neither except against it for being whole which is broken in sacrifice, nor except against it for being broken which is whole in affection."

The names given above do not exhaust the list of writers who have furnished extracts for this Psalm alone, but they are enough to give a slight idea of the wide field of literature traversed in the search for every help in the interpretation of the sacred book.

The 40th Psalm is doubtless one of those sublime compositions referred to in the preface, in dwelling on which the mind is subdued with awe and wondering adoration.

Its inscription, "To the Chief Musician," is held to show that it was to be sung in the congregation, notwithstanding the personal form of expression; and while the words are by the mouth of David, they are of the Holy Ghost, concerning the true "Root of Jesse," David's Lord.

The Psalm opens, "*I waited patiently for the Lord*," and the exposition shows how applicable these words were to our blessed Lord, who, through the agony of Gethsemane, the taunts of His enemies, the buffeting and cruel scourging, and the pangs of the shameful cross, uttered no murmur of reproach or complaint, but with infinite patience bore all things, even to death. "*And he inclined unto me and heard me.*" The figure here is explained as representing God bending down to hear the low cry of one whose strength is nearly spent, and the prophecy as fulfilled when our Lord prayed alone in the night watches on the mountains, and in the garden of Gethsemane. In verse 2, "*He brought me up also out of an horrible pit, and out of the miry clay*," the *horrible pit* is supposed to prefigure the horror of darkness which wrapped round the spirit of the Son of God when he bore for us the bitter curse of sin, in the awful solitude of those closing hours of life: the simile being taken from the loathsome dungeons, deep down in the earth, in which men were sometimes imprisoned in blackest loneliness.

"*Sacrifice and offering thou didst not desire, mine ears hast thou opened: burnt-offering and sin offering hast thou not required*," verse 6. Mr. Spurgeon offers a most beautiful exposition of the words, "*Mine ears hast thou opened.*" He says:—"Our Lord was quick to hear and perform His Father's will; His ears were as if excavated down to His soul; they were not closed up like Isaac's wells, which the Philistines filled up, but clear passages down to the fountains of His soul. The prompt obedience of our

Lord is here the first idea. There is, however, no reason whatever to reject the notion that the digging of the ear here intended may refer to the boring of the ear of the servant, who refused out of love to his master to take his liberty at the year of jubilee. His perforated ear, the token of perpetual service, is a true picture of our blessed Lord's fidelity to His Father's business, and His love to His Father's children. Jesus irrevocably gave Himself up to be the servant of servants for our sake and God's glory."

The affecting words of verse 12—"*For innumerable evils compassed me about; mine iniquities have taken hold upon me, so that I am not able to look up; they are more than the hairs of mine head; therefore my heart faileth me*"—are taken as showing, first, that our innumerable sins were the measure of the pains and woes of the world's Redeemer, and then the awful and mysterious reality of the transfer of he guilt of sinful man to the Sinless One, the unutterable anguish from that dread burden which bore down His soul and shut out His Father's face, so that He could only pray according to the sense of the words, "*Be pleased, O Lord, to deliver me: O Lord, make haste to help me.*" After this manner was the prayer in Gethsemane—"If it be possible, let this cup pass from Me;" and then the words in the concluding verse of the Psalm—"The Lord thinketh upon me: Thou art my help and my deliverer"—were fulfilled in that supreme hour, for "There appeared an angel unto Him from heaven, strengthening Him."

There is a quaint note by Mark Frank on the words in verse 7, "*Lo, I come.*" It is as follows:—As His name is above every name, so this coming of His is above every coming. We sometimes call our own births, I confess, a coming into the world; but, properly, none ever came into the world but He. For, 1. He only truly can be said to come, who is, before He comes; so were not we, only He so. 2. He only strictly comes who comes willingly; our crying and struggling at our entrance into the world shows how unwillingly we come into it. He alone it is that *sings* out, "Lo, I come." 3. He only properly comes who comes from some place or other. Alas! we had none to come from but the womb of nothing. *He* only had a place to be in before He came.

The third volume of the series was not completed till the beginning of the year 1872. Mr. Spurgeon experienced far greater difficulty in finding extracts illustrative of the Psalms herein contained than he had known heretofore. A few of them had been written upon very fully by other expositors, but many appeared to be comparatively unexplored by modern commentators. He was therefore compelled to resort to the Latin writers to a great extent, being assisted in the work of translation by Mr. Gracey, of the Pastors' College, an accomplished classical scholar. Here they met with much disappointment, for often they found only fragments of thought suitable for their purpose, and these scattered over the pages of immense tomes, so that their gleanings were but scanty, although, as they hoped, of sufficient value to compensate them for the time and toil expended. This part of the work involved the expenditure of much money as well as labour; but Mr. Spurgeon was resolved that no effort should be wanting to perfect the work to which he had put his hand, and to that end enlisted the aid of others to supplement his own endeavours.

The cost of publication of this volume promised to exceed that of the first and second numbers, printers were receiving higher wages, and the price of paper and the expense of binding were greater than they had been, but it was hoped it would not be necessary to put an increased charge upon the new volume, and this it was seen might be avoided if a larger number were sold, as was hoped might be the case. Mr. Spurgeon desired no more than that the amount realised by the sale of the book should be sufficient to cover the outlay upon it; he found his own exceeding recompense in the joy afforded by the work itself, and in the hope he cherished of being of service to his fellow-workers.

The fourth volume occupied a still longer time in preparation than either of the preceding ones, for the difficulty of obtaining fresh notes increased as the work advanced; and Mr. Spurgeon noted with great surprise that even in the case of those memorable Psalms, the 84th, 90th, 91st, 92nd, and 103rd, there should be so great a dearth of expository matter.

Although it might seem discouraging to find so little among those old friends of the book-shelves that had furnished supplies for the previous numbers, Mr. Spurgeon was not to be daunted, but gave himself up still more untiringly to a further search till he could obtain what he sought, frequently shortening the hours for his much-needed rest, that he might have a little more time for his labours of research. He remarks, with some satisfaction, that the new volume has not lacked in quantity, as he hopes it has not suffered in quality, in spite of the difficulties he had to encounter, while he thanks God that he has enabled him to accomplish so much of his purpose.

Four years and a half after the publication of the fourth volume of the *Treasury of David* the fifth was offered to the public. In his preface to this volume Mr. Spurgeon apologises for the length of time that elapsed between the completion of the fourth and fifth books; but we think that, considering the enormous quantity of matter contained in each volume, and considering also the marvellous amount of other work that the author had in hand and got through, it is wonderful that such a book should have been produced in the time stated.

Before its appearance many inquiries concerning it were made of the publishers by an interested public, whose knowledge of the value of the former treatises made them eager to become acquainted with the ideas of the writer upon the later Psalms. We can well imagine that students and preachers who had learned to depend upon the *Treasury of David* for the help they needed in preparing lectures, sermons, etc., on the Psalms would feel lost when their attention had to be directed to those upon which this *Treasury* was still locked.

The labour of writing the fifth volume was greater than that which had been entailed in the production of the others, and yet it gave its author scarcely as much satisfaction when it was completed as had the former books. Greater research was required to obtain a smaller amount of information than had been the case in dealing with the earlier Psalms.

Few writers have written at length upon many of the Psalms commented upon here, and as the supply of material was meagre, so there was less variety of choice; and while for the previous books many rich and suggestive extracts had been found, for this such valuable matter was not obtainable.

There have been many commentators upon the Psalms, but none have been so thorough as Mr. Spurgeon. Others have either grown tired in their work, or, having said their cleverest things at the beginning, have left nothing fresh to say. Then, too, instead of taking each passage as it stands, they have constantly referred to parallel passages, which means a continual turning back on the part of the student, and entails much loss of time.

Another difficulty encountered arose from the fact that most expounders have written with great fulness upon the Psalms or parts of Psalms with which they have been most familiar, and which have appealed to them with the greatest force, while other passages have been almost entirely overlooked, as if they were not equally God's words to man. Of all parts of the Old Testament the Psalms are best known and most read, and therefore it is singular to find how very much has escaped the notice of many who have made them their special study. While thousands of commentators express their ideas upon certain verses and passages, other parts are as much neglected as if they were not part of Scripture at all.

Another reason why this volume was rather slow in appearing was because its author wished to put into it only his best work, and not, in his hurry to complete it, bestow less thought upon its last than upon its first pages. He says that often he sat down to comment upon a Psalm and found himself not exactly unequal to the task of writing, but unable to do so without *forcing* his mind to the work, in which case its production would not be characterised by that freshness and richness, as if it were the outcome of a mind thoroughly in sympathy with the subject to be discussed, and overflowing with ideas concerning it. Months sometimes elapsed during which he lingered over a Psalm, waiting till he should be inspired with thoughts concerning it. The 109th Psalm was a case in point. Mr. Spurgeon felt as if he should never be able to treat it successfully had it not been for the terrible bloodshed in Bulgaria, which so filled him with righteous indignation that he could no longer restrain himself. The words of David seemed exactly applicable to the times, and he poured out his soul upon them. There were difficulties to be met in dealing with other Psalms, but in comparison with those of the 109th, they were easy to overcome.

That perhaps grandest of all sacred poems, Psalm 104, was not easily despatched; indeed the remarks upon it occupy forty closely-printed pages, and if bound separately, would form a fair-sized volume, which would in itself constitute a "Treasury" to its possessor, though its writer declared that, after bestowing his best efforts upon it, he was not satisfied with the result.

Only fifteen Psalms were commented upon in this fifth book, against an average of about twenty-five in each of the first four; but the 119th Psalm was too long to be included in this volume, which was therefore ended with the Psalm preceding it.

We cannot but admire Mr. Spurgeon's determination to do every part of his work as well as possible, even though God should call him home before it was completed. Work of this kind is never as well done as it might be if it is executed like mechanical work, by the piece, or at so much per hour.

Only those who have been occupied in a similar way can form any conception of the enormous amount of labour entailed before a book similar to the one before us can be produced. We might call the system employed by the author and his co-workers by the name of "Thorough," for no pains have been spared, and no stone has been left unturned, to procure the best thoughts of the greatest thinkers of all nations and all ages upon the Psalms of David. These have been thoroughly sifted, and that which is true separated from that which is error, and to the best and most applicable truths have been added the best and most applicable words of one of the most inspired of God's ministers.

In the fifth volume, as indeed in the production of all the others, many willing hands and active minds were employed to assist Mr. Spurgeon. An enormous amount of translation was done for which this book is very little the richer, but which nevertheless had to be done. By far the greater part of all that was translated from the Latin was of no use, a few extracts only being retained. And this is far more the case with the volume before us than with the earlier ones. Latin writers, like English commentators in most instances, show signs of having grown more tired of their work the further they have proceeded with it, and their comments become more and more scant and valueless. Then again, some of the most voluminous writers were evidently possessed very largely with the organ of imagination, and this has led them to weave very wonderful and impossible stories upon small evidence, and to give almost ludicrous interpretations of the text. Worse than all, their translations are doubtful, and as a rule they contrive to make things of least importance teach what they consider most important lessons.

The great expenditure of labour for small returns made the production of this book especially difficult; but though, as we have already said, it was scarcely as satisfactory to its author in its completed form as its elder brothers, we who have opportunities of proving its usefulness have nothing but words of commendation to say on its behalf. And our admiration is, if possible, increased for him who, in his determination to leave no single passage unexplained, spared so much time and care and thought for—not worldly gain, not that he might be praised of men, but that he might give the best help that he could to all seekers after the truth. God gave him great gifts, and these, whether as writer, as preacher, as philanthropist, must be used to their very fullest extent for His glory and for the enlightenment and the raising of his fellow-men.

It was evidently a source of much satisfaction to Mr. Spurgeon to feel that this great work which he had undertaken, and in the completion of which so many of his best years were being spent, would not end with his life, but long after he had ceased to render active service here would remain to guide and instruct those who should labour in the cause of Christ. But he felt, as every truly great man must feel, that this large production was, after all, a small matter, and that though he had penetrated as far as was possible to him into the depths of the Word to find its hidden meaning, his best comments were superficial when compared with its fathomless abysses. He believed that the very words of the Scriptures were inspired, and that in order to find their real significance one must know as far as possible what were the actual words which God inspired His servants to write. These are of utmost importance to us, for it is by them that we understand God's will concerning us. Jesus said, "These are they which testify of Me."

Still another volume of the *Treasury of David* was issued from the press in the autumn of 1882. The enthusiastic reception which the five previous volumes had had must have left little doubt in the author's mind as to the success of this, while it must have been a continual source of comfort and encouragement to him as he proceeded with his great self-imposed task. Comparatively few men in this age, in which ambition seems to be one, if not the chief, of the ruling spirits, are so little affected by mere public opinion as was this king of Nonconformity. His ambition was not to receive the plaudits of men, but to entice and compel, and by any and every means to stimulate them to praise their Maker. Yet he must have been made glad by the many expressions of gratitude he received, which showed him that God accepted the service he had thus rendered Him.

In the volume to which our attention is now directed only five Psalms—those from cxix. to cxxiv. inclusive—are considered. The Psalm cxix. goes by the name of the longest Psalm, and it equals in length twenty-two of the Songs of Degrees by which it is followed. It might almost have formed a complete book itself, but this would scarcely have been of uniform size with those already published, while in the last the matter must have been considerably compressed to include all the remaining Psalms.

This the author was not willing to do. The nearer he got

to the end of his task the more anxious he became that there should be no signs of weariness or slovenliness, but that it should, if possible, be even more excellent at its close than at its beginning.

The production of this sixth book was not unattended by many difficulties—what work that is of high value is easy?—but these only made Mr. Spurgeon and his willing helpers the more diligent, and the greater the difficulties the more zealous were they in overcoming them.

No less than 397 pages are devoted to Psalm cxix. We speak of it as the longest Psalm, but unless we have studied it with great earnestness and with the aid of the *Treasury of David*, we have probably not realised that not only does it exceed all other Psalms in length, but in depth and breadth of meaning also. To our expositor it appeared like a great prairie, boundless in extent, and bewildering in its boundlessness; or like a mighty ocean, in comparison with which other Psalms are lakes; or like a continent of holy thoughts; or like a vast extent of fields filled with an abundance of ripe corn, ready to yield its rich grain to satisfy the needs of man. With such a revelation of its immensity it is little wonder that this most indefatigable of workers hesitated as he surveyed the task before him.

A few of the leading characteristics of this Psalm, which, in addition to its length, make it unique, may be mentioned here. First, its arrangement is peculiar; it is alphabetical, the first eight stanzas beginning with the first letter of the Hebrew alphabet, and each succeeding eight with a new letter right through the twenty-two letters of which it is composed. The subject of the Psalm is the law of God, and in every verse but two throughout its entire length this is distinctly mentioned. It is curious to notice the various names given by the Psalmist to God's law; there are no less than ten—law, testimony, way, commandments, precepts,

A TRIUMPHANT CONCLUSION.

word, judgments, righteousness, statutes, faith; and these recur in generally regular order.

Some commentators discern in this Psalm the form of a diary, and evidences that it was written at different parts of the author's life. Matthew Henry speaks of it as "a collection of David's pious and devout ejaculations, the short and sudden breathings of his soul to God, which he wrote down as they occurred, and towards the latter end of his time gathered them out of his day-book, where they lay scattered, added to them many like words, and digested them into this Psalm."

As to its value, one of the ancient fathers describes it thus :—" It applies an all-containing medicine to the various spiritual diseases of men—sufficing to perfect those who long for perfect virtue, to rouse the slothful, to refresh the dispirited, and to set in order the relaxed;" and it has been called "The Alphabet of Divine Love," "The Paradise of all the Doctrines," "The Storehouse of the Holy Spirit," "The School of Truth," "The Deep Mystery of the Scriptures, where the whole moral discipline of all the virtues shines brightly."

Mr. Rogers, Mr. Keys, various ministers who had formerly been students in the Pastors' College, and others again came to the assistance of their most esteemed friend and minister, who, having the care of so large a church and so many important institutions, could scarcely have completed his work unaided. But not only was the sixth volume finished, but the seventh and final volume was begun, and after four more years of earnest labour the last word upon the last Psalm was written, and the date appended to the preface, October 1885.

Very little can be told concerning this last book beyond what has already been said with regard to the former volumes. The chief difficulties were as before mentioned; those which arose from the fact that so few commentators had written at length upon the later Psalms, and therefore greater research had to be made without much valuable information being gained. The same industrious helpers continued their services to the end, except that Mr. Gibson, whose work was ended here, had been called away to labour in a higher sphere, leaving behind him very full and useful notes translated from Latin authors.

It was with mingled feelings that Mr. Spurgeon wrote his seventh preface. Great and laborious as his task had been, he had derived much pleasure and help from it, and there was more than a little of regret when it was concluded. In describing his experiences while engaged in his work he quotes the following from Bishop Horn:—

"And now, could the author flatter himself that any one would take half the pleasure in reading the following exposition which he has taken in writing it, he would not fear the loss of his labour. The employment detached him from the bustle and hurry of life, the din of politics, and the noise of folly. Vanity and vexation flew for a season, care and disquietude came not near his dwelling. He arose fresh as the morning to his task; the silence of the night invited him to pursue it; and he can truly say that food and rest were not preferred before it. Every Psalm improved infinitely upon his acquaintance with it, and no one gave him uneasiness but the last; for then he grieved that his work was done. Happier hours than those which have been spent on these meditations on the Songs of Zion he never expects to see in this world. Very pleasantly did they pass, and they moved smoothly and swiftly along; for when thus engaged he counted no time. The meditations are gone, but have left a relish and a fragrance upon the mind, and the remembrance of them is sweet."

In the summer of 1878 Mr. Spurgeon's fertile brain, and alike fertile pen, produced a book—one of a series of works, uniform in size and price—called *The Bible and the Newspaper*. Small as to bulk and clear as to style (which goes without saying), it has had a large circulation, and in 1890 the publication had reached its twenty-second thousand.

The title is curious! What have the Bible and the newspaper to do with each other? Very little, if any, most of us would say, but Mr. Spurgeon, to whom everything in nature and art was a means of instruction in the ways of God, found much to be learned from the thoughtful reading of these records of everyday events. In his preface he says that his object in writing the book was not simply to provide entertaining reading, but to encourage Sunday-school teachers and "all other servants of the great parable-making Master" in finding instructive similes from even the most ordinary surroundings.

With this worthy object in view Mr. Spurgeon wrote forty-six charming little papers on current topics of the day. Many of the incidents which form the bases of the articles will be still fresh in the minds of readers, but few who have not read the book will form any idea of the amount of spiritual teaching which a mind constantly alert to discover some new means of adding to the Kingdom of God could obtain from them.

The loss of the *Eurydice* forms the theme of the first paper, which is entitled, "A Voice from the Sea." All England was filled with dismay at the terrible disaster which befell this good ship just as it had reached home, and the truth was brought closely to many sorrowing hearts that "In the midst of life we are in death." In the *Bible and the Newspaper* we are warned against feeling secure before we are actually safe in Christ, and we are bidden to beware of the sudden temptations which assail us when our sails are set, and we are going smoothly on before a fair wind; also, no matter how prosperous we may be, we should be always prepared for emergencies. Above all things, we should keep our eyes looking towards God, who sleeps not, but is ever regardful of the needs of His children.

The "Calling out of the Reserves" during the time of the Zulu war led Mr. Spurgeon to observe that not only in the army, but also in Christian churches, there are many who belong to the "Reserves." Indeed, in the churches the reserves are so numerous when compared with the active soldiers of the army of the King of kings, that they greatly hinder the holy war, and the enemy is not conquered.

The various characteristics of those who form the "Reserves" in the church and the need there is for their activity are discussed with such power, that surely "inactive professors" who read will no longer merit such a title.

A tirade on the costly dress worn by women, and a burst of righteous indignation against the wicked waste of money in which some people indulge, resulted from the trials of Madame Rosalie and another "Madame." The former brought an action against a gentleman of large means, to compel him to pay an enormous debt incurred by his wife for dress, and the latter was herself sued, because it was found that while professing to make ladies "beautiful for ever," she really disfigured them for life. The papers are called "Ladies' Dress" and "The Deceiver and the Victim." Many texts of Scripture are quoted to show how, both under the old and new dispensations, the outward adornment of women is condemned; and besides this, Mr. Spurgeon says how much more profitably the money which is spent on *over*-dress might be used, and how childish it is to think so much of personal decoration, besides being altogether inconsistent with the following of the lowly Jesus.

An amusing little story, culled from an American newspaper, led to the writing of "Religious Sluggards." Here is the story:—"A Sunday school boy, at Maysville, Kentucky, was asked by the superintendent the other day if his father was a Christian. 'Yes, sir,' he replied; 'but he is not working at it much!'"

"Sympathy created by Kindred Experience" was written at the time when there was a great strike among the Lancashire operatives, who refused to accept a reduction in wages which their employers declared to be absolutely necessary. An article in the *Daily Telegraph* upon this strike mentioned one feature in which it differed from strikes as a rule. It appears that many of the artisans were themselves small tradesmen belonging to co-operative spinning concerns, and these realised the bad condition of trade, and were able to understand the position of affairs and explain them with great clearness to their working brethren.

Referring to this, Mr. Spurgeon pointed out that no one can fully sympathise with a suffering brother or sister unless he has had the same kind of trial. Even Christ Himself needed the suffering which He endured to make Him a perfect Saviour; but He did suffer, and we know that "in all our afflictions He is afflicted." And it is in order that they may the better comfort those who are in sorrow that God's servants are often called upon to endure great afflictions. The more varied a person's experience the better able will he be to carry out the Apostle's injunction to "Rejoice with those that do rejoice, and weep with those that weep."

The *Daily News* of May 15th, 1878, recorded the fact that the Queen had sent a telegram to Mr. John Bright expressing her deep sympathy in the irreparable bereavement which he then sustained. Mr. Spurgeon dwells upon the honour of receiving royal sympathy, but reminds us that we may continually enjoy the sympathy of the King of kings. Mourners upon earth have access to the courts of Heaven by a secret system of telegraphy, and the message that passes from the Highest to the most lowly is "When thou passest through the waters I will be with thee."

A brief but, to some one, very important advertisement stands at the head of another paper—" H. C. wants money ; " and " Tests for diamonds," " Pearls," " Deserters," " Want of stamina," " Home-sickness," " Life and Machinery" form the subjects of others. In the last-named Christians are warned against trusting to the various organisations of churches instead of helping in the many necessary works themselves. There is no doubt that secretaries, committees, missionaries, and many others do most important work, but these do not exempt private individuals from responsibility.

Every one of these many interesting articles bears beneath its title two or three texts of Scripture which are exactly *apropos* to the subject in hand. As one reads through these bright little discourses one is struck with the close connection which temporal and spiritual matters had in the mind of the great preacher, and even more so with the fact that the latter always had the pre-eminence. He was truly ever about his Father's business.

Another book which has been even more popular than the *Bible and the Newspaper* is called *All of Grace*. The fourth edition and the fortieth thousand of this book was published in 1889. That it should be popular is not at all surprising, since it deals with that most important of all topics, the salvation of human souls. Ministers, Sunday School teachers, those interested in mission work, and indeed all who are engaged in the grand crusade which has set out to win the world for Christ, if they have not already read *All of Grace*, should most certainly procure it. It is eminently suited to all who are seeking Christ, for it takes up every difficulty, doubt, and indeed almost every phase of experience through which an inquirer can pass. In the introductory chapter Mr. Spurgeon says that his sole purpose in writing the book is the eternal salvation of the reader, and that he himself will suffer great disappointment unless the object he has in view is realised. In order to accomplish this, and so that even the most ignorant may thoroughly understand, the very plainest language is used, and nothing can be more direct than the teaching given This book is only one more proof of Mr. Spurgeon's great faith. He did not depend upon his own words at all, but he believed in the power of the Holy Ghost to make them abundantly fruitful, even to the saving of millions of souls, and there is not the least doubt that the simple words which he thus sent forth to the world, trusting the result to God, have been the means of the conversion of many.

On the cover of the book we are told that it is "A Word to those who are seeking Salvation by the Lord Jesus Christ," and one of the first things we learn concerning salvation, as we peruse its pages, is that it is "All of Grace," and costs nothing at all; that salvation is not something that we have to give, but that is given to us, and the receiving of which will fill us with joy now and for ever. Then the ungodly are instructed in the way by which they may become justified. These ungodly ones are dealt with most tenderly, and the greatest sinner, as he reads, may feel that he has abundant cause for hope; ay, he may be certain that salvation is for him. The illustrations are all of a most homely character, and are taken from our ordinary life, and so they appeal to the simple in a special way.

What it is to believe in Jesus Christ is very clearly explained; and the sinner is told that if he believes he cannot be lost; and again and again he is assured that he is not saved because of any merit of his own, but "All of Grace."

How we are to be delivered from sinning is the subject of one chapter, what faith is that of another, while in another are words of comfort for those who mourn their lack of strength and power to keep themselves.

The sinner is not left to himself when he has been clearly taught what salvation is and how he is to obtain it, but how he may be kept from again falling, and how his faith may be confirmed, are fully told; and as one reads one cannot but feel that the writer is speaking only of what he knows and has experienced, and thus his words are of threefold power.

This book, though it is only small, will surely outlive its writer by many years; we hope as long as there are in this world sinners in need of its awakening power and its comforting truths.

Every one will be glad to hear that we are very far from having seen the last of the works of Charles Haddon Spurgeon, for there is a commentary on the Gospel of St. Matthew now in the press, which will be welcomed by many thousands who can imagine what they may expect from that which they have already seen from the prolific pen which has now been laid down for ever.

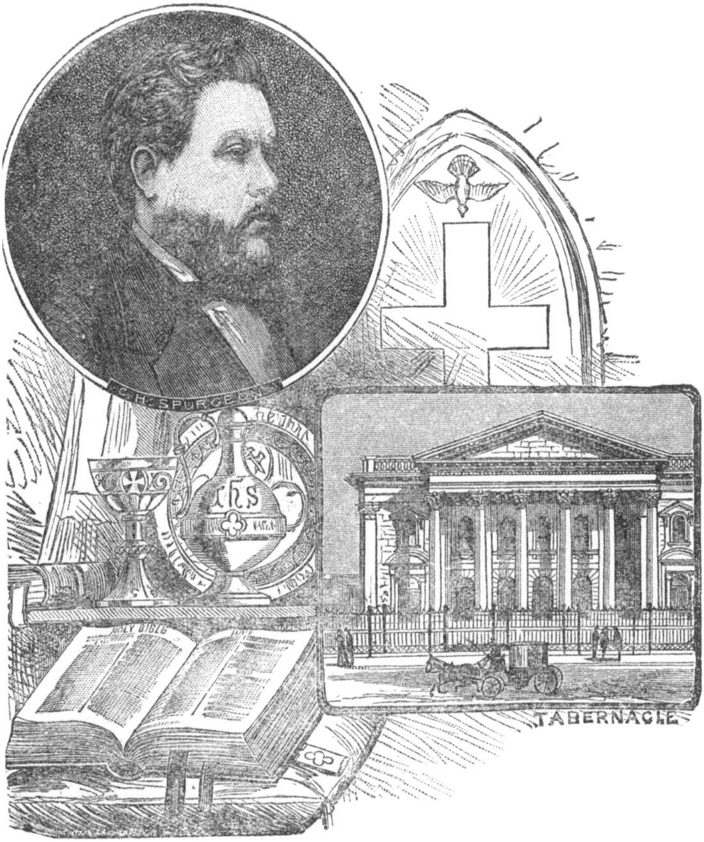
C. H. SPURGEON
ihs
HOLY BIBLE
TABERNACLE

CHAPTER XVIII.

GREATLY BELOVED.

Is there one, among all the good and great of our land, that the influenza—that plague of modern times—has not made more or less to feel its scourge? To count up the number of England's losses during the last few years which may be directly or indirectly traced to its attack would be impossible. Influenza and anxiety have become synonymous terms, and we have grown to dread the mention of its name in connection with those near and dear to us as that of some noxious reptile, ever crouching in hiding in readiness to rise and sting.

For some time the epidemic had spared the dearly loved pastor of the Metropolitan Tabernacle, but during the latter part of the month of May 1891 he also was stricken down. In his case the fever was not so cruel as it had been in some others. True, he had a sharp attack, and was left, as all who suffer from the ravages of this disease are left, in a most trying state of prostration. But that the attack had been of comparatively short duration is proved by the fact that on the first Sunday in June he occupied his place in the Tabernacle as usual. On this occasion Mr. Spurgeon appeared to be suffering from weakness; but that was no more than was to be expected, and while his people felt every sympathy, they also felt that they might congratulate both him and themselves that the illness which had stricken so many down to rise no more had passed him over with comparative leniency.

On the day following (Monday, June 7th), Mr. Spurgeon went into the eastern counties for the few days' rest and change which he needed to recruit his health. The weather was cold, and during the time of his stay Mr. Spurgeon was a good deal exposed to the ravages of the east wind, for he was in the vicinity of Stambourne, among the scenes of his childhood and early youth, and was naturally anxious to revisit as many of them as possible. Alas! it was here that he took the chill which eventually led to such fatal results. He returned home to Westwood feeling unwell, and on Friday June 12th, kept his room, hoping that a few days' quiet and nursing would put right all that was wrong, and he might be able to preach on the following Sunday. Little did he, or any of those who loved him so dearly, think that when he entered that room he entered it for twelve long weeks of terrible suffering, and for a protracted struggle between life and death such as has hardly ever been witnessed.

On Thursday, June 18th, it had been arranged that the pastor should join the children of the Orphanage, as usual, in their annual celebration of his birthday; but when the day came he was far too unwell to be able to leave his room, and the references made on that occasion to his condition showed that it was giving his friends very grave anxiety. He was at this time suffering greatly from prostration and debility, and each day, instead of the longed-for improvement, his attendants had the grief of seeing him grow weaker and weaker.

On Tuesday, June 23rd, it had been arranged that Mr. Spurgeon should preach at the opening of the Surrey Gardens Memorial Hall, in the building of which he had taken the deepest interest. The opening had already been once postponed on account of his former illness, and on

A SAD HOLIDAY. 295

Sunday, May 24th, he had written from his sick-room to the congregation at the Metropolitan Tabernacle:—"I do not propose to put off the collection for the Surrey Memorial, because your love is just as generous in my absence as in my presence. I want £270 still to complete the £3000 which the ground and buildings have cost. You will not allow me to have any trouble about that. . . . If this amount is supplied while I am ill, I shall come out with a double smile upon my face."

It was on the day of the opening of this building, which had been the object of so many trustful prayers, that Dr. R. M. Miller, of Norwood (Mr. Spurgeon's usual medical attendant), first considered his patient's condition to be so critical that he desired to consult with Dr. Kidd. The opinion of this gentleman was that there was danger, though he did not give voice to this thought till some days afterwards. He made a point of seeing Mr. Spurgeon on Wednesday, the day after the consultation, when it was patent to all that he was hourly getting worse instead of better. This day was one to which the children at the Orphanage had long looked forward with the greatest delight, as it was the date of their annual outing. The teachers and friends strove to prevent the heavy clouds which hung over their own spirits making any difference to the children's enjoyment, but there were none among the elders whose hearts were not heavy as they wandered about Whitstable in charge of their flock; and for them the one event of the day which brought any comfort was a prayer-meeting, which was held on the beach, on behalf of him who was so near and dear to them.

Thursday came, bringing with it no signs of improvement; indeed, the patient was visibly weaker. When the people gathered for the service in the evening at the Tabernacle consternation was on every face; and Mr. Stott (the assistant minister), instead of preaching a sermon, turned the service into a prayer-meeting. Many and fervent were the prayers offered, for all felt that there was only one Refuge in this hour of sorrow. He who now lay in such distressing weakness had taught by example and precept that in prayer Christians found always their mightiest weapon and their truest consolation. At this meeting it was arranged by Mr. Stott and the deacons that an all-day prayer-meeting on behalf of their suffering pastor should be held on the Monday following.

The people went to their homes on Thursday feeling somewhat comforted, but their faith was greatly tried on Friday, when the bulletin with regard to Mr. Spurgeon's condition stated that the past night had been the worst that he had experienced since the commencement of his illness. He was in such a prostrate condition that all who saw him felt the gravest apprehension as to the ultimate result. On this morning one of the telegrams received at Westwood was from the Conference then being held at Mildmay, asking for news of the patient's condition. The reply sent by Mr. Harrald was so very unfavourable that a gloom was thrown over the whole proceedings. Many were affected to tears, while all felt that in prospect of such a loss as then seemed imminent there was nothing that would avail but " effectual fervent prayer." The meeting at once agreed to the proposal that all business should be suspended, and that the time should be spent in offering prayers to God on behalf of the sufferer.

On Saturday the London papers were eagerly sought after for news of the progress of Mr. Spurgeon's illness. All sorts and conditions of men were alike anxious to obtain the latest particulars; and papers of every shade of political opinion were agreed in their expressions of sorrow for the trouble which had fallen upon the whole Christian world. In the *Standard* a long leader appeared, which spoke in most eulogistic terms of Mr. Spurgeon's life and work, and

AN ALL-DAY PRAYER MEETING. 297

deprecated as a loss which would be unspeakably heavy to Christians of all denominations the fatal termination of a life so valuable. On this day, however, Dr. Kidd, for the first time, allowed himself to express an opinion on the case; it was to the effect that, as a consequence of Mr. Spurgeon's having taken cold, gout had been forced in on the internal organs. In spite of the intense suffering, Dr. Kidd was of opinion that during the last two days some slight progress had been made.

The next day, Sunday, June 28th, will never be forgotten by those who took part in the services at the Tabernacle. The latest news of the pastor was posted on the outer gates, and tears of joy were shed by some as they saw that, for the first time in a whole long, anxious week, the words gave a glimmer of hope. The bulletin by Dr. Miller was as follows:—"Westwood, Sunday, June 28.—The Rev. C. H. Spurgeon has slept well, and is refreshed thereby. The improvement in the symptoms noticed yesterday by Dr. Kidd and myself is fully maintained, and even a little more marked." In the pews of the Metropolitan Tabernacle, and throughout many other London churches that Sunday, the following notice was circulated:—

"ILLNESS OF PASTOR C. H. SPURGEON.

"It is generally known that our beloved pastor is suffering from the results of a serious relapse following upon a recent attack of influenza. The best advice has been sought and acted upon, and although there is still cause for anxiety, the hope is fervently cherished that a life so precious will be spared, and that the Lord will bless the means employed for his speedy restoration to health.

"The officers of the church have arranged for an all-day prayer-meeting on Monday next. The meeting will commence at seven o'clock in the morning, and will be continued throughout the day. It is earnestly desired that those who cannot join in the meeting for prayer at the Tabernacle will arrange for special united supplication at some period of the day.

"'And this is the confidence that we have in Him, that if we ask anything according to His will He heareth us.'

"METROPOLITAN TABERNACLE,
"*June* 28*th*, 1891."

The services at the Tabernacle on this memorable Sunday were conducted by Dr. Sinclair Paterson in the morning, and by the Rev. W. Stott in the evening, both of whom endeavoured to make them as bright and cheery as possible under the sad circumstances.

The all-day prayer-meeting, which took place the next day, was one of the most remarkable gatherings which has ever taken place in that building, so noted for wonderful meetings. It commenced, as had been announced, at seven o'clock in the morning, and was conducted by Mr. William Olney, Rev. W. Stott, Rev. J. A. Spurgeon, Rev. W. Williams, of Upton Chapel, and Mr. J. T. Dunn successively. From the early hour named until nine o'clock at night members of the Tabernacle and friends who sympathised with them, and who loved their pastor "for his work's sake," continued to pass in and out. There were men and women present of different nationalities as well as of all shades of religious belief, and notably some who had taken prominent exception to Mr. Spurgeon's opinion and action during the ever-to-be-regretted "Down-grade controversy," and all were evidently in the deepest earnestness as they prayed that the life so dear and so useful might be spared. A telegram arriving from Westwood about noon was the cause of great thankfulness, as it stated that the patient was still slowly improving.

During the whole of the day letters, telegrams, and messages continued to arrive at the Tabernacle, telling how in other places as well as here prayer was ascending to God for the recovery of the great preacher. Among other telegrams were two which came from Canon Fleming and the Secretary of the Wesleyan Conference respectively, while letters were read from Dr. Angus, Rev. J. R. Wood, Rev. S. Pearson, the Secretary of the Peace Society, and many others. In the morning Mr. Thomas Olney and Professor Gracey addressed the meeting, and in the afternoon Mr. Henderson, of Ware, gave an address on "Praying truthfully." At about four o'clock the meeting was augmented by as many as one hundred and fifty poor mothers, who entered in a body.

At seven o'clock in the evening a very large number of people were present in the chapel. The Rev. W. Williams first presided, and he read from the prophet Isaiah the narrative of the sickness of Hezekiah, and drew a parallel between the case of the prophet and that of their beloved pastor. Hezekiah was stricken down just at the time when his work seemed most to need him, and their pastor was also, it seemed to them, as much needed as, or more than ever then, by their church with all its adjuncts of Christian service. In the prophet's case, God had given him fifteen more years in which to labour on earth for Him; and Mr. Williams felt that it might be that a similar mercy would be vouchsafed to themselves.

Rev. W. Stott alluded to the large number of friends who had joined their own members in earnest prayer to God that day, and spoke of the comfort it had given them to feel that all denominations had been in unity with them, referring particularly to a clergyman of the Church of England who, among others, had lifted up his voice in prayer within those walls that day. He told the assembly the good news that the improvement in Mr. Spurgeon's condition was maintained, and quoted Mrs. Spurgeon's remark when she had heard of the projected meeting—" If you do have such a day of prayer, it will prove to be a day of praise." God had been very good to them, and had allowed her prophecy to come true, for among all the other letters and telegrams was one from Mr. Spurgeon himself asking them to praise God for his partial recovery. At nine o'clock this remarkable meeting closed, having been open without intermission for fourteen hours.

Thankful indeed were thousands of hearts in this and other countries as day after day during the whole of that week the news of Rev. C. H. Spurgeon continued to be of steady improvement. Each day was felt to be a gain, and although it was known that he was very weak, it was felt that the probability was that Mr. Spurgeon would ultimately be raised up to take the place which it seemed impossible for any one else to fill. But, alas! dark and anxious days were coming for the members of the Tabernacle, and the many others who held him dear. The sunny days of the first fortnight of this July dragged by heavily indeed in the now silent home at Westwood, for the patient had a very serious relapse in the beginning of the month, and the darkened chamber in which the dear master of the house lay was the scene of a struggle which every day seemed to grow more and more unequal.

The first note of alarm was sounded on Saturday, July 4th, when the bulletin of Mr. Spurgeon's health was not nearly so favourable; and on Sunday, when the Rev. John Robertson, of Edinburgh, occupied the pulpit of the Tabernacle, he had nothing but bad news to communicate. There had been a return and increase of kidney congestion, which had induced nausea, drowsiness, and prostration. Dr. Kidd, who had been again called in, reported on this day: "On the most careful examination of the Rev. C. H. Spurgeon, I can testify that everything which medical art and skill can do is being done for the patient. The case is a very dangerous and difficult one. The most watchful care is given to his case day and night."

Before the sermon was preached, a letter from Mr. Harrald was read, which, however, did not give a ray of hope. "I need say little, except that Mr. Spurgeon is no better. He is in greater need of an all day of prayer than he was last Lord's Day. Let all plead day and night."

After a most touching and earnest prayer, Mr. Robertson preached a striking sermon on the rather singular subject (considering the circumstances of the time), "How to be Happy," basing his remarks on Psalm i.

The news of the pastor which reached the congregation at the evening service was still very mournful. The enormous building was full to overcrowding, many persons having to stand during the whole of the service. There seemed to be a spell over the vast assembly, and as the preacher urged upon the unconverted the solemn necessity of immediate decision for Christ, he was listened to in breathless silence.

It was resolved that the Tabernacle should be open for prayer the whole of the day following. Four prayer-meetings were held, and from morning till night many hundreds passed into the building to join in the supplication. The evening meeting was announced to be for members only, so there were not many strangers present, but among the visitors was the Rev. Newman Hall. At the end of this day a telegram reported a very slight improvement, but in the evening of the next day the news was worse.

The interest and sympathy felt in Mr. Spurgeon's critical condition did not abate, but rather increased as the time went by. Daily meetings for prayer were held at the Tabernacle, which continued to be attended by hundreds of anxious friends. The telegrams and letters of sympathy received at Westwood were innumerable, and it was said that at the Westwood post-office one man was solely employed in answering telegrams of inquiry. The most touching was a telegram from "son Tom" in Australia, who felt very keenly the necessity of being parted from the loved ones at home at such a time as that. The beloved wife of Mr. Spurgeon was wonderfully upheld during the whole of her husband's illness, but the strain of watching and anxiety began to tell upon the weak frame. It was thought advisable to call in the aid of other eminent physicians; not because Mr. Spurgeon's friends had not the greatest confidence in Doctors Kidd and Miller, but that the outside public might know that everything possible was being done. Sir Andrew Clarke and Sir Richard Quain being unable to attend, Doctor Russel Reynolds met the other doctors in consultation, and entirely concurred with their view and treatment of the case.

Towards the end of the week it was felt on all hands that the great worker was almost beyond human recovery. The *Baptist*, published on Friday, July 10th, said:—"Baptists are this week united in a common sorrow. They suffer together a terrible ordeal in awaiting new tidings from Mr. Spurgeon's bedside. And we have the sympathetic company of the whole Christian world. Moreover, outside the boundaries of the churches and of religious profession, a multitude of men manifest the keenest anxiety in the doctors' bulletins. The interest has at last become painfully intense. As an evidence of the place the patient holds in the affections of the people, this watchfulness and concern are strikingly suggestive. He has won his way to the hearts of men. His abilities may have served him to arrest and maintain popular attention, but only the power wielded by wonderful devotion to the noblest of aims will in any measure account for the widespread demonstration of sympathy witnessed within the last few days."

The *Record* (the chief organ of the Church of England) said: "His removal by death would, humanly speaking, be almost a national calamity He towers far and away above all his Nonconformist brethren in personal power and attractiveness, and his religious influence in the world is probably more widespread than that of any other living man. His unswerving fidelity to the cardinal truths of the gospel amidst the falling away that is unfortunately too obvious in his own and other Dissenting bodies, has had a most salutary effect, and his loss from this point of view would be a heavy blow to religious as distinguished from political Nonconformity."

Sunday, July 12th, was another day remarkable for its sadness at the Metropolitan Tabernacle. In the widespread anxiety that was experienced it was felt that the latest information was sure to be obtained there, and when the seats in the Tabernacle were thrown open they were immediately filled. No bulletin had as yet been posted outside the gates, and the coming of the minister and deacons was looked for with the most strained anxiety. When, however, Pastor H. O. Mackey entered with the deacons no bulletin had arrived. The ordinary routine of service was departed from, and as one after another lifted up his voice in prayer the feelings of many found vent in tears.

When at length the bulletin came the short sentences were listened to in breathless silence:—" Rev. C. H. Spurgeon passed a restless night. The waste of albumen is still very great, notwithstanding a fresh outburst of gout." Mr. Mackey delivered a discourse upon the Lord's Prayer, and announced that prayer-meetings would be held, as before, twice a day in that building.

The afternoon was remarkable for a meeting of upwards of two thousand Christian workers connected with the Tabernacle, and in the evening, instead of following the usual plan of service, the vast congregation resolved itself into a prayer-meeting. A message which arrived to the effect that the sufferer was, if anything, a trifle better than in the morning, was hailed with hearty ejaculations of "Thank God!" and the service closed in silent prayer.

During the day the following notices from the church officers were circulated :—

"In this time of the church's sorrow and anxiety the officers desire to acknowledge with gratitude to God the widespread and loving sympathy which the pastor's illness has called forth. The hearts of all have been touched, and united supplications have been constant and fervent. At the special meetings held at the Tabernacle all classes have been represented, and the presence of so many ministers at these gatherings is gratefully acknowledged. In the severe trial which they are called upon to sustain, Mrs. Spurgeon and the members of the family have been comforted by the loving sympathy of friends in all parts of the world; and their faith has been strengthened by the knowledge that prayer has been made unto God without ceasing for the recovery of one who is so dear to them, and whose ministry has been so graciously followed with such marvellous results."

A further announcement was as follows:—"To the church and congregation,—The officers of the church very earnestly appeal to the members of the church and congregation to accord a most hearty welcome to the honoured brethren who have so readily consented to occupy the pulpit during the lamented absence of our dear pastor. Assured of the love and loyalty of their fellow-members to our suffering pastor, they rely upon the hearty co-operation of all in maintaining the funds of the church. It is most important that seat-holders should renew their seat-tickets without delay, and that the free-will offerings towards the support of the institutions so dear to us all should not suffer any abatement. In this time of great anxiety and sorrow to us as a church we do well to bear in mind the gracious promise of our covenant-keeping God: 'Bring ye all the tithes into the storehouse, that there may be meat in mine house, and prove Me now herewith, saith the Lord of hosts, if I will not open you the windows of heaven, and pour you out a blessing, that there shall not be room enough to receive it' (Mal. iii. 10)."

The public interest during this week rose to a pitch of painful anxiety. The bulletins issued spoke almost uniformly of loss of strength, delirium, and prostration, and it was known that if a change for the better did not soon take place all hope would be over. The Prince of Wales instructed Colonel Knollys to write to Dr. Kidd for particulars, and gave him a message to convey to the great preacher if he had opportunity. Many ladies and gentlemen called at Westwood; among others the wife and daughter of the Archbishop of Canterbury, Lord and Lady Kinnaird, Mr. George Williams, Sir Charles Lawson, Sir Frederick Perkins, and Rev. W. Arthur. The telegrams which poured in from all parts caused a complete block on one morning at the Beulah Hill Post Office. It is impossible to enumerate the associations and societies who in this way showed their interest, but among others telegrams were received from the committee of the Baptist Missionary Society, the Nonconformist ministers of Wrexham, the South London Presbytery, the Primitive Methodist General Committee, the Denbigh, Flint, and Merioneth Baptists in session at Festiniog, the British and Foreign Sailors' Society, an assembly of ministers at Grimsby, a meeting of the Loyal Orange Institution at Netley Abbey, the London Wesleyan Council, the Chesham Sunday School Alliance, the Lambeth Auxiliary of the Sunday School Union, the Baptist ministers of Hitchin, the Council of the Evangelical Alliance, and by General Booth, from four thousand salvation officers assembled in council.

The sympathy expressed by eminent churchmen was very marked; the Bishop of Rochester telegraphed to Mrs.

Spurgeon, "As I am myself ill and unable to call and inquire for Mr. Spurgeon, I am anxious to express to you my warm sympathy with you in your anxiety," and received the reply, "I am deeply grateful for your kind message of sympathy. My dear husband is no worse to-day. I regret that you also suffer so much. May the Lord comfort you." Doctor Maclagan, Archbishop-Designate of York, sent "prayerful sympathy." Canon Sinclair, in asking the prayers of the congregation at St. Paul's on Sunday afternoon for the Rev. C. H. Spurgeon, referred in a feeling manner to his life and work. The Rector of Newington (the parish in which the Tabernacle is situated), between whom and Mr. Spurgeon the most kindly feeling always existed, wrote most sympathetically to the wife of his afflicted friend.

At length, when even the most hopeful had begun to despair, the dark cloud began to show signs of lifting. After two terribly anxious days on Wednesday and Thursday, July 15th and 16th, a decided change for the better took place. Mr. Spurgeon was able to take some natural sleep, which resulted in a visible gain of strength on the Friday, while Saturday's bulletin stated that for the first time in four weeks he had been able to take solid food. At first the improvement seemed almost too good to be true, but as hour after hour went by, and there was no falling back, the watchers in that stricken household felt that they might "rejoice with trembling," and the thousands who almost as one man had scanned the papers for tidings, dreading each day the worst, drew a long breath of relief.

On the first day when there was felt to be a ray of hope (Friday, July 17th), Mrs. Spurgeon received an expression of sympathy which she appreciated most highly, in the form of a letter from Mr. Gladstone. We give the letter and its reply, the latter enriched with a line in Mr. Spurgeon's own handwriting:—

"CORTON, LOWESTOFT, *July 16th*, 1891.

"MY DEAR MADAM,—In my own home, darkened at the present time, I have read with studied interest the daily accounts of Mr. Spurgeon's illness, and I cannot help conveying to you the earnest assurance of my sympathy with you and with him, and of my cordial admiration, not only of his splendid powers, but still more of his devoted and unfailing character. May I humbly commend you and him in all contingencies to the infinite stores of the Divine love and mercy, and subscribe myself, my dear madam, faithfully yours,
"W. E. GLADSTONE."

The reply contained a postscript by Mr. Spurgeon himself:—

"WESTWOOD, UPPER NORWOOD, *July 18th*, 1891.

"DEAR MR. GLADSTONE,—Your words of sympathy have a special significance and tenderness, coming from one who has just passed through the deep waters which seem now to threaten me. I thank you warmly for your expression of regard for my beloved husband, and with all my heart I pray that the consolations of God may abound towards you even as they do to me. Although we cannot yet consider the dear patient out of danger, the doctors have to-day issued a somewhat more hopeful bulletin. I feel it an honour to be allowed to say that I shall ever be your grateful friend, "S. SPURGEON.

"P.S.—Yours is a word of love such as those only write who have been into the King's country, and have seen much of His face. My heart's love to you. "C. H. SPURGEON."

The bereavement which Mr. Gladstone and his family had suffered (referred to in the above letters) was the loss of his eldest son, Mr. W. H. Gladstone, who died suddenly on July 8th.

During the whole of Mr. Spurgeon's illness only those to whom he was accustomed were allowed to be in attendance upon him. The labour of love was shared among his own family and by a faithful man-servant "George," who, with other men-servants, took turns in watching at night. Mrs. Spurgeon was most wonderfully upheld through the trying time, and in answer to countless prayers she received "special grace for special need."

It may be interesting here to give a few extracts from

newspaper articles which appeared about this time, as showing the high and universal esteem in which Mr. Spurgeon was held. The *St. James's Gazette*, a paper representing advanced Conservative principles, had the following:—" In spite of a less pleasant report this morning, we may almost hope that Mr. Spurgeon has taken a turn for the better. Yesterday he was able to take solid food, and the doctors then considered that his progress, though slow, was satisfactory. The universal feeling would be one of thankfulness that a valuable life had been spared, and that an eloquent preacher and an earnest worker had been snatched from the jaws of death. His long and still anxious illness has served to show how much his sterling honesty of purpose is appreciated by those who differ from his theological views. Archbishops and bishops have sent messages of sympathy, while religious organisations in all parts of the world have testified their concern at the dangerous illness of the great minister."

The *Inverness Courier* said:—" Very great interest is taken in the North of Scotland in the health of Rev. C. H. Spurgeon, whose sermons enjoy a wide circulation both in town and country. It is now over twenty years since he preached in Dingwall at the opening of the fine new Free Church built for the late Dr. Kennedy. There are many, however, who still remember that visit with pleasure, and who have never ceased since to take a personal interest in Mr. Spurgeon's health and labours. They will be sorry to see that the reports of his condition are of such an unfavourable character."

The *Western Morning News*, alluding to Mr. Spurgeon and the demonstration of feeling around his sick-bed, said: —" He had in his early days, perhaps, to win his right to be considered as a leader. His critics saw nothing in him save what they were pleased to call his vulgarity, and we are bound to add that he repaid them in kind. At one time he regarded a bishop of the Church of England as a God-forsaken fraud, and looked upon a bishop with horror. But of late years he and the Archbishop of Canterbury have been personal friends, and the grounds at Addington were always as much open to Mr. Spurgeon as to the Primate of all England himself. There was a time when Bishop Wilberforce, whose sense of humour sometimes ran away with him—as it did with Mr. Spurgeon—could at the dinner table reply to an expression of a wish that there was a Spurgeon in the Church of England, by raising his episcopal finger, and saying with the mock solemnity of fatherly rebuke, 'Thou shalt not covet thy neighbour's ass.' But now all the bishops who have been brought into personal relation with Mr. Spurgeon, even the slightest, show their personal interest in his welfare. The outburst of feeling around Mr. Spurgeon's sick-bed has been one of the most gratifying signs of the times."

It is needless to say that the service at the Tabernacle on the Sunday following the improvement in Mr. Spurgeon's condition was characterised by a spirit of great joy and thankfulness. The Rev. D. M'Ewan conducted a bright service in the morning, and in the evening Mr. Stott preached to the young.

The next week (the last in July) was one of fairly steady progress. The public interest felt in the course of the illness by no means abated. The Prince of Wales again made inquiries. The Earl and Countess of Aberdeen, Sir W. and Lady Lawson, and many others, called at Westwood. Messages of inquiry and sympathy came from the Bishop of Worcester; Archdeacon Taylor, Liverpool; Canon Sidebotham, Mentone; Rev. W. Hay Aitken, Dr. Rainy, Dr. John Hall, New York; Dr. T. Smith, Moderator of the Free Church General Assembly; the Congregational Churches of the Northern District of London, the Stratford District Nonconformist Churches, the London Baptist

Board, the Association of Free Ministry, Hanley; the Baptist Home Mission of Scotland (Dr. Landels, chairman); the Welsh Congregational Union at Wrexham; Messrs. Evan Spicer and J. Carvell Williams, on behalf of the Liberation Society, etc.

From this time forward Mr. Spurgeon made slow improvement each week. The long days of August crept slowly by, each day bringing with it a very little more strength to the invalid. Throughout the weary period of convalescence his spirits kept wonderfully bright, and his messages to his dear flock were characterised by great faith. On Sunday, August 2nd, he wrote to them:—" Loving thanks for your prayers, which I believe God is hearing every day for me. My head will not act, but my heart does. God bless you all!"

The doctor's reports, however, in spite of the gain of strength (which was of course a wonderful advantage), stated that the serious malady from which Mr. Spurgeon was suffering was by no means cured, so that his friends in the midst of their joy felt uneasily apprehensive.

At the end of August he was able to pass part of each day sitting in a chair, which relieved the monotony of lying in bed; and during the first fortnight in September he took exercise in a wheeled chair in the garden at Westwood. A letter which was written to his people at the Tabernacle about this time will give an idea of his condition :—

"*September* 13*th*, 1891.

"DEAR FRIENDS,—I cannot write much, but I cannot withhold my heart and my pen from saying, 'O bless the Lord with me, and let us exalt His name together.' This week has, by its fine weather, set me free from a three months' captivity. Those believers of all denominations who so lovingly prayed for me will now help me to praise the Lord. Verily, the loving God heareth prayer.

"I fear my doctors would have a mournful tale to tell of my disease, and from inward consciousness I must agree with them; but I FEEL better, and I get into the open air, and therefore I hope my face is turned toward recovery. Reading, writing, thinking, etc., are not yet easy to me. I am forced to vegetate. I fear it will be long before I can be at my beloved work.

"I send my hearty love to you all, and my humble gratitude to that great army of praying people who have been heard of the Lord in their cries for the prolongation of my life. May we believe more, pray more, and therefore receive more.—Yours, in bonds of true affection,
"C. H. SPURGEON."

By the beginning of October Mr. Spurgeon had so far advanced as to be able to go to Eastbourne for a fortnight's change of air and scene. The sojourn by the sea wrought wonders for him, and he returned home in remarkably good spirits. It was thought quite safe for him to entertain the idea of going to Mentone, and arrangements were made with that end in view. In the meantime it had been decided that during the pastor's long absence his place should be occupied by Dr. Pierson, of Philadelphia, a most able preacher and zealous Christian worker. It is remarkable that before receiving Mr. Spurgeon's letter asking him to occupy his pulpit, Dr. Pierson had written offering to come. In a loving letter of farewell to his people, Mr. Spurgeon wrote:—

"I have called Dr. Pierson, from America, with the view of an advance all along the line. I was bearing the cause on my heart, and thinking that as you had heard so many different men, it might be well if, before my return, some one would be with you for a season—the same preacher for a time. No one suggested Dr. Pierson to me; it came from my heart, and I think I was led of the Lord. This beloved brother is the author of several powerful works on the side of the truth, and a man of burning missionary zeal. I have had the closest fellowship of heart with him as a champion of the faith. Long ago he said to me that he would give up every occupation to serve me, and I believed him. I sat down and wrote him, but the remarkable fact is that he had already written me, so that the next day I heard from him, hinting that a time had come when his former offer might be renewed. I believe it is of the Lord. I am responsible for the action, and I look not for blame, but for the manifest approval of my Lord. Let nothing flag. There may be some deficiencies to be made up on my return, but let these be as light as possible. If friends took the seats there would be none. I am not going to burden myself with any care. I leave the flock with the great Shepherd of the sheep, and I feel that you will be both led and fed. The Lord grant that, whether I speak or am silent, rejoice or suffer, live or die, all may be to His glory and the progress of His Gospel. I am a debtor now to all the churches and to all classes of society. The sympathy shown me every day almost breaks my heart with gratitude. What am I? One thing I know, I am your loving servant in Christ Jesus, and the Lord's messenger to many, many souls who never saw me, but who have read the sermons. To you at the Tabernacle I am very near of kin. God bless you all.—Yours in One Head, C. H. SPURGEON."

On Monday, October 26th, Mr. Spurgeon, with his dear wife and brother, and Mr. Harrald, his private secretary, set out for Mentone. The journey was regarded by Mr. Spurgeon's friends with a good deal of apprehension, but everything that could be thought of was done to relieve its tedium. As an instance of most delicate forethought and kindness, it may be mentioned that Baron Rothschild placed his special carriage at the disposal of Mr. Spurgeon for the long railway journey, an attention which was gratefully appreciated, and which no doubt helped very considerably to make the time of travelling more pleasant and easy. So well was the journey borne that Mr. Spurgeon telegraphed on reaching Mentone—" Not wearied, but improved by thousand miles' journey. Almost miraculous. Hallelujah! Spurgeon."

Thankful indeed were thousands of hearts when this news was received, and most earnestly and prayerfully did they hope that the improvement might continue, and that the people's preacher might be fully restored. For many weeks this seemed probable. True, Mr. Spurgeon's condition varied, but on the whole the news that came through November and December was of a hopeful character. At the end of the year the pastor wrote to his people:—" I have nearly finished thirty-eight years of my ministry among you, and have completed thirty-seven volumes of published sermons preached in your midst. Yet we are not wearied of each other. I shall hail the day when I may again speak with you."

CHAPTER XIX.

REST FOR THE WARRIOR.

It was a great pleasure to both Mr. and Mrs. Spurgeon that they were for the first time able to be together at Mentone. After so many years of suffering and weakness, it was not to be expected that the delicate companion of all the best years of his life should be able at the last to be with him; but so it was, and it will ever be a joyous memory to the bereaved widow that he had the gladness, during those three delightful months, of pointing out to her the beautiful scenery, and all the places and views which he especially admired.

All the world knows of the two addresses delivered at Mentone on the last evening of 1891 and the first morning of 1892. They are printed in full in the *Sword and Trowel* for February, under the pathetic title, "Breaking the Long Silence." In the last he told the friends assembled what he saw in the picture—A Pathway Made, A Guide Provided, Strength for the Journey Given, and a Power Over-ruling All. The following are the closing words :—

"One thing more, and this is brightness itself: this year we trust we shall see *God glorified* by us and in us. If we realise our chief end, we reach our highest enjoyment. It is the delight of the renewed heart to think that God can get glory out of such poor creatures as we are. 'God is light.' We cannot add to His brightness; but we may act

AT THE GATES OF THE CEMETERY.

as reflectors, which, though they have no light of their own, yet, when the sun shines upon them, reflect his beams and send them where, without such reflection, they might not have come. When the Lord shines upon us, we will cast that light upon dark places, and make those who sit in the shadow of death to rejoice in Jesus our Lord. We hope that God has been in some measure glorified in some of us during the past year, but we trust He will be glorified by us far more in the year which now begins. We will be content to glorify God either actively or passively. We would have it so happen that, when our life's history is written, whoever reads it will not think of us as 'self-made men,' but as the handiwork of God, in whom His grace is magnified. Not in us may men see the clay, but the Potter's hand. They said of one, 'He is a fine preacher;' but of another they said, 'We never notice how he preaches, *but we feel that God is great.*' We wish our whole life to be a sacrifice; an altar of incense continually smoking with sweet perfume unto the Most High. Oh, to be borne through the year on the wings of praise to God; to mount from year to year, and raise at each ascent a loftier and yet lowlier song unto the God of our life! The vista of a praiseful life will never close, but continue throughout eternity. From psalm to psalm, from hallelujah to hallelujah, we will ascend the hill of the Lord; until we come into the Holiest of all, where, with veiled faces, we will bow before the Divine Majesty in the bliss of endless adoration. Throughout this year may the Lord be with you! Amen."

The fact that Mr. Spurgeon was able to deliver these addresses greatly encouraged the Tabernacle friends, who hoped, as he did, that they would soon be together again. The month had much that was overwhelmingly sad in it. The death of the young Duke of Clarence, almost on the eve of his marriage, touched every heart with grief. Mr. Spurgeon sent the following telegram :—

"Prince of Wales, Sandringham, England.—Grateful memories of generous kindness to me in my affliction constrain me respectfully to present assurance of tender sympathy with you and the Princess. Fervently I pray God to sustain and bless you both.—Spurgeon, Mentone."

He scarcely expected a reply, but the response came—

"Spurgeon, Mentone.—We send our heartfelt thanks for your kind message of sympathy.—Prince of Wales, Sandringham."

The nation sorrowed also for the death of the great good man Cardinal Manning, and before January was ended came the news that Mr. Spurgeon was again seriously ill, and with no strength to battle against the attack.

"I shall be home in February," he had said.

He was pleasantly occupied in preparing a little volume, *Drives at Mentone*, for which friends were preparing photographs.

On the 17th of January Mr. Spurgeon again conducted service at the hotel. The last hymn he gave out was Rutherford's—

"The sands of time are sinking,
The dawn of heaven breaks."

And his closing prayer was most impressive. It is good news for the entire Christian world that he had prepared a Commentary on Matthew, and he read a portion of this to the little assembled company.

The next day he took his last drive, and that evening he became seriously ill.

"My work is done," he said to Mr. Harrald; and his last message to his people was this—"*£100 hearty thank-offering toward Tabernacle expenses. Love to all friends.*"

It had to come at last—the death that had been fought back by prayer—the agonised prayer of a multitude no man can number—"Spare this useful life for future usefulness." Were the prayers then in vain?

THE LAST SUNDAY.

"Heaven was besieged with prayers, nor was one vain,
God's great light shone when lights of earth grew dim
And the 'abundant entrance' was for him
And God's 'Well done, good servant,' quenched all pain."

A great gloom hung over the Metropolitan Tabernacle on Sunday, January 31st. Even on Saturday the people could not rest. Some men and women as they went to work in the morning held a prayer-meeting in the little lecture hall. Another meeting was held later in the day, when fervent prayers were again offered that the pastor's life might be spared. Mr. Dunn, one of the deacons, presided. He reminded them of what Mr. Spurgeon often said—"Speak not of C.H.S. but of I.H.S.—Jesu Hominum Salvator,"—but they could not be unmindful of the many who had need to cry for his restoration to health. Then came more prayers until one o'clock had sounded. Three in the afternoon saw another gathering, at which the same deep and earnest supplications ascended; and then, when the shades of evening had fallen, came the largest meeting of the day, the usual Saturday gathering for prayer.

In the deep shadow of that never-to-be-forgotten Sunday the Church stayed itself on God. Dr. Pierson, whose ministrations during the sad time were, by Divine help, wonderfully efficient, read a letter which Mr. Harrald had written on the 28th, saying how ill the pastor was, and begging the people to pray earnestly still. The service was intensely solemn, and was made more so by the few minutes of silent prayer in which all engaged. The following telegrams arrived during the day:—

"MENTONE, *January* 31*st*, 11 A.M.

"The Rev. C. H. Spurgeon has had another very restless night, and his condition this morning gives cause for the greatest anxiety. He can still take a small quantity of milk.   (Signed) FITZ HENRY.

"3.30 P.M.—The Rev. C. H. Spurgeon is now insensible, and much weaker than he was this morning.   (Signed) FITZ HENRY.

"6.30 P.M.—Mr. Spurgeon's condition this evening is extremely critical. The rev. gentleman does not recognise his wife, and appears to be quite unconscious. He refuses food. Milk is forced down his throat, but is not retained. Telegrams of sympathy are being received from all quarters, and a large number of persons have called to inquire the latest news during the day.

"10 P.M.—Mr. Spurgeon is sinking fast, and all hope of his recovery has been abandoned. He is quite unconscious, and suffers no pain."

As the time for the evening service drew near an immense crowd gathered outside the Tabernacle, and almost immediately after the gates were opened they filled every seat in the place. The service was a very solemn one, and the tones of Dr. Pierson's voice, as he again besought of God to spare the life that was so unutterably dear, vibrated with emotion. The service was short, and after the telegram had been read it resolved itself into a prayer-meeting. But when the congregation broke up every one felt that the calamity was impending, and the deacons remained at the Tabernacle in case further news should arrive.

No one can say in how many churches throughout the kingdom, and indeed in all parts of the world, the prayers of the crowds were joined to those of the Tabernacle. The afternoon telegram was read, and everywhere a sense of loss began to be felt.

In the meantime the watchers around the deathbed in a small bed-room on the first floor of the Hotel Beau Rivage, at Mentone, knew that the end was come. He had been unconscious for several days, although when he spoke it seemed that his thoughts were running on his beloved wife and his work at the Tabernacle; but there were no parting words, for he did not recover consciousness at the last. Mrs. Spurgeon watched by his side, as did also Miss Thorne, Mr. Harrald, his faithful secretary, Dr. Fitz Henry, his con stant medical attendant, and two other friends.

At eleven o'clock on Sunday night, in perfect peace, the end came.

Mr. Harrald, the "armour-bearer," as Mr. Spurgeon called him, immediately knelt down and thanked God that the dear sufferer was at rest, and prayed that strength to bear the sorrow might be given to those who had to bear it in all its keenness. And then Mrs. Spurgeon softly raised her voice in praise for the beloved one whose love and companionship had been hers for so long, and in prayer for the help which she so greatly needed now.

Early the next morning printed copies of the following telegram were affixed to the rails of the Metropolitan Tabernacle:—

"SPURGEON'S TABERNACLE, LONDON.
"MENTONE, 11.50.
" Our beloved pastor entered heaven 11.5 Sunday night.
"HARRALD."

The black-bordered newspapers were not needed; the news itself brought mourning to millions. It will never be known—indeed it does not matter—how many voices were raised in his praise, but seldom has there been such a consensus of opinion in regard to any man as was expressed when the news spread that Charles Haddon Spurgeon had passed away. The newspapers were almost unanimous in their testimony. "For more than one generation Mr. Spurgeon has been the foremost of Nonconformist ministers, fitted for his position by a rare union of qualities," said the *Times*. " His removal is not only a terrible loss to the vast congregation he had gathered round him at the Metropolitan Tabernacle, and a serious blow to Evangelical Nonconformity, but it leaves a blank that can hardly be filled in the pulpit oratory and the ministerial energy of the day," said the *Daily News*. "A great, a fearless, and a faithful minister of the Gospel," said the *Daily Telegraph*. "There was only one Spurgeon," said the *Daily Chronicle*. " Mr. Spurgeon's fame while he lived belonged to a sect, but a larger and, as we think, a more liberal world will claim the right to place a wreath upon his hearse," said the *Standard*. And the *Christian World* said:—" The great career is now consummated, and we can survey it from end to end. ' Call no man happy till he dies,' said the classic proverb. Mr. Spurgeon is happy in his death, crowning, as it does, a life lived in the full blaze of publicity, but against which no man's finger can point a reproach, and which, beginning with predictions of failure from numberless critics, ends amid the universal esteem of his countrymen and of Christendom."

There was scarcely a church or chapel in the kingdom where, on the following Sunday, there was not some reference made to him and the lessons of his life; and loving, grateful, regretful words were spoken by preachers of every shade of thought and theology. The feeling of the universal Church was: "A Prince is fallen in Israel: who can ever fill the place that he has left vacant?" And yet all hearts were filled with thankfulness for his marvellous life and labour.

All sorts of affectionate stories were told of him in print during the few days that followed. His great kindness and tenderness of heart and manner were remembered with loving regret. One told how once, when his dog had misbehaved himself, Mr. Spurgeon threw his stick at him; but the dog could not believe that he meant it, and, picking up the stick, he carried it between his teeth and laid it at his master's feet, wagging his tail, and looking into his kind face for the usual response.

Another told of the humour that lighted up everything, even when trouble was upon him. Mr. Mackey said that when Mr. Spurgeon's son Thomas was visiting him once in indifferent health his father wrote—" Take care of him. I now wish him at the other end of the earth, for he coughs a good deal."

Many said " The poor orphans will be doubly orphaned now," and they remembered a story told of his kindness to one of them. It was visiting-day at the Orphanage, and the mothers and aunts and other relatives were there with the boys. The president was sitting on one of the seats in the grounds when a little boy came up to him.

"Mr. Spurgeon," said the child, "I want to sit up there between you two gentlemen, because I have something to say to you."

"Come up, and say on then."

"Mr. Spurgeon, if there was a little boy who hadn't got any mother or sisters to see him and give him things, when all the other little boys had, don't you think somebody ought to give him a penny?"

The quick tears came into Mr. Spurgeon's eyes, and he said, "Here is sixpence for you, my boy; run off and enjoy it."

Yet another tells the story of how Mr. Spurgeon had received a present of a five-pound note to help toward his expenses at Mentone. When happening to meet a young man who was there also for his health, he said, "Ah, that note is for you. You are getting rather hard up, aren't you? Take this."

But indeed a whole volume might be filled with such reminiscences, for scarcely a friend met friend who had not something good to tell of that vivid personality which had passed away from earth.

But one thing should not be forgotten. An interviewer from one of the worldly society journals of the day once went to see him, and Mr. Spurgeon talked so simply and sincerely of God and his goodness, Christ and his salvation, that the man was wonderfully impressed. We are not sure that Mr. Spurgeon did not even propose to him that they should have a little prayer together, for it would not have been unlike him.

"He is the last of his kind," said more than a few; but if he were, there would indeed be even more reason to lament his death.

There were some extraordinary scenes at the Tabernacle. Fears were at first felt lest the remains of their beloved pastor should be buried at Mentone, but the news speedily came that he was to be brought " home to rest."

There was, however, a very interesting memorial service held in the Scotch Presbyterian Church at Mentone, at the opening of which Mr. Spurgeon had preached a year before; and representatives of all sections of the Christian Church gathered round the olive-wood coffin which contained the body of him whom they had loved and esteemed, Canon Sidebotham, the Rev. A. M. Topp, the Vicar of Clifton, and many others being present. The Rev. J. E. Somerville delivered an address, and they sang " For ever with the Lord," while the coffin was borne from the church to the railway station.

On the Sunday at the Tabernacle Dr. Pierson so conducted the services as to still more endear him to the hearts of the people, and after the communion service Mr. Thomas Olney announced that the Rev. James Spurgeon had consented to continue as pastor-in-charge, and that Dr. Pierson, in response to an earnest appeal, was willing to remain the officiating minister.

The body arrived in London on Monday, February 8th, and was borne to the College. Beautiful flowers had covered the coffin at Mentone, but Mrs. Spurgeon had sent a number of magnificent palm branches, which waved above it when, during the next day, more than fifty thousand persons passed through the College common room. Exquisite floral tributes were also there—one from Scotland in the shape of an anchor, composed of lilies and hyacinths, and bearing some words from Mr. Spurgeon's letter, " The sun shines at length;" and another a large floral harp of lilies, with one broken string, from Ireland, accompanied with a sword and trowel in violets. On Wednesday there were services all day: in the morning for the members

MEMORIAL SERVICE IN THE TEBERNANCE

of the Tabernacle Church, in the afternoon for ministers and students, and in the evening for Christian workers of all denominations. Mr. Ira D. Sankey was present at this meeting, and sang four lines which touched all hearts—

> "Sleep on, beloved, sleep and take thy rest :
> Lay down thy head upon thy Saviour's breast ;
> We love thee well : but Jesus loves thee best—
> Good-night ! good-night ! good-night ! "

When this service was over the most remarkable of the series commenced, for at 10.30 on Wednesday night the Tabernacle was packed chiefly with men who resided in the neighbourhood, and who thus showed their love for the departed minister.

The funeral the next day was one of the most impressive that even the metropolis has ever witnessed. More than sixty societies sent representatives. The Legation of the United States was represented. The Baroness and Mr. Burdett-Coutts, M.P., and several members of Parliament were present, with many well-known clergymen of the Church of England and all denominations. After a short service in the Tabernacle the coffin was borne down the aisle to the hearse while the Orphanage children sang—

> " Though art gone to the grave,
> But we will not deplore thee."

The coffin was placed in an open hearse. On the top of it, "as both breastplate and pall," was the open Bible, with a scarlet ribbon marking the text, " Look unto Me and be ye saved," which was the means of Mr. Spurgeon's conversion. The coffin bore the following inscription :—

In ever-loving memory of
CHARLES HADDON SPURGEON,
Born at Kelvedon, June 19, 1834.
Fell asleep in Jesus at Mentone, Jan. 31, 1892.
" I have fought a good fight, I have finished my course, I have kept the faith."

There were forty official carriages, and about two hundred in all in the procession. As it started the voices of the Orphanage children were again heard singing Sir Arthur Sullivan's beautiful setting of the "Hymn of the Homeland"—

> "The Homeland! the Homeland!
> The land of the freeborn;
> There's no night in the Homeland,
> But aye the fadeless morn.
> I'm sighing for the Homeland,
> My heart is aching here;
> There's no pain in the Homeland
> To which I'm drawing near."

All along the route public-houses were closed, shops had their shutters up, flags were half-mast, and the people stood mournful and silent. The bells of St. Mary's, Newington, and of St. Mark's, Kennington, were tolled, and no signs of respectful sympathy were anywhere lacking. Ten thousand persons were admitted by ticket to Norwood Cemetery. The grave, under the shadow of the chapel cloister, had been lined with flowers and mosses; and the coffin, with the Bible and its canopy of palms sent from Mentone, was placed in the vault.

At the special request of the family, conveyed through Mr. Archibald Brown, the spectators did not uncover their heads. The coffin was lowered amongst the palms and flowers of the grave in silence. Then Mr. Archibald Brown gave out a couple of verses of "There is a fountain filled with blood," and it was sung softly by the sad multitude to a familiar tune. The commitment passage, which is part of the Nonconformist ritual, was recited, but there was no symbolising of earth to earth by the sprinkling of dust or ashes. After a brief pause for silent prayer, Mr. Archibald Brown, pointing to the coffin and its open Bible, said:—

"Beloved President, Faithful Pastor, Prince of Preachers,

FAREWELL.

Brother Beloved, Dear Spurgeon,—We bid thee not farewell, but only for a little while 'good-night.' Thou shalt rise soon at the first dawn of the Resurrection Day of the redeemed. Yet is not the 'good-night' ours to bid, but thine. It is we who linger in the darkness; thou art in God's own light. Our night, too, shall soon be past, and with it all our weeping. Then, with thine, our songs shall greet the morning of a day that knows no cloud nor close; for there is no night there. Hard worker in the field, thy toil is ended. Straight has been the furrow thou hast ploughed. No looking back has marred thy course. Harvests have followed thy patient sowing, and heaven is already rich with thine ingathered sheaves, and shall be still enriched through years yet lying in eternity. Champion of God, thy battle long and nobly fought is over. The sword which clave to thine hand has dropped at last; the palm branch takes its place. No longer does the helmet press thy brow, oft weary with its surging thoughts of battle; the victor's wreath from the Great Commander's hand has already proved thy full reward. Here for a little while shall rest thy precious dust. Then shall thy well-beloved come, and at His voice thou shalt spring from thy couch of earth fashioned like unto His glorious body. Then spirit, soul, and body shall magnify thy Lord's redemption. Until then, beloved, sleep. We praise God for thee, and by the blood of the everlasting covenant hope and expect to praise God with thee. Amen."

The Bishop of Rochester, stepping forward, pronounced the Benediction, with right hand uplifted, and thus ended a memorably simple, solemn, and beautiful burial.

Among the last words that Mr. Spurgeon wrote for the *Sword and Trowel* were these:—

"If any one had prophesied twenty years ago that a Dissenting minister—and a very outspoken one, too—would be prayed for in many parish churches, and in Westminster

Abbey and at St. Paul's Cathedral, it would not have been believed; but it was so. There is more love in the hearts of Christian people than they know of themselves. *We mistake our divergencies of judgment for differences of heart;* but they are far from being the same thing. For my part, I believe that all spiritual persons are already one."

It is good to think that he had that pleasure, though he could never have guessed how much his death would do to bring Christian men more closely together.

"What was the secret of Spurgeon's power?" was the question asked in many quarters. And many answers were given, but they were right who declared that "it was his spiritual force which drew men." It was "Christ in him, the hope of glory," which made him what he was. This kept him steady during his forty years of marvellous popularity, and made him humble as a little child through all the love that was lavished upon him; this led him to care for the orphan, and be open-handed and liberal to any who needed his help; this fired his heart and directed his eloquent tongue; this kept his faith clear, and his life in harmony with it; and this it was that gave him such a Gospel to preach as the crowd was dying to hear. He believed, and therefore he spoke. And he, "being dead, yet speaketh;" for the good which such men do lives long after them.

APPENDIX.

No reference has been made in the foregoing pages to the theological controversy into which, in 1887 and subsequent years, Mr. Spurgeon threw his whole nature; but the book would not be a complete history of his life if this part of his work were ignored. He was born a soldier as well as a builder, and believing himself unmistakably called of God to wield his sword in defence of the "Old Truths" as against "Modern Thought," he deliberately took his place in the forefront of the battle, not without counting the cost, though he could not help feeling most deeply the pain. No man was more greatly beloved by the Baptist Union than Charles Haddon Spurgeon. At no time of his life did the mention of his name at its assemblies fail to produce an enthusiastic manifestation of affectionate feeling towards him; and it is possible that if he had continued to attend the meetings, and had seen and heard for himself the spirit which characterised them, instead of having to depend upon reports—however good—he would have found less to fear, and more to hope in regard to his brethren. But he was very jealous for his

God; and all that he did was done from the highest motives, and with a single desire for the glory of his Master.

The Baptist Union in 1883 met at Leicester; and at the public reception of the delegates a Unitarian minister gave an address, and was well received. This grieved some ministers and delegates, who wrote to Mr. Spurgeon about it. He and they considered it a very grave sign, and soon afterward, in the *Sword and Trowel*, Mr. Spurgeon published a strong and yet tenderly-worded protest. He said that though he had a desire to look at things in a favourable light, and though he believed that there was no uniform desire among the brethren to fraternise with those who reckon the Lord Jesus to be no more than man, yet he believed the bond of union had suffered a severe strain, and he for one could have no fellowship with those who rejected the Gospel. This protest brought him hosts of letters from both sides, but especially from those who sided with him and who believed, as he did, that the truth was in danger. Other articles followed the first, until in 1887 the papers known as the "Downgrade" articles were published, and called to themselves the consideration, and awoke the controversy, of the whole religious world.

Of course much feeling was excited, and some stern things were said, and at length Mr. Spurgeon made this declaration, "We retire at once, and distinctly from the Baptist Union."

The times had moved on too rapidly for him; the sturdy Puritan could do no other than abide by the old landmarks; it was his solemn conviction that where there could be no real spiritual communion, there should be no pretence of fellowship; and even that fellowship with known and vital error was participation in sin. He could not feel it right for believers in Christ's atonement to be in declared religious union with those who made light of it, for believers in Holy Scripture to be in confederacy with those who deny plenary inspiration, and hold that there is another probation after death.

Mr. Spurgeon wrote to the Secretary of the Baptist Union on October 28th, 1887, stating that he withdrew from the society, adding, "I do this with the utmost regret, but I have no choice." He requested them not to send any one to him to ask for reconsideration; but a deputation did wait upon him; with very little result.

A most sad time followed, upon which we would not dwell if we might. The Baptist Union accepted his resignation, and words were said on both sides which would now be gladly forgotten. It was feared that there would be a serious secession from the Union, but this was prevented greatly through the intervention of the Rev. James A. Spurgeon, and there was a remarkable meeting in the City Temple on April 23rd, 1888, when nearly two thousand men agreed to a declaration of faith and principle which united almost the whole denomination. It re-stated the common articles of faith, and though it did not satisfy Mr. Spurgeon, it was, at least to a great extent, a peaceful settlement of differences.

Mr. Spurgeon had to suffer the keenest pain in connection with all this, more especially as some of his own students withdrew from him, or he from them; but the President's loving heart was not quite broken, and after a purging of the Pastors' College Association, and a re-adjustment of its basis, and even while the controversy was at its height, the work went on. At the Pastors' College supper, held on April 18th, 1888, the noble sum of £3700 was contributed.

Much of the heat died down during the last three years. That Mr. Spurgeon's protest was needed has been acknowledged on almost all hands; and many loved and blessed, and honoured him yet more abundantly for it. Some who did not agree with his methods have yet rejoiced in that which he accomplished. Nobody loved him the less for the sharp rebuke which he gave them; and this has been abundantly proved by the universal sorrow of the whole Christian Church, and especially by the denomination which will ever claim him as its most honoured leader.